THE CASE
FOR
PROBABLE CAUSE

A STUDY
OF THE
DARREN WILSON
MICHAEL BROWN
GRAND JURY DECISION

KEVIN B. O'CONNELL

Published by Blue Ink Printing

Published in the United States of America

ISBN-13: 978-1505787009
ISBN-10: 1505787009

Cover by Kevin B. O'Connell

FOREWARD

As were so many others, I was both intrigued and disturbed by the shooting of Michael Brown and the incidents to follow. And like most others, I formed an opinion of the events and a perspective of their unfolding before I was fully informed. It is just that easy in our society for a white individual to jump to the conclusion that a young black male from an economically depressed community is involved in unlawful activity, meets up with law enforcement, acts contrary to the expected behavior, and in this particular incident, is shot to death by a police officer who under different circumstances—were Michael Brown white instead of black—may very well have made different choices.

However, I also found it unreasonable to accept without question that a white police officer would show such depraved indifference to human life that he would walk up casually to another human being, black or not, who is down upon his knees, has his hands raised over his head, and is pleading for the officer not to shoot, and that officer responds by emptying the clip of his weapon into that individual's body. Most reasonable people, I believe, would feel the same way and want more information before accepting this is the way Michael Brown died.

Of course, as that information became available, a more clear and accurate portrayal developed as to the events which took place on Canfield Drive in Ferguson, Missouri, on August 9, 2014. And while deep emotional and social components surfaced due to the incident, manifesting themselves in intense and often violent gatherings and protests by the masses, the use of military-style vehicles and weapons, the involvement of the national guard, the destruction of municipal and private property, nation-wide demonstrations, and even the irrational killing of police officers, a very small and select group of citizens was charged to limit itself to the cold and objective language of civilized law and make sense of it all.

That small group was the Grand Jury for the State of Missouri, a collection of 12 individual and private citizens tasked with deciding whether or not there was probable cause to indict Officer Wilson for the unlawful and willful killing of Michael Brown. To reach their decision, they collectively had to weigh the statements of more than 60 witnesses—some eyewitnesses, others expert witnesses, along with the physical and forensic evidence, and either find or not find probable cause that Officer Wilson acted out of self-defense and within legal guidelines when he made the decision to fatally shoot Michael Brown.

Here in this book, you will find synthesized and organized all of the information made available to the Grand Jury. I have read, analyzed and interpreted every statement provided by every witness, all of the reports produced by the various law enforcement agencies, such as the FBI and the St. Louis County Police Department, all reports and statements produced by the medical care providers who treated Officer Wilson, the statements provided by Officer Wilsons' training officer and his sergeant, among others, all three autopsy reports produced by the medical examiner and the two independent pathologists, and every available diagram that seemed relevant and accurate.

I think the reader will find of particular interest the actual statements of the alleged eyewitnesses themselves, most of whom were interviewed multiple times by different law enforcement and official persons. Most intriguing is how the details change over a relatively short period of time, how even the most well-meaning and truthful witnesses modify their recall from one interview to the next, and how some of the most blatant liars stick to their stories in the face of physical evidence that is both contrary and undeniable.

Overall, it is my objective to analyze and interpret the information, which I do throughout the book, and come to reasonable conclusions and logical speculation based on the collective whole of the information available. In addition, I do come to an inclusive conclusion, and it is right there at the end of the book, if you feel the need to go there first. I am confident my perspective will in no way minimize the rest of the text or the content in which it is developed and presented.

As for the book, it begins with an introduction to the three main individuals brought together by the unfolding sequence of events: Officer Darren Wilson, Michael Brown, and Dorian Johnson. The perspective of each with regard to the incident is provided in their own words and the words of others with whom they are in contact immediately prior to and after the incident.

The second part of the book introduces the key witnesses. I first group together those who are in physical proximity to each other and therefore share a similar perspective, at least in terms of location. These are followed by individuals who just happen to come upon the developing situation. The remainder of the witnesses are then presented in lessening degree of credibility, concluding with two who clearly fabricate every detail they provide. Ultimately, for those who have an appreciation of human nature and an eye for detail, the inclusion of a synthesis of each of the separate statements made by each witness will be particularly entertaining and interesting. What at first might appear to be unnecessary redundancy is actually a real-time study in the psychology of the human mind.

The third part of the book presents the testimony of the expert witnesses. These are individuals called upon not because they claim to have seen any part of the actual incident, but because they provide insight through interpretation of the physical and forensic evidence, and the type of training an officer receives when dealing with subjects who respond threateningly, and the protocol the officer is then expected to follow. Included also, are the summaries of various reports, such as DNA findings and the toxicology results for both Darren Wilson and Michael Brown.

The fourth and final part of the book presents the indictments the Grand Jury is charged with deciding upon, an analysis of that process—and of course, my conclusion.

PART 1: THE PROTAGANISTS

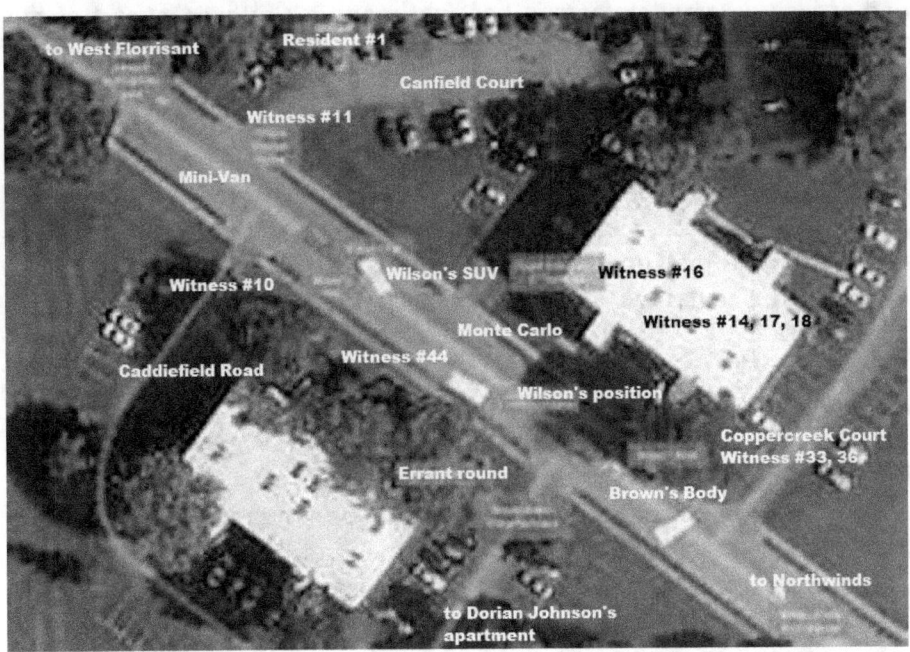

Diagram of the incident scene. Includes position of key witnesses

MICHAEL BROWN

MICHAEL BROWN AND VIRON

Prior to the day of the incident, Michael Brown has been living with one of his two grandmothers in her apartment in Northwinds, east of the Canfield Green Apartments. However, about a week earlier, she is admitted to the hospital and Michael goes to stay informally with a friend of his named Viron. Viron is about a year older.

Viron, however, does not have his own apartment, but is living with his older sister in a two-bedroom unit on the south side of Canfield Drive and between Canfield Court to the west and Coppercreek Court to the east. The apartment is on the Coppercreek Court side of the complex. Viron's sister is not married. She has two young sons, both toddlers, and is expecting a third child.

The night before the incident, Viron reports that he and Michael Brown, to whom, he says, he is related to by blood—cousin of cousins—are together in the living room of his sister's apartment, watching TV or playing video games. As the night grows later, Michael begins to nod out on the couch upon which he has been sleeping for the better part of the week, while Viron, among other things, is speaking to a lady friend of his on his cellphone. At approximately 4:00 am, Viron has the opportunity to tell Michael, who assumedly at this time is awake, that a sudden bad feeling—he infers a premonition—has come over him. Michael tells him it is nothing and suggests he gets some sleep. Viron reports he falls asleep sometime around 5:00 am.

Later that morning, probably around 7:00, Viron receives a phone call from his mother. She is outside the apartment in her vehicle and has come to pick up her grandsons so that their mother can go to work. She would like Viron to help bring the boys down and situate them in the car. Viron, however, is half-asleep still, and instead, Michael Brown volunteers to help. Viron gives Michael his cellphone and tells him to make sure he calls his grandmother in the hospital to check on things and let her know how he is getting along and where he is staying. Viron is aware that Michael and his grandmother had an argument just prior to her going into the hospital. He says it was just one of those things between family members.

At this time, Michael is still wearing the same clothes he wore the day before: a grey-colored shirt, khaki shorts long below the knees, yellow and black socks with green marijuana leaves, and Nike brand sandals or flip-flops. He also has a St. Louis Cardinals baseball cap.

According to Viron, Michael is a big fan of his marijuana socks, of which he recently bought a number of pairs, and wears them routinely. Viron states that Michael recently has started smoking marijuana—within the last four months, and has been doing it routinely since then, but primarily on holidays and birthdays. He acknowledges he too smokes marijuana, and that he and Michael are together practically all the time.

After Michael helps get the boys into their grandmother's car, he comes back up to the third floor apartment and returns the cellphone to Viron. He tells Viron that he and Dorian Johnson are going to the store and asks if he wants to come along. Viron tells him he is going to sleep a little longer and they'll catch-up when Michael gets back.

Viron states that he hears the gunshots only 15-20 minutes after Michael left the apartment to go to the store.

MICHAEL BROWN AND DORIAN JOHNSON, BEFORE THE STORE

At approximately 7:00 am, Dorian Johnson wakes up, takes a shower, and makes the decision to leave his apartment in search of a cigarillo so he can smoke marijuana, something he says he does routinely to get his day started. As he leaves his third floor apartment on the south side of Canfield Drive and east of Caddiefield Road, and more or less directly across from Coppercreek Court, he sees Michael Brown in the parking lot across the street. He is putting some kids in a car.

Dorian states his initial intention is to purchase the cigarillo from a guy he knows in the complex over by Coppercreek Court, but after meeting up with Michael Brown, he decides to go with him to the store. He decides he can buy breakfast for his girlfriend and himself at the same time. He also says that he has only known Michael Brown for a short time—a few months, having only recently moved to the apartments. But he describes Michael as quiet and easy-going, and he states that Michael brought him over one time to meet his grandmother.

According to Dorian, he sees Michael Brown talking to some construction workers there by the building. He describes their conversation as informal, but he says he isn't close enough to hear what it is they are talking about. He says he comes up to the spot where Michael is with the construction workers and they exchange greetings. Dorian tells Michael that he is there to get a cigarillo, and then he is going to get breakfast for him and his girl and then go back to his apartment. Michael asks him if he wants to go to the store with him. Dorian agrees.

Before heading out to the store, Michael and Dorian engage in some extended conversation, this according to Dorian, which includes girls, clothes, and education. Dorian tells Michael that he has some college experience—Dorian was at one time enrolled in Lincoln University—and shares some of the challenges involved. Prior to heading out to the store, Dorian asks Michael to go up and see if Viron would like to go with them. He does so and comes back to say that Viron prefers to get some sleep.

All told, Dorian believes approximately a half-hours passes from the time he meets Michael in the parking lot and they head out to the store.

MICHAEL BROWN AND CONSTRUCTION WORKER #2 (WITNESS #36)

According to Construction Worker #2, it is around 11:00 am and he is working on getting around a particularly stubborn root in order to move forward with a drainage project. He is frustrated, acting out in an angry fashion, and swearing when he notices Michael Brown standing near to the worker's truck and watching. The worker states he acknowledges Michael with a 'what's up'. Michael responds by telling him that Jesus Christ can help him with his anger issues. The worker invites Michael to grab a shovel and hop down into the hole and have a go at the root, if he wishes. Michael shows no interest in doing so. However, he does spend the next thirty minutes or so watching the worker, but without saying too much.

At this point, Worker #2 engages in conversation with Worker #1 about a different strategy for getting around the root, and while doing so, he notices Michael Brown take his leave and climb the stairs back up into the apartments.

A few minutes later—the worker doesn't say how many—Michael Brown reappears in the parking lot and he is accompanied by Dorian Johnson. The two pass-by the worker, and the worker notices that Michael Brown is folding a small amount of marijuana into a piece of lined notebook paper. The worker asks Michael if he is going to smoke the marijuana using the notebook paper. Michael responds that he is going to the store to pick-up some blunts, that he'll smoke the marijuana using the cigarillos. At this time, the worker tells Mike that blunts are no good, and instead, he should try using wax. Michael says nothing in response, but Dorian answers, saying he doesn't know what wax is. The two keep walking. The worker says that was pretty much the end of their conversation, but he does explain to the detective that the wax has marijuana crushed into it, and that the process maximizes the effect of the marijuana when smoked.

Following up on the conversation, the detective asks the worker if he believes Michael Brown is under the influence of marijuana at the time they are talking. He says he sees nothing to indicate as much, but that Michael has a habit of speaking slowly, and when he does speak, he exhibits a sort of tic in which his head lifts back and his eyes flutter. He believes Michael is just "slow in nature", stating, "I just thought he had an issue up there or something."

Worker #2 then states that it is approximately 15 minutes after Brown and Johnson start west on Canfield Drive that he hears the first gunshot.

MICHAEL BROWN AND CONSTRUCTION WORKER #1 (WITNESS #33)

According to Construction Worker #1, he and his partner are working together at the Canfield Green Apartments, trenching and piping out drain spouts. They arrive around 8:00 am and it is approximately 11:00 am when he first sees Michael Brown. He notices Michael come down a set of stairs in proximity to their truck, shortly after which Michael engages in some conversation with Worker #2 while he is trying to remove a stubborn tree root.

Worker #1 hears Michael Brown ask, "One of you two mad about something? I'm getting a bad vibe." Worker #1 recalls his partner saying something light in response, but doesn't recall the exact words. His partner and Michael then engage in conversation for a period of time he describes only as "long", and at some point in which Michael makes a reference to Jesus Christ. Worker #1 says he is working on digging the trench and not really paying attention. At one point, the partner goes over to the truck to get a tool, Michael Brown follows him, and the two of them speak for a while longer.

Worker #1 does recall that when Michael Brown speaks, he tends to lift his head, and he notices Brown often clenches his left fist. In addition, while Brown and Worker #2 are talking about Brown's socks, Brown comments that "you've got to try everything in this life...to figure out where you want to go in this world". Worker #1 thinks that Michael may be under the influence of marijuana at this time. At the end of the conversation, Worker #2 and Michael Brown shake hands.

Michael Brown then climbs the stairs back up into the apartments. When Worker #1 again sees him, it is ten to 15 minutes later and he is with Dorian Johnson. The two stop to speak with Worker #2, but Worker #1 is too far to hear any part of what they say. Shortly after, Worker #1 states that he goes over to Worker #2 to suggest they get back to the task at hand. Brown and Johnson move away and start walking up Canfield Drive towards West Florissant.

Worker #1 says he doesn't see Michael Brown again until after he hears a loud bang, looks up, and Michael Brown is moving at a "good clip" and in his direction.

MICHAEL BROWN AND DORIAN JOHNSON, AT THE STORE

According to Dorian Johnson, while he and Michael Brown are walking to the store, the topic of money never enters their conversation. Dorian assumes Brown has money. He bases his assumption on the style of clothing Brown usually wears, which he refers to as Next Generation and which he considers pricey. He states he has money in his pockets.

Once in the store, Michael Brown moves up to the counter and is face to face with the store clerk, who Johnson recalls is a male. However, there is another clerk, a female, who is by the register. Dorian states that he is standing to Brown's back. There is also another customer, a man, who enters shortly thereafter and goes about his own business.

In response to the male clerk asking Michael Brown what he wants, Brown indicates the cigarillos and reaches over the counter and past the clerk and takes a box of mini-cigarillos, the kind that sell, according to Dorian, at .69 cents per individual cigarillo. The clerk does not respond. Brown then hands the box to Johnson. Johnson states he believes that Brown intends to pay for the item.

However, once Brown hands the box to Johnson, he then again reaches around the clerk and over the counter and grabs an additional handful of loose cigarillos. This time, the clerk responds by attempting to swat aside Brown's hand, but he misses and instead hits the counter top. In the process, he also manages to knock some of the cigarillos out of Brown's hand and to the floor.

Brown responds by picking up the cigarillos that were dropped, and then faces and moves towards the front door of the store. It is at this time that Johnson decides something is not right. Seeing no exchange of money, Dorian Johnson places the box of mini-cigarillos down upon the counter. He says that he often goes to that store and knows that he will be recognized, and that he does not wish to have any trouble with the owner. He also thinks that Michael Brown is playing some kind of prank on the owner, and states that he does not know Brown well enough to assess his relationship with the owner.

By this time, Michael Brown is striding towards the door and behind the other male customer, who Dorian states, momentarily waits, holding the door open for Brown. However, he leaves before Brown gets to the door and allows for the door to swing closed. As Brown grabs for the door and slings it open, the clerk comes around the counter and tries to stop Brown by reaching out to grab hold of him. Michael Brown responds by knocking away the clerk's hand and moving towards him in a menacing manner. Dorian Johnson states that his only concern while this confrontation is developing is to get around Michael Brown and out of the store, wishing to distance himself from the incident and aware of the store's security cameras.

As both Johnson and Brown exit the store, Johnson states that he hears the clerk say that he is calling the police. As they are walking away, Johnson states that he is just staring at Brown and thinking that he doesn't see Brown as the kind of person who would engage in this type of behavior. Brown, however, is just laughing it off and telling Johnson to be cool and calm. In addition, Johnson states that as far as he knows, Brown had not smoked any marijuana that morning, nor did he appear to be high.

According to Johnson, as they leave the Ferguson Market and are on West Florissant and walking back to Canfield Drive, a distance of 4-5 minutes, he and Brown are passed by a Ferguson police vehicle, and Johnson recalls thinking it is an unusually fast response time and that they are both going to be arrested. However, the vehicle drives past without taking any notice of them and pulls into a nearby McDonald's. The two then see two more police vehicles before they reach Canfield Drive.

As they reach Canfield Drive, Michael Brown is in process of dividing the cigarillos between them, and the two are engaged in general conversation, part of which is to decide their next destination, whether to Dorian's apartment or to where Michael is staying.

And that is when they encounter Officer Darren Wilson.

MICHAEL BROWN AT THE STORE, ACTUAL VIDEO

A review of the video produced by the security camera at the convenience store shows Michael Brown enter the store and followed by Dorian Johnson. Brown is wearing a white t-shirt, khaki-colored shorts extending below the knees, yellow and black socks with marijuana leaves and pulled up high along the shin, and a red baseball cap. Dorian Johnson is wearing a black t-shirt with a white or light-colored print on the front, light-colored shorts extending below the knees, and what appears to be brownish-colored shoes or sneakers.

Once in the store, Michael Brown goes immediately to the counter, while Dorian moves three or four feet further into the store and then comes back to a position just behind Brown. Brown reaches over the counter, where his hand moves out of view, and then turns and hands an item to Dorian Johnson, who immediately accepts the item. Brown then turns again towards the counter and may be involved in conversation. Approximately 10-12 seconds later, he then again reaches over the counter, his hand disappearing from view, and then coming back into view, at which time Brown has a handful of some item. Together he and Dorian Johnson move back in the direction of the front door.

As they are again in view of the camera, Dorian Johnson is seen to the left of the front door and approximately five feet from it. The clerk, dressed in a white, long-sleeved button-up shirt and black pants, is seen coming up on Michael Brown's right hand side and moving ahead of him and straight to the door. The door, at this time, is being held open to the outside by a male seen only from shoulder down and wearing a pair of denim jeans and a white shirt. Dorian Johnson is moving to Brown's left and slightly behind him. The clerk reaches for the bar across the door, which has been let go by the other man, and is attempting to pull it closed before Brown gets to it. However, Michael Brown reaches out ahead of the clerk with his left arm and forcefully pushes him away and to the right. Dorian Johnson, at this time, moves ahead of Brown and out the door. Brown, meanwhile, turns back towards the clerk and takes a menacing step in his direction. The clerk moves back and allows Brown to leave unimpeded. The clerk then moves to the door, steps out into the parking lot and watches Brown and Johnson walk away. He then comes back into the store and is seen moving back in the direction of the counter.

DORIAN JOHNSON

INTERVIEW WITH THE ST. LOUIS COUNTY POLICE DEPARTMENT

Dorian Johnson is interviewed by the St. Louis County Police on August 13, 2014, at 3:41 pm. The interview takes place in a conference room at the law offices of Bosley and Associates. Freeman Bosley, Jr. is the attorney representing Dorian Johnson. The interview is conducted by a detective from the Bureau of Crimes Against Persons. Also present are a Special Agent from the FBI, a male who claims to "Know [Dorian's] people...and [is] in charge of his security", and a female who may be Dorian's mother. In addition, mention is made of a warrant for Dorian from Cole County. Prior to the start of the interview, Bosley reminds Dorian that he is speaking with an FBI agent and that it is imperative that he tells the truth. The interview concludes at 5:54 pm.

Dorian Johnson is the 22 year-old male African-American who is with Michael Brown as the two of them are walking down Canfield Drive and are engaged by Officer Wilson. Dorian Johnson is also present at the convenience store when Michael Brown steals the cigarillos. He is a resident of the Canfield Green Apartments. His unit is located across the street from where Michael Brown is currently staying and east of Caddiefield Road. Johnson lives with a girlfriend and he has an infant daughter.

According to Dorian Johnson, he wakes at approximately 7:00 am and around 7:45 leaves his apartment in search of a cigarillo for the purpose of smoking marijuana, something he says he does routinely to start his day. As he comes out of his apartment, he sees Michael Brown across the street in a neighboring parking lot. Brown is placing his "nephews" in a car. Dorian crosses over to Brown and invites him to go along to the store with him to get the cigarillo. After they leave the store, they are walking along Canfield Drive and going back to the apartment to play video games and listen to music. As they are walking, they are talking about girls and the neighborhood.

At this point, Freeman Bosley stops Dorian and encourages him to tell the whole story, including details of the incident at the Ferguson Market.

Continuing, Dorian states there is an incident at the market in which cigarillos are stolen 'by law, but "not in a manner to where it was forceful or, you know, a weapon was drawn." He states he and Michael Brown are at the counter and the clerk asks what they need. Michael Brown then reaches over the counter and grabs a box of Swisher mini-cigarillos, the .69 cents kind, and turns and hands the box to Dorian. Dorian states that the clerk has no reaction. Michael Brown then reaches over the counter a second time and grabs a handful of loose cigarillos. He then turns and heads for the exit. At this time, Dorian states he figures out what is going on and sets the box down upon the counter.

According to Dorian, the clerk is slow to react, but he does manage to move ahead of Michael Brown in an attempt to block the door. Michael Brown uses one hand and moves the clerk aside. The clerk stumbles. Michael Brown opens the door and exits. Dorian Johnson walks out behind him. Dorian further states as his pants have no pockets and he is wearing a white tank top, he has no place to put the cigarillos Michael Brown has taken from the store. Brown continues to hold the cigarillos in his hand.

Johnson and Brown then start to walk down West Florissant and towards Canfield Drive. Johnson states that upon leaving the store he hears the clerk say he is going to call the police, and therefore he is afraid they will be arrested. However, he finds it odd that multiple police vehicles pass them as they are walking without paying any attention to them. He thinks the clerk does not make the call.

As they turn on to Canfield Drive, they move to the center of the road because, according to Dorian, his apartment is on the right hand side and Brown's is on the left hand side. He states there is no traffic and no one is being obstructed by their presence. They are walking single file with Johnson out front.

According to Johnson, Officer Wilson's vehicle appears and it is heading towards them. As it nears, Officer Wilson stops beside them and says, "Get the fuck on the sidewalk." Johnson says that Brown has no response, but that he tells Officer Wilson they are nearing their destination. He and Brown continuing walking, and Johnson is under the impression that "the officer was finished with us".

However, Johnson states he hears the screech of Officer Wilson's tires as he aggressively reverses his vehicle at a rapid speed and puts on his brakes. The vehicle comes to a stop on an angle, nearly hitting both Johnson and Brown, who are required to leap back, and is blocking traffic from both directions.

Johnson and Brown are now face-to-face with Officer Wilson. Officer Wilson says, "What did you say?" Johnson describes Wilson as angry and aggressive. He further states that Officer Wilson attempts to thrust his door open, but due to the vehicle's proximity to Michael Brown, the door hits Brown and comes back and closes on Officer Wilson. Johnson says, "It recalled [sic] so fast, "boom", real quick...I could see how the officer mistook that as a shove."

According to Dorian Johnson, at this point, Officer Wilson's left arm comes out of the window and "...directly on my friend's throat." He then describes Michael Brown as angry and Officer Wilson's arm bulging with the intensity of the grip. Dorian notes that as Michael Brown still has his hands filled with the cigarillos, he cannot at any time get a grip on Officer Wilson. Instead, he is twisting and turning in his attempt to pull away. Dorian further states that Officer Wilson makes no other attempt to exit the vehicle, but is instead trying to pull Brown in through the window, to the point that Brown's head is above the height of the car, but his chest is bowed toward the window. Both Brown and Wilson are cursing at each other.

At some point, according to Johnson, Officer Wilson loses his grip on Brown's throat and has a grip on the back of Brown's shirt instead. Brown uses his advantage to turn to Johnson and hand him the cigarillos he has in both hands.

Continuing, Johnson states that once he has the cigarillos, Brown and Wilson are face to face and engaged in a tug-of-war. Officer Wilson then states, "I'll shoot." Johnson believes Officer Wilson is referring to a taser. However, he then states that Officer Wilson is pointing his gun out of the vehicle window, and because he is much shorter than Michael Brown, Johnson is staring directly down the barrel. Officer Wilson again states "I'll shoot", after which he fires the weapon.

According to Johnson, when the weapon goes off, he is standing to Michael Brown's right and in proximity to the rear door of the driver's side of the vehicle. He also infers that Officer Wilson still has a grip on Brown with his left hand and is pointing the gun with his right. Johnson says that immediately after the shot, he sees blood pool on Michael Brown's shirt, to the right side of his torso, but he doesn't see where he is hit. He then states that he looks at Brown, and Brown at him, both with the realization that Brown has been shot. Simultaneously, they both start to run.

Dorian Johnson acknowledges that there are three cars lined-up to the rear of the police SUV and he takes cover between the first and the second. He at this time sees Michael Brown run past and heading east back towards his apartment building. He also hears a scream from the first car that he passes, and is aware that Officer Wilson is yet to exit his vehicle. As Brown runs by him, Brown says, "Keep running, Bro."

As Michael Brown reaches the third car, Dorian sees Officer Wilson run past. He has his gun drawn. At this point, Dorian states that he tries to enter the second car, a Monte Carlo, which has its windows rolled down, and as he does, he asks the occupants to drive him deeper into the complex. Instead, the car drives up on the sidewalk to get around Officer Wilson's vehicle and leaves him crouching there in the street.

This is when, according to Johnson, Michael Brown runs past the third car, and at which time Johnson observes Officer Wilson shoot Brown in the back. Brown then stops running. At this point, Officer Wilson is positioned behind the second car and Michael Brown is near the intersection of Canfield Drive and Coppercreek Court. They are approximately 15 feet apart or less. Johnson uses the term a 'car length'.

Michael Brown, with his back still to Officer Wilson, then raises both his hands above his head, one higher than the other—due, according to Johnson, to a bullet wound in his back, and turns toward Officer Wilson, at which time he says either "I'm unarmed" or "I don't have a gun". Johnson then states as Michael Brown attempts to get a second sentence out, Officer Wilson "fired several more shots." Continuing, Johnson says, "I heard more than four shots fired. My friend went all the way down in the fatal position...I watched him take every... several more shots. I watched his facial expression." Officer Wilson then takes a couple of steps towards Brown, at which time, Johnson states, he takes off running.

The detective now begins to ask questions for the purpose of clarifying specific details.

According to Dorian Johnson, when Officer Wilson first attempts to exit his vehicle, the vehicle is so close to Michael Brown and Dorian Johnson that it barely opens an inch before the brunt of the door hits Michael Brown and bounces back to close. Dorian states he is hit in the left arm by the handle of the door. From there, the physical confrontation between Brown and Wilson escalates quickly. It lasts, however, no more than 45-50 seconds. During this time, both Brown and Wilson are using profanity, but at no time does Michael Brown attempt to pull Officer Wilson out of the vehicle or put his hand on Officer Wilson's gun.

In response to direct questioning as to the gun, Johnson states Officer Wilson has the weapon inside the car at all times, but its barrel is pointing outward and towards both Johnson and Brown. Johnson reports there is only one shot while he and Brown are immediately outside the vehicle and before they both start running. However, Johnson also states that the bullet hits Michael Brown on the right side and that he sees the blood splatter.

The detective then clarifies the distance Michael Brown moves from the point he stops and turns to face Officer Wilson and then collapses to the pavement. Johnson states, "It's not far. Upon being shot, he was in shock and trying to talk. So, he couldn't run or make a full step, so much as a stutter step. He didn't take a full step." He then states that Brown "did not try to walk back up on the officer".

The detective then asks if Dorian knows of anyone else who may be contacted as a witness, or anyone else that he may have heard from about the incident. Dorian says, "No sir. Since that day I was so scared and feared for my life I couldn't talk to anyone."

INTERVIEW WITH THE GRAND JURY, VOLUME 4

The interview of Dorian Johnson by the Grand Jury takes place on September 10, 2014, at approximately 1:00 pm. The procedure is conducted by Alizadeh and Whirley. All 12 jurists are present. The first part of the interview covers Dorian's early morning routine prior to the incident with Officer Wilson, including prior to meeting up with Michael Brown there in the complex and the incident at the convenience store. However, keeping with the format, only his statement concerning the events of the incident with Officer Wilson are presented at this time.

According to Dorian Johnson, he and Michael Brown are walking east on Canfield Drive, and up until Canfield Court, they are on the sidewalk. At some point, while involved in general conversation, they take to walking in the middle of the street. They are undecided as to their destination. Over the next 30 seconds or so, Johnson states maybe two or three cars come past, and all move around them without issue. Shortly after, Officer Wilson, coming west towards West Florissant, approaches their position, slows his vehicle, lowers his window, and says, "Get the fuck on the sidewalk." Johnson describes Officer Wilson's tone as 'rude'.

Continuing, Johnson states that he told Officer Wilson that he and Brown are nearing their destination and will be out of the road shortly. He states Michael Brown said nothing. Officer Wilson then starts off. Johnson is thinking the issue is resolved. He then states, "A split second later we hear the tires screech." Officer Wilson reverses his vehicle at high speed, nearly strikes Johnson and Brown, and comes to a stop so that Johnson and Brown are immediately at the driver side door and "right in [Wilson's] face". According to Johnson, at this point, he and Brown are shoulder-to-shoulder and facing Wilson. Brown is to Johnson's left. Johnson states he is nearer to the passenger door on the driver's side.

Once the vehicle comes to a second stop, Johnson states, Officer Wilson asks, "What did you say?" Simultaneously, Officer Wilson attempts to exit his vehicle. He opens the driver's door aggressively, but as Michael Brown is standing in close proximity, the door hits Brown and immediately bounces back towards Officer Wilson and "closed back on him".

Officer Wilson does not attempt to open the door a second time, but instead, according to Johnson, reaches out the open window with his left arm and grabs Michael Brown by the shirt around the throat and neck area. Johnson states, "I watched his hands, you know, they really tightened up ... he had a good grip on it."

At this time, with the stolen cigarillos still in his hand, Michael Brown places one hand on top of the cruiser and the other on the lower frame of the open window, and he is trying to push away from Officer Wilson's grip. Johnson states both Brown and Wilson are yelling and cursing at each other, and the expressions upon their faces are intense and angry. He states there is no wrestling or punches thrown, only a "tug-of-war".

At some point, Officer Wilson loses grip on Michael Brown's neck or throat and has hold only of his shirt. Brown is able to twist one direction and the other, but he is not free. According to Johnson, Brown turns to him and hands him the Cigarillos. With his hands now free, Johnson states, Brown has superior leverage and begins to pull or push harder to get away from Officer Wilson. Officer Wilson still is using only his left hand, and he is trying to pull

Michael Brown into the vehicle. Johnson states, however, that Michael Brown's upper torso or hands do not at any time pass through the window. Johnson does acknowledge that the SUV is rocking back and forth during the confrontation. Johnson states he remains beside Michael Brown and in proximity to the driver's door during this time.

Continuing, Dorian Johnson states that Officer Wilson, his left hand pulling on Michael Brown's right arm, and Michael Brown's left hand pushing on or near the driver's side door mirror, says, "I'll shoot." Johnson believes Officer Wilson is referring to a taser.

At this point, the attorney asks for clarification as to the hands of Brown and Wilson.

Dorian Johnson states that as he is in a state of shock, it is possible that Brown's right hand may have passed in through the window due to the amount of pulling and pushing. He does insist, however, that Michael Brown does not make a fist or throw any punches, and that he sees more of Officer Wilson's left arm out of the car than Michael Brown's right arm in the car.

Continuing, Johnson states that he sees the barrel of Officer Wilson's gun. Officer Wilson then says, "I'll shoot." According to Johnson, Brown's left hand, at this time, is no longer in contact with the vehicle. Johnson is still beside Brown. Officer Wilson has his gun—in his right hand and fully within the vehicle—aimed at Michael Brown. No sooner does Officer Wilson finish his sentence, the gun fires.

At the moment the gun is fired, Johnson states that both he and Brown are standing fully upright, and he at no time sees Michael Brown touch Officer Wilson's gun. The bullet exits through the window and strikes Michael Brown in the chest. Johnson states he immediately sees blood.

Now free from Officer Wilson's grip, Brown starts to run, as does Johnson. Johnson states that both he and Brown initially start off in the same direction, east towards Coppercreek Court. (Later, Johnson states that he ran fully around the police SUV.) While Brown continues to run down the middle of the street, Johnson takes cover alongside a gray-colored Sunfire. He states Michael Brown runs past him and says, "Keep running, Bro." Johnson then states he does not see Officer Wilson exit his vehicle, and that there is a short span of time between when he and Brown run and he hears Officer Wilson exit the vehicle and close the door.

According to Johnson, the next time he has a view of Officer Wilson, Wilson has his gun drawn and is striding after Michael Brown. Johnson states Officer Wilson walks past two cars in position behind the SUV and within proximity to the rear of the third. Johnson acknowledges he is, at this time, trying to get into the second vehicle (the Monte Carlo) and asking the driver to take him away from the scene. Instead, the car pulls off. Johnson states he is left standing in the road. From his position, he observes Officer Wilson "pace towards Big Mike. I see him fire the second shot. I see Big Mike turn around and face the officer. And now the officer is past the last car and Big Mike is off the sidewalk, no more in the street."

At this point, the attorney asks specific questions for clarification with regards to details.

Continuing, Dorian Johnson states that he sees Michael Brown running toward Coppercreek Court, and as he reaches the intersection, but not stepping fully off of Canfield Drive, Officer Wilson fires a second shot that Johnson believes hits Michael Brown. He states, "[Brown] kind of jerked and that's when he stopped running." Brown then turns with his hands raised, one higher than the other, without either above head level, and faces Officer Wilson. Johnson states at no time does he see Michael Brown with his hand down upon his mid-section or by his waist.

At this point, Dorian Johnson states that Michael Brown says he doesn't have a gun. As Michael Brown begins to repeat this phrase, Officer Wilson shoots several more times, the last of which is fired, according to Johnson, as Brown is on his way to the ground. Johnson acknowledges that Michael Brown took one step towards Officer Wilson as the shots are being fired and just before he collapses. Johnson states he did not see Officer Wilson approach Brown's body when he was prone in the street, and that the final shots were fired from a distance of seven feet or so.

Following Michael Brown's collapse in the street, Dorian Johnson states that he runs across the field and back to his own apartment, which is east of the Caddiefield Road complex on Canfield Drive, and to the south of Canfield Drive.

While in his apartment, Johnson changes clothes and returns out to Canfield Drive. By this time, he states, Officer Wilson has left the scene and people have started to congregate. He states there is a second officer on the scene and he is putting up tape and keeping people at a distance.

Dorian Johnson then states that he goes down to the Northwinds Apartments and tells Michael Brown's grandmother what has happened. He acknowledges there are other members of Brown's family present, and that at their urging, he speaks with a representative of Fox 2, who is present at the scene. He states he makes no attempt to speak with the police, and that it was three or four days later that he learns authorities want to speak with him, and at which time he had obtained the services of an attorney.

Later in the interview, Dorian Johnson, responding to a question as to the Brown family's private autopsy report and how those details may have influenced his recall, mentions Witness #16, saying, "Not from the autopsy, but from different witnesses ... like the girl (Witness #16) on her third floor." Later, Dorian Johnson, in response to a question as to other possible witnesses present at the time of the actual incident, says, "I only saw one person that was out there...and I only saw her because before the first shot when the police stopped us, she was on her balcony and I just happen to glance up and see her and she stood there." He then provides her name [Piaget Crenshaw (Witness #16)] to the attorney. In addition, he states he met her only recently, seeing her for the first time when she moved in, and that he offered to lend a hand.

ANALYSIS AND INTERPRETATION

There are specific concerns related to Dorian Johnson's statement. He chooses to omit specific details, provide details that other witnesses do not support, and with regard to Witness #16, specifically, clearly provides false testimony.

INITIAL INTERACTION

Dorian Johnson states that Officer Wilson stops his vehicle and without provocation says, "Get the fuck up on the sidewalk." While this is possible, it is unlikely that having done so—and seemingly prepared to be confrontational— that Officer Wilson would then, as Johnson acknowledges, permit Johnson and Brown to continue walking and himself pull away prior to observing some sign of compliance. Instead, it is more reasonable to conclude that Officer Wilson decides to reverse course, having already started forward, due to some other variable that gets his attention—a confrontational or dismissive remark—and in the process notices Johnson's black shirt and the cigarillos in Brown's hands.

PHYSICAL CONFRONTATION BETWEEN BROWN AND WILSON

With regard to the physical confrontation between Officer Wilson and Michael Brown, even if Officer Wilson is overly aggressive and immediately confrontational, it is not reasonable to conceive he has the arm length to reach out and immediately grab hold of Michael Brown by the neck, throat, or the collar of his shirt while Michael Brown, at 6'5", is standing in a fully erect position—or that he would do so with his weaker arm—Brown weighs 289 pounds. It is more probable that in order for Officer Wilson to grab Michael Brown by the neck, throat, or collar of his shirt, Michael Brown would have had to be leaning down and towards the driver's side window, and that Officer Wilson would have motive.

It is also reasonable to conclude that Michael Brown, obviously conscious of the fact that he just stole items from the Ferguson Market, is capable of responding defiantly as a result and initiates the physical contact, or at the least, is in the frame of mind to interpret the incident with the door as aggressive behavior directed at his person, and to which he then responds. In this case, it is probable that Brown makes a conscious choice to engage Officer Wilson, and does so by going through the driver's window.

Further, while it makes sense that Michael Brown would be unable to remove Officer Wilson's grip on his shirt or person when his hands are occupied with the cigarillos, it doesn't make sense that in the position to freely hand the cigarillos to Johnson that he wouldn't be equally as capable of using his size and superior leverage to simply pull away from the vehicle. It is questionable, given all the variables provided by Johnson, that Officer Wilson would be able to control the 289 pound Johnson with only a hold on the sleeve or back of his t-shirt. Logic and reason suggest Brown sustains engagement by choice.

DORIAN JOHNSON'S PROXIMITY TO THE VEHICLE

Dorian makes multiple statements putting himself in close proximity to the vehicle during the physical confrontation between Brown and Officer Wilson, all of which are intended to suggest he is witnessing the entirety of the confrontation. He states—more than once—that he is by the rear door on the driver's side and at no time further than an inch away from Brown.

However, while multiple witnesses place Johnson at various points during the confrontation, none of those locations—other than when the cigarillos are handed off—are in close proximity to either Brown or the vehicle. He is reported to be in front of the vehicle, to the rear of the vehicle on the passenger side, and off to one side of the street or the other.

Further, Dorian Johnson insists that he sees Officer Wilson with his gun in his right hand, and that the weapon is aiming out from the vehicle at both him and Michael Brown. However, his statement at no time provides for Officer Wilson leveling the barrel of the gun at the interior panel of the front door or the firing of the round that shatters the glass and damages the exterior of the door. It is therefore likely that Johnson does not have the unobstructed view of the weapon that he claims, and therefore is not in the location he claims to be in.

Finally, Johnson claims he is at Brown's side when he is shot. He states he sees Brown get hit in the chest to the right side of his upper torso and the resultant spread of blood beneath his shirt. He then looks Brown in the eyes, sees that Brown realizes he has been shot, and they both take off running. However, Brown is hit by the second shot, not the first one. The wound is to his thumb and not to his chest. And witnesses state that Johnson actually runs off following the first shot, meaning he is not at Brown's side at the time of the second shot.

It is reasonable to conclude, then, that Dorian Johnson cannot provide for the actions of either Michael Brown or Officer Darren Wilson from the time of the first shot to the time of the second shot.

THE MONTE CARLO

Dorian Johnson, consistent with the statement of multiple witnesses, acknowledges that he makes an attempt to get into the Monte Carlo, and that the occupants refuse to let him in or drive him from the scene. However, this is also the time in which Michael Brown moves to the corner of Coppercreek Court, turns and is fired upon by Officer Wilson, and therefore a sequence of events unlikely to have been witnessed by Johnson.

According to the statement made by the driver of that Monte Carlo, she sees Officer Wilson pass by her car as she is ducking her head down to the front seat. Shortly after, and with her head still down, she hears the first string of shoots. At this same time, she states that Dorian Johnson is crouched down beside the passenger door of her car and trying to get in.

If as she says she is not in position to see the shots, but only hears them, and Dorian Johnson is in a similar position—she recalls telling him to keep his head down, it is logical to conclude that Johnson does not see the shots either. Therefore, he does not see Michael Brown in the vicinity of Coppercreek Court, does not see him stop and turn around, and does not see him with his hands raised. All of which suggests he learns these details at a later time and from some other source.

THE FATAL STRING OF SHOTS

As for the fatal shots, Dorian Johnson's statement is not consistent with Michael Brown's movements from the time of the first string of shots fired by Officer Wilson to when he collapses in the middle of Canfield Drive.

After fleeing from the police SUV, Michael Brown runs approximately 160 feet to the intersection of Coppercreek Court and Canfield Drive. He then stops and turns, comes away from the sidewalk, and is shot by Officer Wilson. After this first string of shots, Brown moves further towards the center of the road, is again shot and collapses. The distance from the sidewalk to where he falls is approximately 50 feet.

Johnson's statement, however, provides for Michael Brown turning and collapsing within a single step. This would suggest, as multiple witnesses claim, that Dorian Johnson had fled or was in the process of fleeing at this time, and therefore did not see the fatal string of shots. In all likelihood, he puts the details together after he returns to the scene of the incident and sees Michael Brown lying face first in the middle of Canfield Drive.

WITNESS #16

Dorian Johnson, at the end of his second statement, says that prior to the encounter with Officer Wilson at his SUV, he chances to look up to the third floor of the complex between Canfield Court and Coppercreek Court and notices Piaget Crenshaw, Witness #16. This statement, however, is clearly fabricated and contradicts his first statement, in which he says he neither sees nor speaks to anyone during or immediately following the incident.

For her part, Witness #16, whose credibility is questionable, states, first, she did not come to her window or balcony until after the first shot was fired; second, she did not come to her balcony until after the third shot was fired; and third, she did not come to the balcony until after her colleague calls her by cellphone. Regardless, at no time does she state she is at a window or upon her balcony during the confrontation. In fact, in one of her later statements, she acknowledges she does not see any part of the initial confrontation.

It is reasonable to conclude that Dorian Johnson conspires with Witness #16 to provide some degree of support to his statement.

TIME FRAME

Dorian claims to meet up with Michael Brown around 7:30 am. The two construction workers, witness #33 and #36, state they first see Brown around 11:00 am and he spends about 30 minutes in informal conversation primarily with Witness #33, the younger of the two construction workers. Dorian Johnson is not present at that time. Michael Brown then goes back up into the apartment complex and reappears approximately 15 minutes later with Dorian Johnson. Together Brown and Johnson spend an additional 10-15 minutes talking to Witness #33, and then they head off to the Ferguson Market.

The question is where are Brown and Johnson from 7:30 and 11:00 am? And where is Johnson during the half hour or so that Brown is talking with Witness #33?

The toxicology report derived from data obtained from the Michael Brown autopsy indicates that he was under the influence of marijuana during the incident. From the available information, it is known that Brown immediately prior to the incident is in the company of a limited number of individuals: Viron (the roommate), the toddlers and their grandmother, Dorian Johnson, and the two construction workers. Dorian Johnson does, however, reference an additional individual from whom he intends to obtain the cigarillo before he decides to go to the store with Brown.

Viron states that he and Brown did not smoke marijuana the night before or that morning. But then again, Viron does not tell the truth about the Brown shooting.

The St. Louis Police detectives interview Witness #33 about the possibility that he provides "wax" to or smokes "wax" with both Dorian Johnson and Michael Brown sometime prior to them heading out to the store.

Witness #33 acknowledges that he had a conversation about smoking, but denies anything more. (Wax is a THC product chemically derived from the marijuana bud which when smoked delivers an elevated concentration of THC and an enhanced effect.) He volunteers to provide a urine sample, and denies he has possession of wax or any other drug.

Both Johnson and Brown are together and unaccounted for a period of approximately three hours. At no time does Johnson in either of his interviews account for this time, other than a sentence or two where he says they were having conversation. Logic, however, dictates that Johnson, who already has acknowledged he smokes marijuana routinely to start his day, and who states he set out that morning for a particular destination with the objective of getting a cigarillo so he could smoke, does reach his destination, does obtain the cigarillo, and does smoke marijuana, and that Michael Brown is present at that time and also smokes. That Johnson strategically avoids discussing this period of time and refuses to provide the necessary samples to the authorities, it is reasonable to believe that he too was under the influence of marijuana during the incident and may have had marijuana on his person at that time.

CONCLUSION

Given the totality of Dorian Johnson's statement, it is reasonable to conclude that he consciously chooses to omit details which if included would provide a more complete picture to the events leading up to the confrontation. He also has purposely modified other details to either put himself in a better light or to minimize backlash from Brown's family and the community— running away, for example, or failing to intervene before the incident escalates to the extent that it does. And he has conspired with other witnesses to substantiate details of his statement that are otherwise false.

DARREN WILSON

INTERVIEW WITH THE GRAND JURY

Darren Wilson's interview with the Grand Jury takes place on September 16, 2014, at approximately 3:20 pm. The procedure is conducted by Alizadeh and Whirley. All 12 jurists are present. For the record, Darren Wilson is the officer involved in the confrontation with Michael Brown and who fires the shots that took Michael Brown's life. His participation in the Grand Jury process is voluntary.

According to Officer Wilson, he starts his shift on August 9, 2014 at 12:00 am. He is scheduled to work a 12 hour day. At approximately 11:30 am, he is required to answer a call regarding a baby in distress. That call brings him to the Northwinds Apartments, east of the Canfield Green Apartments. Shortly after he responds, an ambulance arrives. No longer needed, he leaves.

While driving in the direction of Canfield Drive, he hears over his car radio a call for officers to respond to a local convenience store which has just been robbed. He hears a description of a suspect wearing a black shirt, and that the item taken is cigarillos. Car 23 responds to the call. Officer Wilson's call number is Frank 21.

As Officer Wilson is heading west on Canfield Drive, he states he sees two individuals walking single-file in the middle of the street. He notes they are interfering with the normal flow of traffic, and specifically two cars that are required to maneuver around them.

According to Officer Wilson, as he comes alongside the two individuals, he slows and stops his vehicle out in front of Dorian Johnson, who is moving towards the vehicle on the driver's side, and out of his window, which is already down, he says, "Why don't you guys walk on the sidewalk?" Wilson then states that Dorian Johnson, as he continues walking, answers, "We are almost to our destination."

At this point, Michael Brown, who is walking behind Dorian Johnson, nears the mirror of the driver's side front door, and Officer Wilson reports saying, "Well, what's wrong with the sidewalk?" Brown responds, "Fuck what you have to say."

Officer Wilson states that Brown's response immediately gets his attention. He looks in his side-view mirror at the now passing Brown and notices the cigarillos in his hand. He then looks at Dorian Johnson and notes the black shirt. At this point, he realizes the connection between Brown and Johnson and the incident at the store. He immediately sends out a call over the radio for assistance. He then puts his vehicle in reverse, passes by both Brown and Johnson, and brings the vehicle to a stop on an angle, both blocking their path and containing their movement.

As he brings his car to a stop, Officer Wilson states that he opens his door with the intent of exiting the vehicle, and as he does he says to Brown, "Come here for a minute." Brown responds by saying, "What the fuck are you going to do about it?" Brown then slams shut the vehicle door before Wilson begins to exit.

Continuing, Officer Wilson states that he tells Brown to get back. Brown responds by glaring with intimidation. Wilson again opens his door, tells Brown to "get the fuck back", and uses the door to push Brown away. Brown grabs the door and pushes it shut, again keeping Wilson from exiting the vehicle.

At this point, Wilson states, Brown's head is above the door frame. However, Brown then ducks forward and with his hands up (in an offensive posture), "he is coming in through the window." Wilson states that Brown hits him in the side of the face with his right fist, but infers that the contact is not full on. He believes he may have deflected the blow partly with his left hand, or the force may have been affected by Brown's choice to hold on to the cigarillos at the same time.

Regardless, Wilson states that Brown then grabs at him once before pausing, moving the cigarillos to his left hand, and then handing them to Johnson. At this point, according to Wilson, he uses his left hand to grab Brown's right hand, and in the process, tries to get the door open in order to get out of the vehicle. He states, however, that Brown is within six inches of the door and uses his weight to keep it closed. Brown then strikes Officer Wilson a second time, and with his right hand.

Officer Wilson then states that he begins to consider his options, and in the process, for various reasons, decides against the mace—it's on his left hip and he can't reach it, his asp—he won't be able to extend it or swing it in such closed quarters, and his flashlight—he can't reach it while still protecting himself, and he doubts it will do him any good. Ultimately, he believes his only option is his gun. He further states that due to the force of the first two punches from Brown, he believes a third, if it lands solidly, will potentially incapacitate him and leave him defenseless.

Officer Wilson draws his gun. He warns Michael Brown, "Get back or I am going to shoot."

According to Officer Wilson, Brown responds by immediately grabbing on to the gun and saying, "You're too much of a pussy to shoot." Wilson then states that Brown is pushing the gun down towards his (Wilson's) hip, and at the same time, he feels "[Brown's] fingers try to get inside the trigger guard with my finger". At some point in the struggle, Wilson states, he uses Brown's own momentum to free the gun up from his hip, and with the gun pointing at the driver's door, Wilson pulls the trigger. The gun fails to fire. He pulls the trigger a second time, and again the gun fails to fire. (Wilson states he assumes that Brown's hand is interfering with the gun.) The third time Wilson pulls the trigger, the gun fires. The bullet pierces the door panel, shatters the glass within the door, and exits. Wilson states he at first believes the bullet hits Brown in the hip.

After the first shot, Wilson states, Brown backs away from the door. He pauses for but a moment, and then comes back at him with his hands, striking Officer Wilson at least one more time. Wilson fires. For the third time the gun fails. Officer Wilson states he then grabs the top of the gun, the slide, racks it, and without looking, fires again. This time the gun goes off. When he looks back to the window, Michael Brown is running from the vehicle.

While Brown is running east on Canfield, Officer Wilson states that as he is getting out of the car, he calls dispatch to request backup. Out of his vehicle, Wilson begins pursuit of Michael Brown. He states they are both running east, but diagonally towards Coppercreek Court and the light pole there on the corner. Wilson states that he runs past two cars stopped to the rear of the police SUV. When Michael Brown reaches the light pole he stops. Officer Wilson stops. Michael Brown turns around to face Officer Wilson. Wilson states he twice tells Brown to get on the ground. Instead, according to Wilson, Brown makes a grunting sound and starts back towards him. According to Wilson, "[Brown] does like a stutter step to start running...his left hand goes in a fist and goes to his side, his right one goes under his shirt, in his waistband, and he starts running at me."

Wilson then states he again directs Brown to get on the ground. Brown continues forward. Wilson then shoots multiple rounds, some of which, he states, miss. However, according to Wilson, he sees Brown's body jerk and flinch, and he assumes at least one bullet hits him. Despite the hit, Brown continues moving forward. Officer Wilson states he starts back-pedaling. As he is doing so, he states, he tells Brown at least twice more to get on the ground. Brown fails to comply. Officer Wilson fires a second volley. He states he doesn't know how many or if all bullets are on target, only that Brown flinches at least one more time. In addition, he states that the shots seem to anger Brown and he appears as if "almost bulking up to run through the shots". At eight to ten feet and with Brown's head down "like he was just going to tackle me", Officer Wilson states he looks down his gun site, sees Michael Brown's head and fires. He states he does not know how many shots he fires, but on the last one, he sees it hit Michael Brown's head, at which point, he says, "The demeanor on [Brown's] face went blank, the aggression was gone, [and] the threat was stopped." According to Officer Wilson, Brown goes down on his face, and due to the momentum of his body, his heels kick up towards his lower back and then fall back to the pavement.

Following the shooting, Officer Wilson states that he makes a call from his shoulder "walkie", soon after which, the second Ferguson police vehicle arrives. He states he leaves the scene in his sergeant's vehicle at the request of his sergeant, the purpose of which is not to incite by his presence the crowd that is already gathering.

Consistent with the procedure of all interviews by the Grand Jury to this point, Alizadeh asks questions for the purpose of clarification, some of which are presented here.

According to Officer Wilson, while pursuing Michael Brown, he more than once directs him to stop. Brown, however, does not comply until he reaches the light pole at the intersection of Canfield and Coppercreek. (Wilson does state that he does not know why Brown stops running at this point.) Wilson states that he does not fire his weapon while Brown is fleeing and has his back to him.

With regard to Dorian Johnson, Officer Wilson states that he does not see him at any time during the incident, and not since the initial encounter at the SUV and prior to putting the vehicle in reverse.

ANALYSIS AND INTERPRETATION

There are five significant events to analyze when looking at Officer Wilson's statement. The first is his initial engagement with Johnson and Brown. The second is Brown beside the driver's side door. The third is the physical confrontation between Brown and Officer Wilson. The fourth is the pursuit. The fifth is the sequence starting with Michael Brown stopping at Coppercreek Court and ending with his death.

Contrary to the statement provided by Dorian Johnson, it is not reasonable to conclude that Officer Wilson, if nothing else is said following their initial dialogue (Wilson/Johnson), would have backed up his vehicle and reengaged Johnson and Brown without cause. It is reasonable, then, to conclude that Michael Brown did respond to Officer Wilson, and in a way that encouraged Wilson to take a harder look. Once Wilson sees the cigarillos and Johnson's black shirt, it is reasonable that he would take additional measures.

Further, although Officer Wilson acknowledges his initial engagement with Johnson and Brown has nothing to do with the robbery at the store, it is reasonable to assume that Michael Brown is sensitive to the fact that his actions will have been reported to the police by this time, and that Officer Wilson will eventually make the connection. This realization on the part of Brown may provide for his extreme reaction to Wilson cutting off their path with his vehicle and the perceived aggressiveness to that act.

With regard to what happens next, it is unlikely, as provided by Johnson, that Officer Wilson without provocation immediately extends his hand out the window and grabs Brown by the neck. With Brown being 6'5" tall, it is improbable that even at 6'4" himself that Wilson, while seated, would have been able to reach that high. Second, Wilson is right handed. It doesn't make sense that he would attempt to immobilize a 280 pound man with his weaker hand and while seated. However, it is possible, that having had his door closed on him twice, that Officer Wilson does take offensive action, and initiate physical contact with Brown, and then the incident escalates from there.

As for Brown remaining outside the window during the physical confrontation, that too is not a reasonable conclusion. Even Johnson states that the first gun shot, at least, originated from within the car, and not with the gun extended out the window. Since the bullet hits the inside panel of the door, well below the lowest level of the window frame, it is reasonable to conclude that Officer Wilson did not have full control of the weapon, and in all probability, that Michael Brown had some direct influence over that lack of control. There is also additional forensic evidence that provides for some part of Michael Brown's hand being inside the vehicle. Combine these two details with Officer Wilson's assertion that at least two other shot attempts failed due to Michael Brown's hand on the gun, and it is reasonable to conclude that while door side, Michael Brown was doing more than pushing himself away from the vehicle. And that's discounting the alleged bruising to Officer Wilson's face.

The pursuit is Officer Wilson's most consistent description of the incident relative to the other witnesses. He provides for the delay noted by others between the time Brown runs from the vehicle and he exits. He places himself east of his vehicle and at the approximate distances provided by others. He describes Brown's actions at the intersection of Canfield and Coppercreek in similar fashion, including Brown's body jerking or flinching. He provides for Brown's movement from curbside to the middle of the road. And finally, his description of the fatal shots, though devoid of sensitivity, are sequentially accurate.

However, despite the consistency in terms of sequence, the actual details as to both Officer Wilson's actions and Michael Brown's leading up to and during the two specific volleys of shots lend themselves to speculation.

First, there seems to be little doubt that at least for a brief time when Michael Brown stops at Coppercreek Court and turns towards Office Wilson, he has his hands raised. However, it is also generally agreed that he then drops them down around his waistline. If, according to Officer Wilson, no shots have been fired since the vehicle, it is not likely that Michael Brown has any other wound at this time than his thumb. Therefore, Brown, when he drops his hands, is not responding to any wound to his lower torso.

Second, if the only wound Brown has at this point is to the thumb, he also would not have had reason to stumble—other than having lost his flip-flops, which according to some of the less credible witnesses, he does there at the sidewalk. It is therefore reasonable to conclude that Brown's initial movement back towards Officer Brown is premeditated and for some purpose other than compliance.

Third, if, as the forensic evidence suggests, Michael Brown had suffered no wounds which account for lowering his hands, is it reasonable to speculate, combined with the stutter step he performs, he is preparing to run past or at Officer Wilson?

Fourth, while there is some evidence that Officer Wilson yells for Michael Brown to stop, there is no witness statement to support his contention that he told Brown to get on the ground. Given that Brown is not at this time mortally wounded, and assuming he does not wish to be, it is not unreasonable to conclude that Officer Wilson does not make this statement, or if he did, he did not do so convincingly.

Finally, with regard to Officer Wilson's claim that Michael Brown remains a threat following the first volley of shots, the forensic evidence does suggest that the last three shots of the second volley, all of which came in rapid sequence, were the shots responsible for Brown's death, and up to that point, the wounds he suffered were non-life threatening, and none were to the torso: thumb, forearm, upper arm, and a graze wound to the bicep. Therefore it is reasonable to conclude that if Brown's intent was to engage Wilson physically at this point, he was well within his physical capabilities to do so, or at least believes he could do so.

RATIONALIZATION

Officer Wilson states he is in fear for his life and that is his rationale for fatally shooting Michael Brown. And while no other person can get inside the head of another to know his thoughts, it is reasonable for Officer Wilson to conclude, following the events at the vehicle, if Michael Brown were to over-power him there in the street and take his weapon, which allegedly he had already tried to do, that Brown would use the weapon on him.

Photo illustrates width of Canfield Drive, angle of Wilson's SUV

Michael Brown flees approximately 200 feet east of the SUV, in the direction of the officer shown.

PART 2: THE WITNESSES

THE MINI-VAN

THE SETTING

The mini-van is the location of four different witnesses. It is driven by Witness #26. Her husband, Witness #30, is seated beside her. There are two other passengers in the seat behind them, Witness #48 and Witness #64—their daughters. The statements provided by Witness #64 are not included. They are redundant, appear to be a compilation of the details provided by the other witnesses in the vehicle, and the witness comes across as both disinterested in the process and questionable as to what she sees. The vehicle comes on to the scene west of the incident and continues to drive around it following a brief pause. Each witness provides a distinct perspective and interpretation of what they see.

WITNESS #26

INTERVIEW WITH THE ST. LOUIS COUNTY POLICE DEPARTMENT

Witness #26 is a mature female. She is driving her mini-van east bound on Canfield Drive at the time of the incident. In the van with her are her husband, two daughters, and another relative. Her interview with the St. Louis County Police Department takes place on August 11, 2014, at 12:33 pm (improperly cited on the document as AM.) The interview takes place at the St. Louis City Central Library. It is conducted by two detectives.

According to the witness, she is in a car with family members traveling on West Florissant. She turns the car to go east on Canfield Drive, and as she approaches the bend in the road, she hears a gunshot. As she approaches Caddiefield Road, she hears two to three more pops, which she at first believes are fireworks. It is at this time that she sees the police vehicle in the road, which she describes as a car, and Michael Brown standing outside it. She describes him as a tall young man, with a white t-shirt and khaki-colored shorts. She also recalls a young girl standing near to her car and on the sidewalk.

Witness #26 states that Michael Brown is standing at the open window of the police vehicle with his arms extended and in contact with the vehicle. Michael Brown then stands up, moves away from the vehicle, and starts to run to the back of the police vehicle and towards the complex—in a direction away from the witness.

Michael Brown reaches Coppercreek Court, and then according to the witness, stops and comes back (in the direction from which he is running). As Brown turns, he raises his hands up momentarily.

At this time, Officer Wilson exits his vehicle and is in pursuit of Michael Brown. His gun is out of its holster and down at his side. As Officer Wilson closes the distance to Michael Brown, he moves to his right and eases up. Officer Wilson has his gun raised and pointed at Michael Brown. Witness #26 states that she hears Officer Wilson tell Michael Brown at least two to three times to get down. Michael Brown brings his hands down and starts "like running at the officer".

Witness #26 states, "I don't know if [Brown] was trying to charge the officer or not. I just know he kind of put his hands down like he was in the running position and he started running, and that's when the officer started shooting." She states Officer Wilson fires three to six rounds. Michael Brown flinches. She then states that Officer Wilson shoots Michael Brown "a lot more times" before Brown falls down. Brown falls face first. The witness sees blood spray from Brown's face prior to falling.

Following the final gunshot, the witness states that Officer Wilson speaks into his shoulder walkie, and by the time she has driven around the apartment complex and comes back out onto Canfield Drive, two other police SUVs have arrived on the scene.

INTERVIEW WITH THE GRAND JURY, VOLUME 11

Witness #26 is the driver of the family van. Her husband, Witness #30, is seated beside her. There are three other passengers in the van, two of whom are her daughters. They are in the back seat. One of her daughters is Witness #48. The interview takes place on October 7, 2014.

According to Witness #26, she is driving the family van east bound on Canfield Drive. The vehicle is cresting the hill just before Caddiefield Road to the west of the apartment complex. She hears two or three shots. She looks and sees Michael Brown standing in proximity to the driver's side door of Officer Wilson's police car. (She later insists it is a car and not a SUV.) She states his back is somewhat to her. She cannot see his hands, other than to say that they appear to be in front of him.

According to the witness, following the sound of the shots, she observes Michael Brown back up from the vehicle and start running east "a good distance" on Canfield Drive. At this time, she observes Officer Wilson exit the vehicle. She states that he seems to be having trouble doing so, but that once out of the vehicle, his gun down by his side, he starts to run after Michael Brown. Officer Wilson is not firing his weapon.

Continuing, the witness states that Michael Brown moves up to [Coppercreek Court]. Brown then stops. He throws his hands up and then brings them back down—a gesture the witness describes as "I can't do this no more". Brown then turns back in the direction of the witness. She states he is shuffling back and forth, as if confused. He then starts to run in the direction of the witness and towards Officer Wilson's position. When asked, the witness states she has the impression Michael Brown is contemplating running past Officer Wilson, but that Officer Wilson might reasonably believe Brown intends to come at him.

At this point, the witness states that Officer Wilson, from a stationary position at a short distance from the rear of the police 'car' and to the passenger side (he had veered off, according to the witness) verbally directs Michael Brown to "get down". Michael Brown, with his hands down in a running position, continues to run in a westerly direction, which the witness describes as towards her position. The witness then hears three to four shots. Michael Brown then starts stumbling, but continues to move forward towards Officer Wilson. Officer Wilson, who the witness describes as "staying back" from Michael Brown, continues to fire. The witness sees blood splatter and spray from Michael Brown's face. Michael Brown hits the ground. Officer Wilson stops firing. The witness hears no further shots.

According to Witness 26, Officer Wilson then uses his walkie-talkie, and within moments two other police SUVs appear on the scene. She waits for them to pass, makes a right onto the Caddiefield Drive, drives around the complex and exits back onto Canfield Road to the east of the complex.

ANALYSIS AND INTERPRETATION

There are three interesting parts to the statements by Witness #26. The first is her impression of Michael Brown's gesture related to his hands and arms. The second is her interpretation of Michael Brown's intent when he starts to run. The third is the actions she attributes to Michael Brown before he actually starts to run.

MICHAEL BROWN'S HANDS

As for Michael Brown's hands, the witness clearly states they do not go up in what would be recognized as the universal gesture of surrender. However, she does infer in her second statement that she believes he is indicating, at least momentarily, that he does not want the situation to go any further—"I can't do this no more". She does add, however, that he later places his hands in a position related to running—a gesture Officer Wilson may reasonably interpret as threatening. This impression is inferred in both her statements.

MICHAEL BROWN RUNNING

As for Michael Brown's intent when he starts to run, the witness takes care to state he is not necessarily running directly towards Officer Wilson as much as west up Canfield. This perception does make sense, in as much as Michael Brown does not move directly towards Officer Wilson from the curbside at Coppercreek Court, but first back towards the middle of Canfield Drive.

MICHAEL BROWN'S ACTIONS AT COPPERCREEK COURT

The witness also states that Michael Brown shuffles his feet in place—no one else makes this observation—while at the intersection of Canfield Road and Coppercreek Court and before moving back towards Officer Wilson. Although she does not offer an explanation, other than, perhaps, that Brown Is confused, it is possible that Brown is thinking about his options. It is also possible that his actions are associated with the loss of his flip-flops, or even an emotional reaction to his hand wound, which he for the first time has the opportunity to stop and take a look at.

OFFICER WILSON'S VERBAL DIRECTIVES

In both her statements, Witness #26 says she hears Officer Wilson tell Michael Brown to get down, and more than one time. Combined with the statements made by other witnesses, it is reasonable to conclude that Officer Wilson does provide verbal directives to Michael Brown and to which Brown does not comply.

PERSPECTIVE

Despite minor discrepancies, such as describing the SUV as a car, the witness' statements present without embellishment and are accurate in the singular events, their sequence, and the general chronology. Furthermore, Witness #26's statement is more consistent with the accepted details than either Witness #30 and Witness #48—both of who are in that same mini-van, which suggests she is reporting only the details she believes she actually witnesses, and not those that she may have spoken about with the other passengers.

In terms of credibility, the witness' statements support the perception that Michael Brown, at some point, may have considered complying with Officer Wilson's directives, and therefore allow for the position that deadly force was unnecessary. However, Witness #26 does not see the initial confrontation at the vehicle and therefore cannot attest to the intensity of the physical confrontation between Brown and Wilson, or speculate within reason as to Wilson's state of mind as a result of that confrontation.

WITNESS #30

INTERVIEW WITH THE ST. LOUIS COUNTY POLICE DEPARTMENT

Witness #30 is an African-American male of mature age. At the time he observes the incident, he is in the passenger seat of a mini-van being driven by his wife. This vehicle is the same in which Witness #48 is a passenger. In addition, the witness acknowledges that he has been convicted of a felony offense, professes no love for law enforcement, believes the officer to have been in the act of doing his job protecting the community, and states that most of what he has heard since the incident is coming from people who could not have witnessed the incident first person.

The interview takes place on August 13, 2014. Both the time and the location of the interview are redacted on the official report document. The interview is conducted by a detective. There is a second detective present. The interview concludes at 1:11 pm. There is a statement by the detective that puts the duration of the interview at approximately 20 minutes.

According to Witness #30, he is in the front passenger seat of a van being driven by his wife. The van is heading eastbound on Canfield Drive. The witness reports that when he first sees Michael Brown, the van is approximately two blocks from the location of the incident (west of Canfield Court).

The witness states that when the incident first comes to his attention, Michael Brown is standing in the middle of Canfield Drive in proximity to the yellow dividing lines. He is facing westbound and towards Officer Wilson. The officer is in position to the rear of and several feet from the police SUV vehicle. The witness states that his attention is drawn to the vicinity of the incident by the shots he hears. He describes hearing three or four shots. At this point, he states that he looks up and sees the flashing lights of Officer Wilson's vehicle.

In his description of the sequence of events, the witness states he sees Michael Brown, while in the middle of Canfield Drive and facing westbound, start to run [back towards Officer Wilson]. (The witness then states later on that Michael Brown is running away when first shot.) He states he hears "one, maybe two shots" while Michael Brown is running towards Officer Wilson. He assumes by the way he staggers that Brown is wounded in the leg by one of these shots. He states Michael Brown is spun around [by the shot], turns again and starts moving towards Officer Wilson. The witness states that from the position of Brown's arms and hands, which he says Brown never raises, other than when he first turns back in Officer Wilson's direction, and then only briefly, he believes Brown to have a gun pointed at Officer Wilson and is concerned about being in the line of fire, as well as for the safety of others there in the residential neighborhood. He does state, however, that from his distance, he does not see anything in Brown's hand.

Continuing, the witness states that while Michael Brown is walking (not running) back towards Officer Wilson following the initial three or four shots, Officer Wilson fires perhaps five to six more shots. The witness further states that Michael Brown is six to ten feet away from Officer Wilson when the final shots are fired. In addition, he asserts that Michael Brown's hands are down by his side.

INTERVIEW WITH THE GRAND JURY, VOLUME 12

The interview with Witness #30 and the Grand Jury takes place on October 13, 2014, at approximately 8:38 am. Ms. Alizadeh and Ms. Whirley are both conducting the interview. The Grand Jury members are present. It is noted that the witness and his wife had come in the week prior, but that the interview does not take place due to the process running beyond the scheduled time.

According to the witness, he is in the mini-van with his wife—she is driving, two of his adult daughters, and he believes, two of his grandchildren. As the van is moving eastbound on Canfield Drive and in close proximity to Canfield Court, he and the other occupants of the vehicle hear three or four gun shots and begin "searching" for the source of the sound. He states his attention is then drawn to a westbound police vehicle with its lights flashing. He states he does not notice if the vehicle is a truck or a car. The vehicle is parked close to the yellow dividing lines in the center of the road and at a 45° angle. The front end of the vehicle is closer to the sidewalk on the north side of the street than the rear end, and the rear of the vehicle is closer to the sidewalk on the south side of the street than the front.

The witness states he does not see Officer Wilson exit the police vehicle. When he first notices him, Officer Wilson is to the rear passenger side of and several feet from his vehicle. He states the officer is moving away from him at a "brisk trot", and due to the angle he has, he cannot tell if the officer has his gun drawn or not.

At this point, the witness notices Michael Brown, who he later describes as wearing a white shirt, blue jeans and tennis shoes. He is standing near the yellow dividing lines of the road and facing Officer Wilson. He states he never sees Michael Brown with his back to Officer Wilson, but later says he sees Michael Brown spin and start to run east on Canfield (thereby turning his back to Officer Wilson). At this time, according to Witness #30, Officer Wilson fires a shot, which the witness believes strikes Brown. The Witness sees Brown stagger and an object fly from Brown's hand which he believes, at the time, to be a gun.

Further prompted by Alizadeh, the witness confirms that he sees Michael Brown start to run eastbound for a distance of approximately 50 feet. He states the officer then fires one time, apparently wounding Brown in the leg—the leg jerks—or the lower side of his torso. Brown staggers and his arms come up and away from his body at an approximately 45° angle (palms forward). The left hand is lifted to the level of his chest and the right to shoulder height. Both hands then drop to his side, hanging loosely. According to the witness, there are other people in the area and they are screaming.

Brown then starts moving back towards Officer Wilson at a pace the witness describes as slow and normal, as if casually walking across a room. He states Brown is not moving fast enough for his actions to be described as a "charge". When Michael Brown reaches a point the witness estimates as 15 feet from the officer, Officer Wilson "unloaded on him"—he fires five to six shots. Michael Brown collapses to the pavement, falling, according to the witness, to his right and upon his back.

ANALYSIS AND INTERPRETATION

There are three statements by Witness #30 which suggest the sequence of events he actually witnesses. First, he places Officer Wilson in a position at the back of the police SUV. Second, he places Michael Brown in the middle of Canfield Drive and facing Officer Wilson. Third, he places the collapsed Michael Brown on his back.

THE SHOTS

The witness states he hears three or four shots before he sees either Officer Wilson or Michael Brown. When he does first see Officer Wilson, Officer Wilson is to the rear of his SUV. However, the witness fails to mention either the Monte Carlo or the Sunfire, or place Wilson in relation to any other vehicle than the police SUV. His statements taken as a whole, then, suggest that it is the first string of shots that he hears, and not the shots that take place at the vehicle, and that by the time he actually locates Michael Brown, he has moved already from the sidewalk and back into the street.

MICHAEL BROWN'S POSITION

The witness states that he never sees Michael Brown in any other place than the middle of Canfield Drive, and always in relation to the double yellow line. Since it is already established that he doesn't become aware of the incident until after the first string of shots, it is accurate to conclude that he does not see Michael Brown at the intersection of Coppercreek Court and Canfield Drive, and he does not see Michael Brown move from the intersection back to the middle of the road. Therefore, he does not at any time see Michael Brown turn and move east on Canfield Drive and he does not see Officer Wilson fire his weapon while Brown is at any time running. These are events he either assumes or that he has derived from the other occupants in the vehicle. If he does see Brown's body jerk, it is a reaction to the shot or shots that hit him prior to the fatal shot and at which time he falls.

THE FATAL SHOT

The witness accurately places both Officer Wilson and Michael Brown in proximity to each other when the second string of shots are fired and Brown collapses. However, he inaccurately describes Brown as falling on his side and then upon his back. It can be reasonably assumed, therefore, that the mini-van is at this time turning off of Canfield Drive and as a result the witness loses his line of sight. From that point on, he is only making assumptions or compensating for what he does not see with details he shares with the other occupants of the vehicle or he learns later.

THE GRAND JURY INTERVIEW

It should also be noted that the witness is led by the attorney to believe that his wife drives past both the police SUV and Michael Brown's body there in the middle of the road and makes a left onto Coppercreek Court. However, the witness himself never says he drives past Brown after he collapses.

Instead, it is more likely that the mini-van makes a right onto the west-most extent of Caddiefield Road, drives along the back road of the complex, and exits further east on Stonefield Road—which is acknowledged by the witness.

PERSPECTIVE

Witness #30 is credible in as much as he is providing the details he believes he sees. However, it is obvious that he merges the sequences of distinct events—for example, insisting that Brown flees east but never leaves the middle of the road, thereby suggesting he is either assuming or compensating with details he learns later from the other occupants of the vehicle or from media sources.

In terms of the objectives of the Grand Jury, Witness #30, at best, provides for the possibility that while Michael Brown on two separate occasions is moving towards Officer Wilson, he is not running or charging at him. However, his testimony also disputes the contention that Michael Brown's hands are at any time in a position to indicate "surrender".

—It is also of interest to note that the witness' own wife, in her statement before the Grand Jury, says he is napping when they first come upon the scene, which though not necessarily calling into question his credibility, would be a detail more useful to the defense than the prosecution.

WITNESS #48

FIRST INTERVIEW WITH ST. LOUIS COUNTY POLICE DEPARTMENT

Witness #48 is an African-American female, probably under the age of 20, but older than 17. She is first interviewed by a detective from the St. Louis County Police Department. The interview takes place on August 14, 2014, at 1:39 pm. The detective is accompanied by a sergeant from the department. The interview takes place at the residence of the witness, who at the time of the incident is in the family van with other family members heading to the Canfield apartments. There are four other individuals in the van, as well as the family dog. The witness is in the seat behind the driver's seat and sitting between two other family members. The van is traveling eastbound on Canfield Drive, having come from West Florissant and destined for Coppercreek Court. The interview concludes at 1:49 pm.

According to the witness, she and other occupants of a car are arriving at their destination at the Canfield Green Apartments and preparing to turn onto Coppercreek Court. She notices a police SUV on Canfield Drive. She states she sees a young man standing next to the SUV. She then hears two shots fired. She then states Michael Brown starts running down Canfield Drive. The police officer then hops out of his vehicle in pursuit of Michael Brown. At some point, Michael Brown, who the witness refers to as "the dude", "turned around and started charging towards the police officer." She states Officer Wilson tells him to stop three times. Brown does not stop; the officer fires three shots. She then says that "the dude kept running." At this time, Officer Brown fires four more times, after which Michael Brown falls to the ground.

At this point, the detective begins the review process.

The witness states the officer's vehicle is parked in the middle of Canfield Drive but angled as if to enter the parking field to the Canfield Green Apartments. When she first notices Michael Brown he is beside the driver's door of the SUV, but she describes him only as "pretty close". She then hears two shots and Michael Brown takes off running. The witness states that Officer Wilson exits the vehicle and starts chasing after Brown. When Brown stops and turns, Wilson stops pursuit. Brown begins to run back in the direction of and towards Wilson. Initially, the witness states, Brown has his hands in a running posture—hands making a fist and at about chest height. The witness states that at one point, Brown has his hands raised up at about shoulder level.

At this point, the detective asks if the witness hears or observes any shots while Brown is running east on Canfield and his back to the officer. The witness states, "No...only when he (Brown) was charging at him (Officer Wilson)."

Prior to the conclusion of the interview, the witness describes Dorian Johnson as wearing a black T-shirt and grey pants, and Michael Brown as wearing khaki-colored cargo shorts and either an olive green or grey shirt. The witness further indicates that Johnson runs south across Canfield Drive.

PHONE INTERVIEW WITH ST. LOUIS POLICE DEPARTMENT

The phone interview is conducted by a detective with the St. Louis County Police Department. The interview starts at 2:39 pm on August 14, 2014. The interview concludes at 2:39 pm. The officer is interested in Dorian Johnson's location at the time of the first shot.

According to the witness, Dorian Johnson is wearing a black shirt and grey pants. Following the first two shots which take place while Michael Brown is in proximity to the driver's door of the police SUV and Officer Wilson is seated in the driver's seat, she observes Johnson running away, moving south towards the apartments on Caddiefield Road.

INTERVIEW WITH THE FBI

The interview of Witness #48 by the FBI takes place at the FBI building on 2222 Market Street on October 29, 2014, at approximately 9:21. Besides the special agent with the FBI, a Department of Justice trial attorney is present. The witness is accompanied by her god-mother who is in another room at the time.

According to Witness #48, she is in a mini-van with four other members of her family. She is seated in the second row of seats behind the front seats and in the middle. She states that she sees a young man who she now knows as Michael Brown standing in close proximity to a police SUV in the middle of Canfield Drive. She states Michael Brown is standing facing the driver's window. His hands are in front of him. She can see the police officer in the driver's seat. She states she cannot say that Brown's hands are in the vehicle.

The witness reports she then hears two shots. At this point, Michael Brown starts running from the police SUV. She also notes that Dorian Johnson, wearing a black shirt and grey jogging pants, starts running south towards [Caddiefield Road].

The witness states that Officer Wilson exits his vehicle and begins pursuit of Michael Brown. He is running behind Brown and yelling stop. His firearm is drawn. At some point, she states, Michael Brown is then charging at the officer and fails to stop. Officer Wilson begins to fire. The witness then states Brown slows and she thinks he is going to stop, but then he starts charging again. She notes his hands come up for a moment, but then lower again. She describes the position of his hands "almost like a tackle (football reference) running."

According to the witness, Officer Wilson starts firing his weapon at Michael Brown, and states, "I don't know. He (Brown) wasn't going to stop."

She states she doesn't know how many shots are fired, but is distracted by at least one bullet that seems to strike Michael Brown in the face. She sees splatter.

The witness describes Michael Brown's movement after the first round of shots as 'staggering', after which he again starts running at Officer Wilson. Following the second round of shots, the witness describes Brown as leaning forward, falling to his knees and smacking his face on the ground.

At this point, the agent seeks confirmation of the point at which Officer Wilson fires the first string of rounds at Michael Brown. The witness acknowledges there is a point at which Michael Brown stops running and turns back to face the officer. She states that from the time the officer exits his vehicle to this point, Officer Wilson has not fired any shots other than the two she reports hearing while he is still seated in the vehicle.

The witness states that before shooting the first string, and while yelling stop, Wilson is additionally backing away from the charging Michael Brown. She states that from the first shots to the last, there are at least seven shots, three the first time and four the second. She states she does not see Officer Wilson approach the body after Michael Brown falls.

INTERVIEW WITH THE GRAND JURY, VOLUME 18

Witness #48 is interviewed by the Grand Jury on November 3, 2014, at 10:15 am. The interview is conducted by Whirley and Alizadeh and before the Grand Jury. This is the fourth interview of Witness #48.

According to the witness, the vehicle in which she is traveling comes off of West Florissant and is heading eastbound on Canfield Drive. This time she refers to the police SUV as a cruiser. She states at the time she first sees Michael Brown and the police vehicle, the van in which she is traveling is approximately two car lengths away. She states she sees Michael Brown on the driver's side of the SUV, but she cannot tell if there is any sort of confrontation or physical engagement taking place between him and Officer Wilson.

The witness makes the statement the she does not see a gun in Officer Wilson's hand when he first exits the vehicle to pursue Michael Brown—his hand is at his waist, nor does she see the gun until Officer Wilson stops in response to Brown stopping and again turning towards him. She states Officer

Wilson does not have his gun drawn while he is yelling for Brown to stop. Once Brown stops running, he turns and starts to run towards Officer Wilson. Officer Wilson responds by drawing his weapon. At the same time Officer Wilson is yelling for Brown to stop running towards him, he is also backing up. She repeats this assertion three times, adding Michael Brown is running with his hands in position as if he is carrying a football.

The witness states that at no time does she see anything in the hands of Michael Brown. She further states that he does at one point look like he is raising his hands, but then brings them back down and continues running towards the officer.

The witness again confirms that she sees blood splatter from Michael Brown's face and assumes he has been hit in the face with a bullet. Further, she states that he first bends at the waist towards the ground and then falls. When reminded she has asserted previously that he falls to his knees, she amends that statement to say, "He like hit his knees and he like just fell."

Later in the interview, the witness is asked if she hears Michael Brown say anything, but specifically, "Don't shoot." The witness states she does not.

Prior to the conclusion of the interview, Whirley asks about how far Michael Brown advances from the time he stops running, turns around and begins to charge Officer Wilson. The witness states two or three feet. She than clarifies that's how far he (Brown) makes it before Officer Wilson starts shooting; Brown then pauses and starts "charging" again. She further states that he does, for a moment, raise his hands to shoulder height, palms forward, before dropping them and moving forward. Here the witness states Officer Wilson fires the second string of shots. Brown advances only a couple of inches more, which the witness describes as "running as fast as he was." She states when the last shots are fired and Brown falls, Officer Wilson is about 15 feet from Michael Brown.

At the conclusion of the interview, the witness states that she feels if Brown is allowed to keep advancing forward he would have tackled Officer Wilson into the back of the police SUV.

ANALYSIS AND INTERPRETATION

Witness #48 is among the most accurate in terms of her statements with regard to the accepted sequence of events that take place during the encounter between Officer Darren Wilson and Michael Brown. If there are concerns, however, it is that she does not engage in her first interview with authorities until almost a full week after the incident—media coverage is extensive, and that she may have discussed the incident with both Witness #26 (mother) and Witness #30 (father). In either case, she may be providing details she herself did not witness.

BROWN'S MOVEMENTS

Despite the fact that Witness #48 is asked numerous times to clarify her definition of "charging"—Whirley asks her if "charging" and "staggering" are synonymous, the witness maintains that Michael Brown is advancing towards Officer Wilson as fast as he could. In addition, she distinguishes between when Brown staggers, when he stops, and when he charges. When it is suggested to her that a single running step performed by someone of Michael Brown's height (6'5") would measure greater than three feet (not referenced above, but in Grand Jury Volume 18), the witness, nonetheless, maintains her position—twice making football analogies. Regardless, it may be that the witness associates "charging" more with the posture assumed by Michael Brown than the actual intensity of his strides.

With regard to distance, given the perspective the witness has from the van, its relation to the position of Michael Brown, and the vehicle's movement, it is not unreasonable that she would express uncertainty. Regardless, her statements describing the sequence of Browns' movements— where he goes when—and the events that take place at each point, are accurate relative to the collective evidence.

THE SHOTS

Witness #48 is one of the few witnesses who accurately state that there are two shots that take place while Michael Brown is beside the police SUV, and that there is a measurable lapse of time between the first shot and the second. Both statements support the claims made by Officer Wilson and the existing forensic evidence.

Furthermore, the witness accurately provides for the two distinct strings of rounds fired by Officer Wilson, the general number of rounds fired for each string, and Michael Brown's locations and movements when each string is fired.

MICHAEL BROWN'S HANDS

The witness at no time makes a statement that suggests Michael Brown's hands or arms are ever raised to a position that one would associate with surrendering. In fact, she emphasizes that his hands go up only momentarily, and then infers that he seems to have a change of mind, lowers his hands—she says he forms a fist, and charges Officer Wilson. In addition, she states that she feels if Brown had not been stopped by force, he would have continued forward and tackled Officer Wilson.

VERBAL DIRECTIVE

The first time the witness states that Officer Wilson is providing a verbal directive to stop to Michael Brown, she suggests it occurs while Brown is moving aggressively towards Officer Wilson. It would suggest, then, that Officer Wilson is warning Brown that he is interpreting Brown's movement as threatening.

In her second statement, the witness states that Officer Wilson is directing Brown to stop while he his fleeing east on Canfield Drive, suggesting that he is telling Brown to stop running. She does not mention a second series of verbal directives, for example while Brown is allegedly moving back towards Officer Wilson.

In her statement to the Grand Jury, Witness #48 clearly distinguishes two different times at which Officer Wilson tells Brown to stop. The first is while he is fleeing. The second is when Brown is moving aggressively towards Wilson, and while Wilson is stepping back from the approaching Brown. The witness does not clarify whether Wilson says 'stop' prior to the first string of shots or the second, but the sequence of events she provides suggests it is prior to the shots that fell Brown.

PERSPECTIVE

Assuming that Witness #48 is basing her statements on events that she actually sees herself, her testimony supports Officer Wilson's claims more so than those of Dorian Johnson, or other witnesses that suggest anything to the contrary. As such, the Grand Jury is obligated to consider that Officer Wilson has cause to believe Michael Brown poses a significant threat to which deadly force is a reasonable response, and that Officer Wilson, given the situation, follows proper protocol.

Photo illustrates the corner of Coppercreek Court and Canfield Drive where Brown stops running and turns back towards Officer Wilson.

THE WORK COLLEAGUES

THE SETTING

Witness #11 and Witness #16 are work colleagues. Witness #16 refers to #11 as both her boss and her manager. Witness #11 is driving her van and heading east bound on Canfield Drive. Her position is west of the incident. She is on her way to pick-up Witness #16. Witness #16 is awaiting her arrival up in her second floor apartment, which is in a building on the north side of Canfield Drive and between Canfield Court to the west and Coppercreek Court to the east. Witness #16 is initially considered a key witness and is heavily involved in the process. Both she and Witness #11 make routine appearances in the media.

WITNESS #11

INTERVIEW WITH THE FBI, GRAND JURY VOLUME 7

The first interview with Witness #11 takes place on August 9, 2014, at 1:53 pm, on Canfield Drive. The interview is conducted by a St. Louis County detective from the Bureau for Crimes Against Persons.

The witness, a female African-American younger than 30 years of age, is the work colleague that Witness #16 states she is waiting for at her apartment on the north side of Canfield Drive and between Canfield Court and Coppercreek Court.

According to the witness, she is driving eastbound on Canfield Drive and west of Canfield Court. She hears the squeal of car tires. She looks up and observes a police SUV stopped in the middle of Canfield Drive. At this time, she says, "I tried to pull my phone out." (Later she states, "[As] a matter of fact, I had my phone in my hand.") She then states that although she does not observe the beginning of the confrontation, she observes Michael Brown being pulled through the window of the SUV, after which he is pulling away from the driver's side door. Then she states Officer Wilson and Michael Brown are wrestling.

Continuing, the witness states she hears a shot and smoke coming from the driver's side window of the police SUV. Michael Brown then starts running. Officer Wilson exits his vehicle. He starts walking in the direction in which Michael Brown is moving and he is firing his weapon at the same time. The witness states that Michael Brown's body is jerking, as if hit with bullets. He turns around with his hands raised and faces Officer Wilson, "and the officer walks up [to] him and continues to just shoot until he falls to the ground."

She states two additional Ferguson police officers then arrive on scene and start taking pictures of Michael Brown lying in the street. Neighbors then start to gather, and she gets on her cellphone and calls both channels 2 and 4.

The second interview with Witness #11 takes place on September 11, 2014, at 3:11 pm. The interview is conducted by a Special Agent from the FBI and an attorney from the Department of Justice. The witness is accompanied by her own attorney. The interview concludes at 4:16 pm.

According to the witness, when she first observes the police SUV, Michael Brown is beside the driver's side door and he is pulling away. Officer Wilson is in the driver's seat and he is pulling in. She states they are wrestling. She then states she goes for her cellphone and at the same time hears a shot. She steers her vehicle to the left towards Canfield Court to place herself out of harm's way. She observes Michael Brown running away. Officer Wilson follows him, shooting towards Michael Brown. Michael Brown turns and puts his hands up. Officer Wilson continues to fire, until Michael Brown goes down.

At this point, the agent begins to question for clarification on specific details.

According to the witness, after the first shot she turns left into the parking lot on Canfield Court. She states she sees Michael Brown pull away from the driver's side of the police vehicle and run away. She does not see Officer Wilson exit the vehicle. As she is parking, she states she loses sight of Michael Brown.

Continuing, the witness states she parks her vehicle in a spot facing Canfield Drive, retrieves her keys, exits and starts across a swath of grass that separates the parking lot from the apartment building. She states the next time she has a line of sight, Officer Wilson is walking up on Michael Brown and the entire time is firing his weapon. She states she does not know how many shots are fired, only that there are multiple, and there is a pause, after which there are again multiple shots. She then states, "Whenever the officer is walking up on him shooting, he (Brown) was turned around with his hands up, and he just went all the way down as the shots hit him." The witness states that Michael Brown's arms are at an angle less than 90° and his hands at head level. She then states on the final shot fired by Officer Wilson, Michael Brown falls forward and "slaps the ground".

Further questioned by the agent, the witness states that Michael Brown goes no further east down Canfield Drive than the spot in the middle of the road that he fell.

ANALYSIS AND INTERPRETATION

Taking into account the entirety of this witness' statements, along with the statements of Witness #16 and Dorian Johnson, it is reasonable to conclude that the details she provides are a combination of what she sees and those she learns or hears later. In her own words, Witness #11 acknowledges she spends two hours with Witness #16 following the incident, and while she states she herself does not know Dorian Johnson, she says she doesn't know whether or not Witness #16 knows him.

AT THE SUV

There is no reason to doubt that while eastbound on Canfield Drive, Witness #11, at some point, sees Officer Wilson's vehicle in the middle of the street and Michael Brown by the driver's side door. It is doubtful, however, that her attention is drawn to the incident by screeching tires—a description used by Dorian Johnson. Instead, it is more likely that the witness has only casual interest in the police SUV until she makes the left onto Canfield Court, and at which time she hears the first gun shot. She immediately stops just within the driveway and looks back in the direction of the police SUV. She then sees Michael Brown start to run east on Canfield.

At this point, she continues into the parking lot and maneuvers her van into a parking space, admittedly taking her eyes momentarily from the SUV. This accounts for why she does not see Officer Wilson exit his vehicle or the initial part of his pursuit. It is also why she cannot account accurately for the chronology of the gunshots to follow.

In addition, the witness does not see Michael Brown pulling or pushing away from the vehicle. These are details she learns from Witness #16, and she from Dorian Johnson—he uses these same words in his interview with the Grand Jury. (Witness #36, by her own admission, doesn't get to her window until after three shots.)

MICHAEL BROWN'S MOVEMENTS

The witness then exits her own car and crosses the lawn in direction of the building and towards the road. As she does so, her line of sight is blocked by the apartment building. As a result, she does not see Michael Brown at or near the intersection of Coppercreek Court and Canfield Drive, and therefore she does not, as she states, see him stop and turn around with his hands up. In fact, Witness #11 states, "Once [Brown] faced the officer, he started going down to the ground as the shots was hitting him." Brown actually falls as a result of the second strings of shots, almost 50 feet closer to Officer Wilson and in the middle of the road.

THE SECOND STRING OF SHOTS

The Witness insists that Officer Wilson is walking up on Michael Brown and firing his weapon until Brown falls. This description, however, is inconsistent with the statements of others that describe Officer Wilson as stationary while firing the first string of shots and backing up as he fires the fatal shots. She also maintains that the fatal string of shots are fired once Brown turns around and still has his hands raised. Yet there is forensic evidence of Michael Brown's blood near to the intersection of Coppercreek Court, more than twenty feet away from where his body ultimately falls. It is clear that Witness #11 is confusing two very distinct events.

PERSPECTIVE

Ultimately, given the witness' willingness to claim to see specific events that she in actuality does not see, and her willingness to embellish and provide false witness, the overall credibility of her statement is questionable. Witness #11 is minimally credible.

WITNESS #16

INTERVIEW WITH DETECTIVE OF ST. LOUIS COUNTY POLICE DEPARTMENT

The interview of Witness #16 with the detective from the St. Louis County Police Department takes place at the scene of the incident, Saturday, August 9, 2014, from approximately 2:19 pm to 2:52 pm. The interview is conducted in an unmarked police vehicle on Canfield Drive. The age of the witness is established as not more than age 20 and not less than age 18. The witness claims to live in the Canfield Apartments, on the west side of the complex between Coppercreek Court and Canfield Court, on the third floor and with a female roommate who is not present at the time of the incident. The witness claims to have been joined by her boss in or near her apartment shortly after the conclusion of the event.

According to the witness, she is waiting in her apartment for her boss to show up so that they can drive to their place of employment in Illinois. The witness works as a sales clerk. She states that she receives a phone call telling her to come outside and at the same time hears tires squealing in the street outside her window, and almost immediately after three gunshots. In her own words, she states, "It was like 'skirrr', phone call, 'boom, boom, boom'—it was all just together."

Before she can say anything further, the detective asks her the whereabouts of her boss at this time. The witness states she is in her van and the van is in the parking lot (on Canfield Court). She identifies the van as a Ford. She then states that her boss witnesses the event from the van, while she herself witnesses it from above, meaning her third floor apartment.

Following further clarification of her position relative to the windows of her apartment, the witness repeats she hears the squeal, assumes it is her boss, and goes to grab her things to leave. She states she then looks out her window to make sure it is her boss, and it is then that she sees Officer Wilson running towards Michael Brown, who at the time she does not recognize, but refers to as a friend of a friend. She states that she does not see the hassle at first, but does see Officer Wilson exit the vehicle and run off in a hurry. She then notes that she moves from her bedroom window to the door in the living room that leads to her balcony. She states she does not go out on the balcony, but only moves aside the blinds to look out. She sees Officer Wilson running and hears shots. She also mentions at this time that the window of the lady who lives across from her is shot out. (She later amends this statement, saying that this was something she is told by others while down on the street and prior to the arrival of the additional police presence. She admits she doesn't know exactly which apartment or which window.) She then states she sees Michael Brown turn around to face Officer Wilson and raise his hands in the air, at which time he is shot. At first she uses the expression "after resisting", but then changes it to "I mean non-resistance, after being compliant to the law".

At this point, the witness recalls that she comes out onto the balcony to record the events that transpire after. She uses an LG Optimist cellphone. She acknowledges that she has already sent the videos and photos to her Facebook page.

The detective then asks her how many officers are present at the scene. She states there are two, but only Officer Wilson during the actual shooting. In response to further questioning, the witness states that she hears the squeal of the tires—a sharp turn—and then almost immediately afterwards three shots. She states she hears as many as four other shots while seeking shelter behind the door of the balcony and within the apartment. She acknowledges this action as the reason for not being able to record the actual shooting of Michael Brown.

She then looks south out the window and sees Officer Wilson running east at full speed. She moves to the next window in the apartment to follow the action. Officer Wilson is running to the right of her line of sight. It is then that she notices Dorian Johnson, who she knows only as DJ, and the black, two-door Monte Carlo. The Monte Carlo is located behind the police SUV and both are pointed west. DJ, according to her recollection, is ducking "scared for his life" behind the rear passenger side of the Monte Carlo for cover from the shots. It is determined that the two individuals in the Monte Carlo have simply happened by the incident and are unknown to the witness.

From the window of her living room, the witness sees Michael Brown. She states that she sees him "get down, like arms up and then get shot afterwards." She claims the door to the balcony is open at this time and she is stepping out onto the balcony. By this time, Michael Brown is already face down on the pavement with his arms at his side and at an angle she describes as 90°.

At this point, the detective goes back to the chronology of the shots. The witness emphasizes it is tire squeal, phone, and then three shots. It's at this point that the witness states that as "she heard it", Michael Brown is shot while trying to pull away from Officer Wilson there beside the driver's side of the car, and at which time the detective tells her he is only interested in what she sees first-hand.

The questioning then returns to the witness' visual perspective from her location on the balcony and what she sees. She states that Michael Brown is fleeing with Officer Wilson in pursuit. She hears multiple shots. Brown then stops "dead in his tracks" (words of the detective to which the witness agrees) and turns to face Officer Wilson. According to the witness, he has been shot at least once by this time, but she doesn't know which shot actually hit him. She states he then raises his arms and is shot at least twice more by Officer Wilson, one of which hits him in the head or face. She states the shots are fired from an approximate distance of three yards. He then falls to the pavement. She confirms that all shots are fired while Brown is upright and that no shots are fired when he is down.

Prior to concluding the interview, the detective asks the witness to show him the videos she took, which she agrees to do. The audio of the recordings includes in her voice the following phrases: Got no gun, they just killed this nigger. They just killed this nigger. Outside my apartment where he ain't armed. He don't got no gun; and, Fuck the police. Ultimately, the witness fills out a consent form allowing the authorities to access the contents of her phone, and surrenders the phone to the detective.

INTERVIEW WITH THE FBI

The witness, referred to only as #16, is responding to interview questions presented by a special agent for the FBI. The attorney for the witness is present, as is a Department of Justice Trial Attorney. The interview takes place on September 11, 2014 at the FBI building on 2222 Market Street in St. Louis. The witness has spoken to a detective from St. Louis County prior to this interview and immediately following the incident. The witness is a black female, employed in sales, and recently graduated from high school. She lives in a third floor apartment in a complex along the north side of Canfield Drive. Her view is looking east down Canfield Drive and from the passenger side of the police SUV.

According to the witness, she is in her apartment getting ready for work and waiting for the individual—her employment manager—with whom she made arrangements for a ride. The manager is running two hours late. The witness states that her phone rings and as she answers it, she hears the screech of a car outside her window. She states both happen simultaneously. Later, she adds that her manager doesn't respond when the witness answers her call because she (the manager) is in the act of accessing the video camera to record the incident.

In response to the screech, which she presumes at the time is a car accident, she looks out her window and sees a white police SUV in the middle of the road, facing towards West Florissant. In addition, she notes that the car of her manager is also present and located in front of the police SUV. She believes the manager's vehicle is facing eastward, but states that she has trouble discerning directions. She uses the lease office of the complex as her landmark.

When she looks, she notes Michael Brown standing outside the driver's door of the SUV. She describes him as being close to the door, so much so that she cannot see his body, but just the top of his head. She says that she cannot see what is going on at the time, other than a lot of movement. At this moment, her attention is distracted by her manager's car which is pulling into the driveway of the complex. She believes this is when she hears the first shot. She states that she then turns back into her apartment, gathers up personal belongings and puts them in her purse. She then returns to the window, at which time she notes that Michael Brown is running down the street. He is being pursued by Officer Darrin Wilson. She the refers to Dorian Johnson, who she calls DJ, who she claims is ducking in front of a Monte Carlo which is also in the middle of the street. She states that the doors on both sides of the car are open and there are two occupants. She states that during the chase, Officer Wilson runs past Dorian, paying him no heed.

Witness #16 then states that in order to continue to view the incident, she is required to move to a second window in her apartment. She moves from the bedroom to the living room. As she does so, and without a line of sight, she hears the second shot. Once again with a clear line of sight, she notes that Michael Brown turns to face the pursuing officer. His hands are in the air. She hears two more shots. Brown then starts to fall forward, leading first with his hands, then to his knees, his face, and then prone to the ground, face down and his hands by his sides. She states up to this point, she has not seen Brown move toward Officer Wilson at any time.

Once Michael collapses to the pavement, the witness reports going to her phone which is charging. She is intent on filming the incident. By the time she exits out onto her balcony, there is a second officer on the scene. She describes the shooting officer, Darrin Wilson, as tall and skinny. The second officer is described as shorter and darker. She says of herself that at the moment she is both crying and videoing the scene. She states that Wilson appears unsettled and not projecting the type of confidence she associates with police officers. She notes he is pacing back and forth, and that from what she can determine, has not suffered any physical injury.

The witness claims that she doesn't realize that she knows Michael Brown, having met him at in informal social gathering sometime prior. She also acknowledges socializing routinely with Dorian Johnson, limited mostly to chance encounters and small-talk conversation.

Upon further question for clarification, the witness acknowledges stating that she believes that Michael, while standing beside the driver's door of the police SUV, is involved in some sort of physical interaction with the officer. She describes what she sees as a tussle and as Michael Brown trying to yank away. It was at this point that she states she hears a couple of gun shots, and then she observes Brown running away. In addition, she claims that she witnesses the very first shot come out the window (of the SUV), and sees a shot hit the building. She later amends her statement to say that she sees the damage done by the bullet after it hit the building.

The witness further states that she believes Wilson was pursuing Brown in anger, noting the redness of his face, which when emphasized by the interviewing detective, she insists is not due to the physical confrontation between the two. She states unequivocally that she does not associate the redness of the officer's face with having been struck by Brown. When asked by the detective if she believes the redness is related to bruising, she says no.

In relation to the fatal shots, the witness states that she does not see Officer Wilson actually fire these shots. He is not in her line of sight, blocked by the structures of her apartment separating one window from the next. She does, however, state that she has a clear line of sight to Michael and that he had his hands up in the air while at least two shots are fired. He has his hands raised when he falls to the pavement.

Upon further questioning, the witness acknowledges that she doesn't actually observe Brown with his hands above his head, or even raising his hands. She sees his hands at shoulder height, his knees bent and in the process of descending. In addition, she states that she does not observe Brown moving forward towards Wilson.

At this time, the Federal Attorney concludes the preliminary part of the interview and states that his purpose for the remaining time is to follow-up on the witness statement for further clarification or details of specific points. His first concern is distinguishing between details the witness actually sees versus those she may have heard from a second person. As a result, he references specific statements given to the detective at the scene which contradict the witness' statements during this interview.

As an example, the Federal Attorney refers to a statement the witness makes to the detective that questions her at the scene and time of the incident—approximately 2:29 pm—where she claims to have seen a neighbor's window shot out by an errant bullet. She then modifies her statement to say that she does not actually see the bullet pass through the window, but is told by someone else that it happens—but that she does hear the bullet. She does not initially say if she hears the shot and then the impact with the window pane, but later states that it is this particular shot that is the loudest and the closest to her position.

The Federal Attorney moves from this point to focus on the witnesses' recall of the screeching tires and the first gun shots. On follow-up questioning, the witness states that the phone ringing in her apartment, the screeching of the tires, and the first shots all happen in close proximity. At this time, the Federal Attorney intentionally uses the plural of the word "shot" and repeats it to the witness multiple times. In response, the witness asserts that the screeching and the shots take place at the same time, but states that she does not see the police SUV come to a stop; but she does see and hear the shots exit the driver's side window of the vehicle.

At this point, the Federal Attorney's focus is on the time frame inclusive of the witness gathering her belongings and returning to her window to see Officer Wilson in pursuit of Michael Brown. The witness confirms that she is in her bedroom, which has two windows side by side, moves to the living room and over to the door out to the balcony. The glass panes of the door are covered by venetian-type blinds. The witness acknowledges that while moving from one room to the next that she has no line of sight to the incident, and further that she does not raise the blinds, but simply moves them as to see outward.

The Federal Attorney then asks about a seemingly contradictory statement the witness makes previously to the on-scene detective in which she states she hears that Michael Brown is trying to pull away from Officer Wilson when the first shot occurs. However, the witness confirms that although she doesn't have a clear view of that part of the incident, she does see it with her own eyes and again describes it as a tussle. She acknowledges she does hear similar talk from others witnesses.

The Federal Attorney then asks about the second round of shots. Here the witness changes her account of the events in terms of retrieving her phone and what she sees, claiming at this time that Michael Brown is already lying dead in the street.

At this point in the interview, the Federal Attorney refocuses on the statement the witness makes to the detective on scene. He reminds the witness that at that time she states she does not see the physical confrontation which took place between Officer Wilson and Michael Brown at the driver's side door the police SUV. He reminds her that in her statement she says she hears the squeal of the tires, thinks someone may have been in an accident, hears three gun shots and then comes to the window. He then states that if this were so, she would not have seen the physical confrontation, as it would have taken place prior to the shots.

The witness, in return, makes the assertion that although her view is limited, she does see Michael Brown yank away from the driver's side door of the vehicle, but as she can only see the top of his head, she makes the assumption there is a tussle of some sort. She further states that her phone rings and the car screeches simultaneously, and that her intent is to illustrate the close proximity of the singular events.

At this point of the dialogue, the witness' attorney interjects, supporting the witness' recall of the events and her testimony, reinforcing the notion that she does witness the events as she states, but that her line of sight is limited.

The Federal Attorney then reads from the witness' initial statement to the detective in which she states, "I heard three gunshots. Boom. Boom. Boom. And then I came to the window." It is his intention, which he states clearly, to distinguish between what it is the witness actually sees and what it is she is filling in having heard details from others or other sources at a later time and date, but did not actually see herself. In her initial statement, the witness says, "As I heard it, Brown was shot while tryin' to pull the guy." At which time, the detective tells her he is only interested in what she sees first-hand.

The witness states that she makes the effort to write down the details of what she witnesses so that she would have it all straight in her head. When asked by the Federal Attorney if she still has that document, she states that she burned it.

Shortly after, the witness' attorney asks for a break in the proceedings. The tape recording is pre-empted. The attorney speaks privately with the witness for 15 minutes. The proceedings continue, as does the recording.

At this time, the witness states that she chose only to give general and vague responses to the detective's questions, inferring that she is concerned, at the time, about not having an attorney present. But that she is being truthful and wants to be helpful. As evidence, she states that she surrenders her phone to the detective for viewing of the video.

In addition, the witness clarifies that all she sees is Michael Brown's head, covered by his ball cap, moving, and that she cannot clearly see anything below that level. She then sees Michael's arm jerk back from the driver's window.

INTERVIEW WITH THE GRAND JURY, VOLUME #9

The interview of Witness #16 with the Grand Jury takes place on October 2, 2014, at the office of the St. Louis County Prosecuting Attorney's Office, 100 South Central Avenue, Clayton, Missouri. The presiding attorneys are Ms. Kathi Alizadeh and Ms. Sheila Whirley. Prior to interviewing the witness, the attorneys, as well as the Grand Jury, listen to the audio of the interview Witness #16 has with the FBI on September 22, 2014.

Witness #16 begins by stating she is waiting for her boss to pick her up so that they can drive to work. She states she works as a sales consultant. When questioned further, she states that she conducts door to door sales. She is involved with energy regulation through Ameren. She clarifies that she calls her boss around 8 or 9:00 am to arrange for a ride, and while waiting she is cleaning her apartment. She states that while doing so, she hears the screech or squeal of tires on the pavement of the road outside her apartment, and as she and her boss had been in an accident only a week or so earlier, that she moves to her window thinking the sound is made by her boss. It is at this time that she sees the police SUV in the middle of the street and facing west towards West Florissant. It is at an angle.

She notices from the angle she has a red hat sticking up over the driver's side door of the SUV. She then sees a jerking movement of an arm of Michael Brown, who at the time she does not recognize. Later during the interview, she states she believes it is Michael Brown's left arm that she sees pull away. She adds that she does not actually see him run from the vehicle, as she believes it is at that time that she goes for her purse. She then recounts the description of her phone ringing, the squeal of the tires and the shots, emphasizing that they happen in close proximity of each other. She notes that the shots are coming from the direction of the police car, that they are right outside her window and loud. Asked if she believes Michael's pulling away is in response to the first shot fired, she said she doesn't know, but that the time frame is consistent.

At this point, the witness acknowledges looking away and going for her purse with the intent to go out to her boss' waiting vehicle, but she decides against it due to the gun shots. She instead moves back towards the windows, specifically the door to the balcony, which is referred to as a big, glass sliding door. At this time, she notes that Officer Wilson is running in the direction opposite that of his parked SUV, but she cannot see that he is in pursuit of anyone. Shortly thereafter, her attention is drawn to the black Monte Carlo, which she states may have been dark blue, and to Dorian Johnson, who she claims to recognize. She states she is hearing shots being fired at this time.

Eventually, Officer Wilson reaches a point just short of the intersection of Canfield Drive and Coppercreek Court where she can no longer see him. It is a point beyond the length of the Monte Carlo. She notes that Michael Brown has just about reached the intersection, and that in all likelihood he too has been running, but that she does not actually see him running. In addition, she states that she at first does not make the connection between Michael Brown at or near the intersection and the person that she sees at the driver's side window of the SUV, stating that by this time he has lost his red hat.

At or near the intersection, she sees Brown turn to his right and in a direction from which Officer Wilson is approaching. She notes that he has his hands raised to about shoulder height and the palms facing outward. In addition, she states that she does not at this time see any blood. She then states that she is in some way momentarily distracted, her sight taken from Brown. When she again looks, he is falling to the pavement, hands first, and lands on his face. She states he goes down in the same place that he is when he first turns to face Officer Wilson. At that point, the witness states she starts crying and goes back into her apartment to grab her phone and starts recording the event.

At this point, Whirley asks if she is inside the apartment or out on the balcony when she sees Michael Brown fall to the pavement. She states she is inside and not yet out on the balcony, and later acknowledges that she does not come out on to her balcony until after the shooting has stopped. She further states that she does not see Officer Wilson while the shots are being fired and cannot tell how far he is from Michael Brown. She also amends her previous statements with regard to the number of shots she hears prior to Brown falling to the pavement, saying she does not know how many shots there are, but that two or three is an accurate guess.

Alizadeh assumes the questioning from this point. She questions the witness about the document she creates listing the details of what she remembers. The witness states that she does so at the request of her attorney, and that she later discards the list out of paranoia. She states she does not burn it—a statement she makes previously. She says her motive is to keep it from reporters—a different one of whom is at her door every day—and other visitors to her apartment. She further states that she does not give the document to her attorney, nor does the attorney make a copy of it or read it directly. She says she may have told her attorney about it, or even have read to her brief excerpts.

ANALYSIS AND INTERPRETATION

There are numerous contradictions and modifications to the statements Witness #16 provides. In addition, there is reason to conclude that she speaks with Dorian Johnson shortly after the incident and before she has an opportunity to speak with authorities.

THE TELEPHONE CALL

Witness #16 provides multiple statements regarding the phone call from her work colleague, Witness #11. In her first statement she says she receives the call and looks out her window to see Witness #11's van in the parking lot on Canfield Court. In her second statement, she says her phone rings and she looks out her window, but this time Witness #11's vehicle is still on Canfield Drive and west of Officer Wilson's SUV. In her third statement, she states she hears the sound of the tires which brings her to the window, and it is then she sees Witness' #11's vehicle. She makes no reference to her cellphone or a call.

Given these variations, along with what can be derived from the statements of Dorian Johnson and Witness #11, it is reasonable to conclude the witness has collaborated with both Johnson and Witness #11, and that were it available, the document that she creates and then destroys would substantiate this collaboration. Regardless, it is clear the witness does not see Michael Brown while he is involved with Officer Wilson at the vehicle, and does not see any of the events prior to the shots at the vehicle.

MICHAEL BROWN AND THE POLICE SUV

In her first statement, the witness says she goes to the window of her apartment to verify the presence of her boss, who is to the west of her location. There she sees Officer Wilson already out of his vehicle and in pursuit of Michael Brown. In her second statement, she says she sees Michael Brown beside the driver's door of the police SUV, although only the top of his head, and there appears to be some physical interaction taking place. She then takes her eyes from the SUV to watch Witness #11 turn into the parking lot on

Canfield Court. She then turns back to see Michael Brown running and Officer Wilson in pursuit. In her third statement, she claims she sees Michael Brown— he's wearing his red hat—jerk his left arm away from the police SUV. However, this time she does not see Brown run from the vehicle, as she is retrieving her purse. Her phone is yet to ring.

Examining each of the statements, it is clear that the witness continues to change and develop her story, and that the details have changed over time depending on who she has spoken to and other sources she may have accessed, such as the media. Her first statement is most consistent with the original details she provides. The second statement seems to have been derived from conversation, perhaps, with Witness #14. He, too, has a similar angle to the incident, and similarly describes seeing only the top of Michael Brown's head. Her third statement is made in collaboration with Dorian Johnson; Johnson acknowledges speaking to her shortly after the incident occurs. He is also the only other witness who consistently describes Brown's actions at the vehicle as trying to pull or push away from Officer Wilson's grip.

FIRST SHOTS

In her initial statement, the witness says that she hears the screech of tires, her cellphone rings, and she hears three shots in succession. In her second statement, she hears the first two shots while watching Witness #11 pull into the parking lot. Later in that same statement, she says she sees the first shot come out of the police SUV and break a window across the street. She then later amends that statement, saying she hears about the errant shot from another observer. However, she does state that she hears a second shot before Brown runs from the vehicle. In her third statement, she reverts to a general reference, saying only that the screech, the phone ringing, and the shots happen in proximity to each other. However, she does add that Officer Wilson is firing while in pursuit of Brown.

The only reasonable conclusion is that Witness #16's first statement is the most accurate, which substantiates that she does not see Brown in proximity to the police SUV, she does not see him running, and she does not see Officer Wilson exit the vehicle and pursue. She hears the first string of shots while she is inside her apartment. By the time she gets to her windows, Michael Brown already has moved back into the middle of Canfield Drive, where she sees him shot, and he falls. The rest of the details she reports come from other sources.

As for the errant shot, that particular round is retrieved from the wall of the apartment across the street where it became embedded. No windows were broken. There is also no forensic or supporting evidence that Officer Wilson was firing while he was running.

MICHAEL BROWN'S MOVEMENTS

In her first statement, Witness #16 states that while Michael Brown is running toward Coppercreek Court, she hears a string of shots, after which Brown stops running and turns with his hands raised to face Officer Wilson. He is then shot multiple times, one shot of which hits him in the head; Officer Wilson is firing from three yards away. In her second statement, the witness says that while Brown is fleeing Officer Wilson, she moves from one window to another and in the process loses sight of both. She then hears a second shot. Now with a clear line of sight, she sees Michael Brown turn with his hands up in the air. Officer Wilson fires two shots and Brown falls to the pavement. She then reports going to retrieve her phone, which is charging, as to record the rest of the incident. Later in the same statement, she acknowledges she doesn't actually see Brown raising his hands or having his hands raised. In her third statement, she says she sees Officer Wilson in pursuit of someone, but she doesn't know who. She then moves through her apartment, and when she again has a line of sight, she sees Michael Brown—she doesn't realize it's him without his hat—in the vicinity of Coppercreek Court. She assumes he runs there, but doesn't actually see him running. She sees Brown turn to his right. His hands are raised to shoulder level with the palms facing forward. She is then momentarily distracted—she doesn't say by what—and when she again looks, Brown is in the process of falling. She insists he turns and falls in approximately the same location.

Examining the witness's statements, it is curious that she doesn't associate the first string of shots with Michael Brown's proximity to Coppercreek Court, but instead to a time in the sequence when Officer Wilson is running. And while she does describe Brown as turning with his hands raised—which occurs at Coppercreek Court, the supporting details she provides are sequential with regards to the events that occur while Brown is once again standing in the middle of Canfield Drive and almost 50 feet from the intersection with Coppercreek: Brown's hands down, Wilson firing two to three shots, and Brown falling. In fact, in her testimony of October 2, 2014, she tells the Grand Jury that Brown turns and falls in the same spot. In addition, she states her line of sight doesn't include Officer Wilson while he is firing, but she states he is 9 feet away from Brown while doing so.

The most logical conclusion, given the sum of her testimony, is that Witness #16 doesn't see Michael Brown in the vicinity of Coppercreek Court, doesn't see Brown stop, turn and raise his hands, and doesn't see the first string of shots fired by Officer Wilson.

PERSPECTIVE

Witness #16 is credible in as much as she does see some of the sequences which make up the events of the incident between Michael Brown and Officer Wilson. However, given the sum of her statements, it is apparent that she is a minor witness at best, and has only partially witnessed the incident.

At worst, in her eagerness to have a greater role, Witness #16 embellishes what she herself sees with details obtained from other sources, which unfortunately, includes collaboration with Dorian Johnson, which she does not to fill in the missing pieces, but to distort the truth and to provide false witness for the purpose of substantiating the subjective motives of Dorian Johnson.

With regard to the objectives of the Grand Jury, Witness #16's statements are not applicable to the two sequences most relevant to the case: Michael Brown's actions at the Police SUV and at the corner of Coppercreek and Canfield where he may or may not have indicated a willingness to surrender. As these are the two areas where her statements consistently deviate and breakdown, she would be fairly easily discredited by the defense.

TWO BROTHERS AND THE SISTER-IN-LAW

THE SETTING

Witnesses #14 and #17 are brothers. Witness #18 is the wife of Witness #17. Witness #14 has a second floor apartment in the same building as Witness #16. His brother and sister-in-law are in their vehicle and pulling into the parking lot outside his complex when they come across the incident. By the time they exit their vehicle and make their way up to Witness #14's front door, the incident has escalated. With regard to the investigation, Witness #14 comes forth voluntarily and before the participation of his brother and sister-in-law. He serves initially as the group's spokesman. However, both #17 and #18 eventually provide statements of their own, and with some interesting deviations from each other and Witness #14.

WITNESS #14

FIRST INTERVIEW WITH THE ST. LOUIS COUNTY POLICE DEPARTMENT BUREAU OF CRIMES AGAINST PERSONS

Witness #14 is a black male. The interview takes place on August 12, 2014 at New Horizons Seventh Day Christian Church at 206 Emerling Drive, Cool Valley, Missouri, at 3:55 pm. There are two detectives present. The witness states he resides in the Canfield Green Apartment complex off of Caddiefield Drive. He states that his perspective of the incident is from the passenger side of the police SUV, but actually it is from the driver's side. (The way the vehicle is angled confuses the witness.)

Witness #14 states that he does not come forth initially due to concerns for his safety, explaining that if he were to go against what others from the area are saying in terms of what happened during the incident, they might "nut up"—go crazy, meaning become aggressive towards him. However, as what he is hearing is not consistent with what he and other family members see, his reluctance to come forward begins to "weigh on" him. Ultimately, he decides it is more important that the family of Michael Brown know what really happened, and so he comes forth.

The interview is concluded at 5:03 pm.

According to Witness #14, he is in his bedroom on an upper floor of the complex and looking west towards West Florissant Avenue. He notices two young people walking in the middle of the street. He then notices the approach of the police SUV, which he states at first drives a few feet past the two young men in the street, then backs up. The witness states he expects the situation to escalate, so he exits his apartment out onto the porch outside his front door. By the time he reaches his porch, a period of time in which he does not have a view of the street below, he states that Michael Brown already appears to be engaged in a physical confrontation with Officer Wilson, whose position remains the driver's seat of the vehicle. The witness describes what he sees as "tussling" and "wrestling". He states he does not see if Brown reaches into the vehicle or if Wilson has pulled Brown into the vehicle. The witness then notices an item fly from the truck, which he thinks may have been Michael Brown's baseball cap. He then hears a pop. Michael Brown backs up from the truck and runs.

Witness #14 then places Michael Brown at a spot 25-30 feet from the vehicle, but does not describe any events that take place from the point that he backs up from the SUV and arrives to that spot. He does state, however, Michael Brown, standing on or near the grass at the intersection of Canfield and Coppercreek, turns and faces the officer with his hands raised, but not raised up all the way. The witness states he sees something on Michael Brown's hand. Brown then looks down at his own side.

By this time, Officer Wilson has exited the vehicle and moves to a position relative to the rear of the SUV, but not quite to the passenger's side, and assumes a shooter's stance.

Michael Brown then takes two steps towards Officer Wilson, at which time the witness states, Wilson shouts, "Stop." He then fires three shots. Michael Brown is hit at least one time and is momentarily staggered—the witnessed describes it as "kinda wiggled". The witness then states that Brown "came back up with the weirdest look on his face [having looked down at the right side of his upper body] and he started coming forward, not like he was trying to attack him ... [but] like to [plead] with him to stop." He asserts he does not interpret Michael Brown's forward movement as menacing.

At this time, Officer Wilson shouts "stop" three times, after which Officer Wilson again fires. Brown, however, continues to move forward slowly, rocking back and forth, hunched over and no longer in a fully upright position. As Officer Wilson continues to fire, Michael Brown falls forward on his face. He does not at any time fall to his knees.

The witness then notes that Michael Brown falls almost directly on the two yellow dividing lines of Canfield Drive, after which he states his attention is drawn to his two family members, and then when he looks back towards the scene, Officer Wilson is moving back towards the police SUV.

The witness then states that others from the neighborhood start to gather. He hears multiple people saying that Michael Brown had his hands raised and was saying "don't shoot, don't shoot, don't shoot." The witness states that Michael Brown never "uttered a word".

He further states that people are stating that Michael Brown is on his knees while he is shot, and that Michael Brown is shot in the head at close range while lying prone on the pavement. The witness goes on to speculate (at the time), if Michael Brown has a head wound, it occurs as he is bent forward and prior to actually falling.

At this point in the interview, the detective reviews specific details provided by Witness #14.

Witness #14 states that the police SUV is heading west on Canfield Drive, but then the detective convinces him it is heading east. (It is possible, however, that the detective is referring to the direction the SUV is moving when it starts to back up towards Michael Brown and Dorian Johnson.)

After establishing Michael Brown's location relative to Coppercreek Court and about 25-30 feet from Officer Wilson, the witness states that Brown, after stopping and turning, takes three to five steps towards Officer Wilson. At this time, he has his hands raised up, palms forward, out in front of his rib cage and not quite shoulder level. Brown is then hit with the first volley of shots. He pauses momentarily, hands down at his side, as if he realizes he has been wounded, then takes additional steps—two to three, his upper torso is bent forward at the waist at an angle of 60-75°, and is shot again. He estimates the time of the incident from the point Brown flees from the SUV to the fatal shots to be no more than five minutes.

The witness then clarifies that most of the people who had gathered were not there during the incident, claiming that at one point he looks around and asks himself if he, his brother and his brother's wife are the only ones seeing what is going on. He states he sees no one else on the road, outside their apartments or on their balconies.

While reviewing the start of the incident at the SUV, the witness states he sees Michael Brown right at the driver's door, with one or maybe two hands or arms within the vehicle, and his head above the height of the door frame and above the roof of the SUV.

The witness, when furthered questioned, states that Dorian Johnson, during the encounter, has moved to the north side of Canfield Drive and is positioned near a tree on the sidewalk. He indicates he recognizes Dorian Johnson as someone he sees all the time. Following the first shot, he states that Johnson flees west towards West Florissant. He further speculates that Johnson gets into a white car which is stopped on Canfield and heading west towards West Florissant. However, he adds that he does not see Johnson get into the white car, only run westward down the sidewalk, after which the white car drives off in the same direction. He does state that Johnson then returns sometime later and exits the white car with a female companion over by the apartments by Caddiefield Road.

As part of his final statement, Witness #14 states, "He (Brown) didn't have [his hands] all the way up, but he did have them up enough...this officer knew he was not threatening him, he was not in imminent danger. He was not charging. He was struggling to stay on his feet."

SECOND INTERVIEW WITH THE FEDERAL ATTORNEY FROM THE DEPARTMENT OF JUSTICE AND A SPECIAL AGENT

This second interview takes place on September 24, 2014 at 10:10 am. The attorney acknowledges in the opening statement that Witness #14 has previously spoken with the county police. The attorney states the objective of the second interview is to distinguish details the witness knows versus those that he might have been assumed or heard from others. The interview concludes at 11:48 am.

According to Witness #14, he assumes Officer Wilson stopped his vehicle and said something to Michael Brown and Dorian Johnson, at which time he sees Michael Brown approach the driver's door of the SUV. The witness emphasizes that his perspective is from the passenger side of the vehicle. He then states that Brown and the officer appear to engage in "tussling". Following further questioning by the federal attorney, the witness states he sees Michael Brown's head above the roof of the SUV and then it ducks down and out of his sight for a brief period of time. He claims from his vantage point, Brown's head is clearly not inside the driver's side window of the truck, but is at the same level and in close proximity to the head of Officer Wilson. He then states that he cannot tell if any part of Brown's torso or upper body is inside of the SUV, nor can he tell if it isn't. He acknowledges both Brown's hands and arm are through the window, and that from what he can see, there is a physical confrontation taking place. Officer Wilson's upper body is clearly visible to him, and it is rocking back and forth as if there is a "tug of war" going on.

The attorney then asks the witness as to the amount of time which lapses between the first shot, fired while Officer Wilson is still in the vehicle, and the time he exits the vehicle. The witness states it is a matter of two or three seconds, but there is a noticeable expanse between the two events.

Continuing, the witness states that Michael Brown runs east, at first down the middle of Canfield Drive and then over towards the north side of the street and to the intersection with Coppercreek Court. The officer, meanwhile, exits the police SUV, moves towards the rear, and then to the rear bumper on the passenger side. A step or two away from the vehicle and towards Michael Brown's position on or near the sidewalk on the north side of Canfield Drive, Officer Wilson stops and assumes a defensive posture, pointing his weapon at Brown. According to Witness #14, he has not fired the weapon since leaving the vehicle.

The witness then states that as soon as Michael Brown takes one step off of the sidewalk, and after which Office Wilson directs him to stop, the officer fires three shots. He further states that Michael Brown is in the process of giving up: "We are looking at him. He is giving up. But then as soon as he stepped on the street … he (Wilson) fired three shots." Upon further prompting, the witness then says that Brown may have taken as many as three steps.

Continuing, the witness states that after the first volley, Brown takes a step back and then staggers as if trying to stay on his feet. He further states that Brown looks down at himself and then back towards the officer. He says at this time, he and those with whom he is gathered (brother, sister-in-law, and a third person), are telling Brown to "stop dude", but they don't believe they could have been heard from that distance. He then states that his sister-in-law makes the comment "They are getting ready to kill him." At this time, Michael Brown is staggering forward, his arms out ahead of him and his knees buckling, with his head lowered and ready to fall, and that is when, according to the witness, Officer Wilson fires the second string of about four shots. Brown falls to the pavement face first with his hands and arms to his side.

At this point, the attorney informs the witness that he/she would like to review the details provided in the first interview in relation to the details provided here in the second.

At this time, the witness describes the angle of Michael Brown's upper torso during the second string of shots as bent 45° to the pavement and his hands coming slowly down. He then states that Michael Brown has been effectively stopped at that point and that his forward movement towards Officer Wilson is due to staggering while attempting to stay on his feet. He states Michael Brown's head is bent, but his focus remains on Officer Wilson, and that Brown is already on his way down to the pavement when Officer Wilson fires the final volley.

In response to the rumors that spread within minutes of the shooting, the witness states that it is not true that the officer shoots Brown in the back, Brown's hands are high in the air, Brown has taken Officer Wilson's gun, Brown is shot while on his knees, or that Officer Wilson walks up and shoots Brown in the back of the head while he is prone on the pavement.

In his final summary, Witness #14 states that Michael Brown stops, turns, steps one foot back onto Canfield Drive, and then a second foot. When his second foot hits the pavement, Officer Wilson starts to shoot. Brown stops, then starts to stagger forward. At this time, still maintaining his defensive posture, Officer Wilson takes three steps back from his position. Officer Wilson then starts to fire again. Michael Brown falls flat on his face, his arms limp to his side.

INTERVIEW WITH THE GRAND JURY, VOLUME 8

The interview with the Grand Jury takes place on September 30, 2014 at 11:33. Prior to the formal start of the interview, Witness #14 verifies that he lives in a second floor apartment on the south side of Canfield Drive. His apartment has a clear and unobstructed view of Canfield Drive both from his front door, which he accesses from wooden stairs to a small porch, and his second floor balcony, which is a communal balcony.

According to the witness, he is in his apartment, and at the same time that his brother and sister-in-law arrive—his brother's truck is pulling into the complex, his attention is drawn to two men walking down the middle of the street exchanging dialogue with some plumbers working nearby. In response to the attorney's query, he states they are walking towards West Florissant. (It is probable that the witness is simply agreeing with the attorney at this time since it has been established that Brown and Johnson were coming from West Florissant and heading east. At the end of the interview, the attorney shows the witness photographs of the scene which shows the police SUV was heading west and the two boys east. She then infers that it was the witness who made the mistake. However, in his previous interviews, his perspective regarding the general movement of both the two boys and the SUV is correct and does not vary.)

The witness goes on to say that his brother arrives, parks and exits his vehicle just ahead of the arrival on scene of the police SUV. He states that when his brother exits his vehicle, he hears Officer Wilson say something to Michael Brown and Dorian Johnson, but that he is too far away to hear what it is. In addition, the witness states he is at this time out of his apartment and on his porch at his front door. He then sees the police SUV roll past Brown and Johnson and then stop and roll back towards them, cutting off their path. His perspective is from the passenger side of the police SUV and looking through the passenger side window into the cab.

Once the officer's vehicle stops, the witness states that Michael Brown is saying something, and then he approaches the driver's door of the SUV. He says that it is his brother that first notices the tussling. At this point, Dorian has backed up onto the sidewalk. Shortly after, they hear the first shot. Dorian then runs to the north side of the street and Michael runs east towards Coppercreek Court. The officer exits the vehicle, moves towards the rear of the vehicle and then across to the bumper on the passenger side, where he takes three or four steps forward in the direction in which Michael Brown runs, and he assumes a defensive posture, stopping and pointing his gun. At this point, Michael has stopped and is standing at the intersection of Canfield and Coppercreek. He has one foot on the grass on the sidewalk and the other on the pavement of Coppercreek. He is looking down at himself.

As Officer Wilson maintains his defensive posture, Michael Brown slowly turns counter-clockwise (to his left) to face Wilson, raising his hands palms forward and approximately shoulder level. Officer Wilson directs Brown to stop. Brown responds by taking a few steps into Canfield Drive. Officer Wilson again directs him to stop and then fires three shots. At this point, Brown stops for a moment and then begins to stagger forward in the direction of Officer Wilson. His hands have not changed position. He is approximately 30-35 feet from Officer Wilson. (The attorney later states that it is 48'2" from the intersection of Canfield and Coppercreek where Michael Brown stops running to the spot in the middle of Canfield where his body falls.)

At this time, Officer Wilson takes three steps back from his position. Three times he tells Michael Brown to stop [moving]. Brown's head is down, he is bent forward at the waist, and his knees are wobbling. Officer Wilson fires four more times. Michael Brown falls forward on his face.

Asked by the attorney as to Officer Wilson's actions following the shooting, the witness states that he is distracted by his sister-in-law, but when he looks again, Officer Wilson has moved away from the body and towards his SUV. There is a second officer already on the scene. He further states that no one moves or disturbs the body.

At the close of the interview, the witness is asked and answers, in his opinion, Michael Brown is disabled by the first round of shots, is not charging towards Officer Wilson, and is not acting in a threatening manner towards Officer Wilson.

ANALYSIS AND INTERPRETATION

MICHAEL BROWN'S HANDS AND ARMS

The primary focus of the questioning by the detectives and attorneys following the first interview by Witness #14 is the location of Michael Brown's hands once he stops running at the intersection of Canfield and Coppercreek and turns to face Officer Wilson. Though it does not bear-out in the text above, the line of question infers that the witness changes his initial statement with regard to the direction of Michael Brown's palms, but not the height at which he has raised his hands.

The witness, however, maintains without variance that Brown's palms are facing Officer Wilson, and at no time does he state, as suggested by the attorney, that Brown's palms are facing skyward or in towards himself. It is uncertain what it is that the attorney is attempting to establish, but it is fair to say he is suggesting a correlation between the direction and elevation of the hands and a gesture which would be clearly interpreted as surrender or compliance.

However, with regard to this same topic, It is also worth noting, at no time does the witness state Michael Brown has his arms or hands in a position that suggests he is surrendering. However, Witness #14 does describe the action as an attempt to balance while staggering, and suggests that the position of Brown's hands by his waist is a response to having been shot, and not to be interpreted as going for a weapon.

MICHAEL BROWN'S MOVEMENT

The second concern is the witness' estimation of the number of steps Michael Brown takes from the moment he stops and turns to face Officer Wilson, the length of those steps, and the aggressiveness with which they are taken.

According to the witness, his estimation changes depending on the reaction of the interviewer. He initially states that Michael Brown takes only a single step; he then modifies his recall to say a step with one foot to the pavement and then the other; and then modifies his statement a third time, saying the number of steps from the curb are sufficient to bring him out onto Canfield Drive. The witness then continues to insist from the point that Officer Wilson fires the first string of shots to the firing of the second, Michael Brown only manages to stagger a few feet, but he does, in his statement of September 30, 2014, state that Brown, after getting his balance, walks several steps towards Officer Wilson. In addition, he does estimate the distance to be 35', which is a close approximation to the actual distance of 48', which he learns from the attorney.

LOCATION OF OFFICER WILSON

Witness #14 consistently places Officer Wilson in proximity to the rear of the police SUV when he delivers the first string of shots. Doing so, he makes no mention of the three cars that are halted in the road and immediately to the east of the police SUV. However, it is understood that Officer Wilson is actually in the area of the second of those three cars when he first fires. In addition, he places Officer Wilson at upwards of 30 feet away from Michael Brown when he fatally shots him, while the actual distance is closer to 8-10 feet.

While the omission of secondary details and inaccurate estimations of distance are consistent throughout the statements of all of the witnesses, combined with other elements of Witness #14's statement, it is not unreasonable to speculate that he sees certain events of the incident and is compensating for what he might have missed with details from conversation with his brother, his sister-in-law, and other members of the complex.

FAMILY MEMBERS

Although from the first interview to the last, the witness' brother figures more prominently in his response, it should be noted that in his original interview, the witness expresses a concern for protecting the identity of his brother and keeping him out of the process. In addition, his sister-in-law, in his statement to the Grand Jury, infers that Witness #14 is unreliable due to his age, and she states that he did not come out of his apartment during the incident, but remained at the door, and thereby inferring he doesn't see the full sequence of events. This statement bears up to a degree based on the first statement by Witness #14 in which he states he first notices Brown and Johnson while in his bedroom. He does, however, state in the second interview the he also notices his brother's vehicle approaching at this time, and goes to the front door in anticipation of greeting him. Contrary to his sister-in-law's assertion, he states he does go out on his porch and to the railing. While collectively these details seem insignificant, a defense attorney will connect the statements of all three family members and emphasize the discrepancies.

PERSPECTIVE

Witness #14 is credible in as much as his statement concerning the incident itself does not vary from one interview to the next, and in as much as he consistently provides for the sequence of events as they are most generally believed to have occurred. In addition, his interpretation of Michael Brown's actions during his final moments—staggering, falling, non-threatening—allow for the speculation that Officer Wilson, at that point, acts with excessive force.

The concern remains, however, how much of the incident did Witness #14 actually see and how much of the details he provides are a compilation of the conversations he has had since with his brother, his sister-in-law, and his neighbors, or information he has gleaned from the media.

WITNESS #17

INTERVIEW WITH THE GRAND JURY, VOLUME 9

The interview with Witness #17 takes place on October 2, 2014, at approximately 1:07 pm. The procedure is conducted by Alizadeh and Whirley. All 12 jurists are present. Witness #17 is in his black colored SUV with his wife and heading eastbound on Canfield Drive coming off of West Florissant. It is approximately 12-12:30 pm. The day is sunny. His destination is the Canfield Green Apartments. He is going to visit his brother, who is a resident on the north side of the street and up on the second floor.

According the witness, as he enters the parking lot on Canfield Court, he observes both Michael Brown and Dorian Johnson walking in the center of Canfield Drive and Officer Wilson's police SUV moving west bound. The witness states he then parks his vehicle and he and his wife make their way over to the stairs leading to his brother's apartment and begin to ascend.

Continuing, the witness states he observes Officer Wilson slow his vehicle and briefly engage Brown and Johnson. Brown and Johnson continue to walk eastbound. The witness notes there is a white vehicle to the back of Officer Wilson's SUV. The witness then states that Officer Wilson moves momentarily forward, but then reverses his vehicle, and stopping at an angle, blocks the path of Brown and Johnson. The witness estimates a time frame of approximately 10-15 seconds.

From the moments Officer Wilson reengages Brown and Johnson and the witness reaches his brother's second floor porch, Brown and Wilson have already engaged physically. However, due to his perspective from the passenger side of the vehicle and the time he is climbing the stairs, the witness does not see if Brown reaches in to Wilson or Wilson grabs out at Brown. He states only that the vehicle is rocking and he could tell something was going on. He then hears a gun shot, and approximately 15-20 seconds later, a second gun shot. (The witness states between the first and second shots, he, his wife and brother momentarily take refuge in the house. They come back out after the second shot and there is a discernible pause in the shooting.)

At this point, the witness observes Michael Brown move from the vehicle and begin to run east on Canfield Drive. Brown gets as far as Coppercreek Court, where he stops running and looks down at the left palm of his hand or his left side.

While Brown is moving east on Canfield, Officer Wilson exits his vehicle and is in pursuit of Michael Brown. He moves towards the back of the police SUV, and at a distance approximately 20 meters (65'), he assumes a defensive stance with his gun raised and pointed at Michael Brown.

According to the witness, Michael Brown then turns and with his hands by his waist and palms forward starts back towards the middle of the street and towards Officer Wilson. (His pace, according to the witness, is a normal walking pace and not charging.) Within the first few steps, Officer Wilson fires at least one shot. Michael Brown stops momentarily and then continues multiple additional steps towards Officer Wilson, a distance of 5-10 yards. Officer Wilson fires four to six more times, and Michael Brown falls to the pavement. At no time does the witness hear either Wilson or Brown say anything.

ANALYSIS AND INTERPRETATION

It is not possible to examine this witness' statement independent from the statement of Witness #14, his brother, or Witness #18, his wife. First, they are all present together at the time of the incident and have the same perspective—at least there on the second floor porch. Second, they acknowledge that they discuss with each other their individual perceptions of the incident and its specific events.

This said, there are two statements by the witness that standout as interesting. The first is that he does not hear Officer Wilson give any verbal directives to Michael Brown. The second is that he states Officer Wilson holds his ground while firing the second volley.

In his multiple statements, Witness #14 states that he is standing beside both his brother and his sister-in-law during the entirety of the incident. He states he hears Officer Wilson direct Michael Brown to stop at least three times. In addition, he states that as Michael Brown is moving towards Officer Wilson prior to the fatal shots, Officer Wilson is retreating, and it is in the process of retreating, or shortly thereafter, that Officer Wilson fires the fatal shots.

It would seem, that given their proximity, if Witness #14 clearly hears Officer Wilson shout "stop", not once, but at least three times, that Witness #17, too, would have heard it. As for the witness not accounting for any backward steps by Officer Wilson, it is reasonable to conclude that his attention is fixed on Michael Brown at that time, or as his statement logically infers, he may have been verbally engaged with his wife—as he claims, and therefore doesn't notice.

Nevertheless, it is puzzling that neither Alizadeh, Whirley, nor any of the jurists ask either of the brothers for clarification on either point.

Witness #17 is credible. His account of the incident is consistent with the events of the incident, the sequence of those events, and the chronology of those events as supported by other witnesses and the forensic evidence as it pertains to the events, their sequence and chronology.

WITNESS #18

INTERVIEW WITH THE GRAND JURY, VOLUME 10

The interview with Witness #18 and the Grand Jury takes place on the morning of October 6, 2014. A specific time is not provided. The witness is the wife of Witness #17. She is with her husband on August 9, 2014, at the time of the incident.

According to Witness #18, she and her husband first encounter Michael Brown and Dorian Johnson while they are driving east bound on Canfield Drive and in the vicinity of the Canfield Green Apartments. Brown and Johnson are in the middle of the road, and outside of being mindful of their presence, the witness does not pay any particular attention to either one of them. She states they are simply two boys not doing what they should be doing, meaning walking on the sidewalk. The witness states that once passed Brown and Johnson, her husband turns onto Caddiefield Road.

Continuing, the witness infers her husband parks the car, they exit and move towards the brother's second floor apartment. (The residents consider units below ground as the first floor; there are actually two floors of units completely above ground. The brother's apartment is one flight of stairs above ground level.) The witness states that going up the stairs, she observes the vehicle of Officer Wilson traveling west on Canfield Drive. She states that as she is up on the patio, the vehicle slows and there is interaction between Officer Wilson and Brown and Johnson. The interaction lasts less than a minute. Brown and Johnson continue walking east. The police SUV proceeds a short distance forward, and then stops and backs up to reengage Brown and Johnson. It stops on an angle ahead of Brown and Johnson, so that Brown and Johnson are even with the driver's door. The vehicle does not squeal or screech. In addition, the witness states that her brother-in-law is at this time inside his apartment.

At this point, the witness is asked by the attorney as to the perspective she has of Officer Wilson's vehicle. She says she is viewing the incident looking down on the driver's side.

Continuing, the witness makes no reference to any struggle going on between Officer Wilson and Michael Brown. She states only that she hears two shots. Michael Brown backs away from the vehicle and moves towards the rear. He then starts to run towards Coppercreek Court. He reaches the grass there at the sidewalk and stops. He then looks down at his hand. He then turns around and starts "going back towards the police officer".

According to the witness, as Michael Brown is moving towards Coppercreek Court, Officer Wilson exits his vehicle in pursuit. He is walking quickly. His gun is drawn, held in two hands, and extended out before him and in the direction of Michael Brown. Officer Wilson then assumes a defensive posture, which he maintains throughout the remainder of the confrontation.

At this point, Michael Brown, still in the vicinity of the intersection of Coppercreek Court and Canfield Drive, steps fully onto Canfield Drive, and with his hands raised to shoulder level, out to his side, and with the palms down, moves back towards the middle of the street and in the direction of Officer Wilson. Officer Wilson fires three to four shots. Michael Brown continues to walk towards Officer Wilson. At a point when Brown is approximately 20' from Officer Wilson, Officer Wilson fires three to four more shots. Michael Brown collapses face first to the ground. The witness further states there are no shots fired while Michael Brown is running from the vehicle or after he collapses. She states there are two strings of shots following the two shots at the vehicle, and that there is a definitive pause between the two strings.

The witness also states that her brother-in-law is inside during the incident and infers he only sees part of it.

ANALYSIS AND INTERPRETATION

Witness #18 is probably the most reliable and credible witness to the incident. Throughout the interview, she steers clear of embellishment, acknowledges when she is making assumptions, acknowledges when there is a question relative to something she did not notice or see, and sticks to only the details she recalls clearly.

In addition, unlike both her husband and brother-in-law, she rightly identifies her line of sight as to the driver's side of the vehicle. She understands that regardless of the angle on which the police SUV came to a stop—which from her brother-in-law's apartment would suggest they are looking at the passenger side, in terms of which way the SUV is facing—west bound on Canfield, and the location of the apartment—the south side of Canfield, the driver's side remains to the left. While this recognition does not indicate she is telling the truth or accurately describing the incident, it does indicate she has an eye for detail and the ability to orient herself—both of which are useful when reporting as a witness.

The witness' statement is the most consistent in terms of the most probable sequence of events and their chronology.

THE MONTE CARLO

THE SETTING

The Monte Carlo is driven by Witness #32. Witness #13 is a passenger. The vehicle encounters Officer Wilson's police SUV east of the incident and is still trailing behind it when the confrontation between Wilson and Brown begins. The two occupants of the car have a front row seat, as it were, but as the first shots are fired, duck down to the seat, after which it becomes questionable as to the sequence of events they actually witness. However, they do have a face-to-face encounter with Dorian Johnson which places parts of Johnson's statements in doubt.

WITNESS #13

INTERVIEW WITH THE ST. LOUIS COUNTY POLICE DEPARTMENT

Witness #13 is an African-American male. He is interviewed by the St. Louis County Police Department on August 22, 2014, at 12:56 pm. The interview takes place in a conference room at the St. Louis Chapter of the NAACP. The procedure is conducted by a detective from the Bureau of Crimes Against Persons. Also present are two additional detectives from the police department and two agents from the FBI.

Witness #13 is the passenger in the white Monte Carlo that Dorian Johnson attempts to enter during the incident.

The interview concludes at 1:36 pm.

According to Witness #13, he is in a white Monte Carlo being driven by a female companion. They are heading west on Canfield Drive, having come from the Northwinds Apartments. It is approximately 11:55 pm. As they head out of the complex, a police SUV, moving "like real quick" comes up upon them and then by-passes them. Moments later, the witness states that they see Officer Wilson stopped in the road and talking to Michael Brown and Dorian Johnson. The witness states, "I guess they didn't comply or what not. I guess he (Officer Wilson) said stop."

The Monte Carlo comes to a stop just east of Canfield Court. There is no other vehicle between the Monte Carlo and Officer Wilson's SUV.

From his location, Witness #13 describes the SUV as parked diagonally. He uses the term caddie-cornered. Michael Brown is up at the window. Dorian is to Brown's back. (The witness then makes the statement that Dorian Johnson was saying [Officer Wilson] pushed the door up on [Michael Brown].) Dorian, according to the witness, looks scared, kind of stumbled and then ran off to the south side of the road.

From the angle he has, the witness can see only beneath the SUV to the driver's side. He sees Michael Brown's feet moving as if he's dancing and reports that the truck is rocking back and forth. He assumes there is an altercation taking place. The altercation lasts about 15 to 20 seconds, at which point the witness hears a gunshot.

At this point, the witness states that he tells his female companion to back the car up and open the doors. He's afraid they are in harm's way. By the time the car again stops, Michael Brown is running past the driver's side, breathing hard, and seemingly having lost one of his flip-flops. The witness hears a second shot and he ducks his head down towards the seat. He doesn't know where Officer Wilson is at this time. However, he reports Dorian Johnson is suddenly there beside the passenger door of the Monte Carlo, inferring only that Dorian has run from wherever he was and over to the car. Four to six seconds later, the witness sees Officer Wilson walk by the driver's side of the Monte Carlo. He is carrying his duty weapon. It is down by his side.

At this point, Witness #13 states that he is looking out the back window of the Monte Carlo and his companion is looking out the rearview mirror. While he's watching, he presumes Officer Wilson says something to Brown— although he doesn't hear it, because Brown stops, and turns "with his hands kinda up...they didn't go fully up." However, Brown then flinches and lowers his hands. The witness hears three shots, after which Brown falls. The witness further states that Michael Brown at no time moves away from the center of the road, and is at all times in proximity to the double yellow line. In addition, he states he sees Michael Brown go no further east then the point in the road where he falls. He states Officer Wilson was approximately 15 yards from Brown at the time he hears the three shots.

Between the time of the second shot and the three shots, Dorian Johnson is crouched down by the Monte Carlo. He attempts to get into the car and asks for a ride. The witness states he tells Dorian that he doesn't know him, and he does not let him into the car. He then tells his companion to leave. She moves the car around Officer Wilson's SUV and continues west on Canfield. At this time, the witness states, he observes the arrival of two additional Ferguson police vehicles.

ANALYSIS AND INTERPRETATION

AT THE POLICE SUV

Early in his statement, Witness #13, while referencing the confrontation at the police SUV, attributes a statement to Dorian Johnson, a person, who up to the time of the incident, he says he does not know and has never seen. This statement, then, immediately suggests that the witness has since spoken to others about the incident, or at the least, as he acknowledges, has watched or read related news stories. For the remainder of his statement, then, it is reasonable to question whether the details he provides are those that he actually witnessed or are they details he learned at a later time.

However, the witness does substantiate that Dorian Johnson distances himself from Officer Wilson's vehicle much sooner in the sequence of events than he himself reports, and as far away as beyond the sidewalk on the south side of the street and to the passenger side of the SUV.

SEQUENCE OF EVENTS

There are two specific events during the incident which Witness #13 omits or provides out of proper sequence. The first is the timing of the second shot. The second is the point at which Michael Brown stops and turns.

The witness clearly states that he is in position to observe the incident from the moment Officer Wilson backs up the SUV. However, he reports the second shot doesn't take place until after Michael Brown runs past the Monte Carlo. Forensic evidence, as well as statements from other witnesses, including Officer Wilson, indicate the first two shots occur while Officer Wilson is still in the vehicle, and while Michael Brown is there beside the driver's side window. How is it, then, that the witness hears one shot but not the other?

Further, the witness states multiple times that Michael Brown stops, turns with his arms up, and is fatally shot there in the middle of Canfield Drive;

he fails to provide for Brown's proximity to Coppercreek Court; and, he makes no mention of the two separate strings of shots fired by Officer Wilson.

It is reasonable to conclude, therefore, that Witness #13 spent a longer period of time ducked down in his vehicle than he thought, looks up and out the back window of the Monte Carlo in time to witness the second string of shots, and fills in the missing sequences using details he learns at a later time.

PERSPECTIVE

Witness #13 is credible relative to the sequence of events which he actually sees. However, as he acknowledges he spends most of his time ducked down in his vehicle and in a position in which he cannot see what is happening around him, his statements in terms of the Grand Jury's task to indict or not are largely irrelevant. There is also the concern that by the time the witness is first interviewed, almost two weeks following the incident, that his statement is skewed by details he has learned since then. Multiple times, for example, he prefaces his statements with the word "guess; and at least once, he relates something that he obviously hears from Dorian Johnson himself, whether first-person or via the media. In terms of the task presented to the Grand Jury, his statements are non-conclusive.

WITNESS #32

INTERVIEW WITH THE ST. LOUIS COUNTY POLICE DEPARTMENT

The interview with Witness #32 takes place at 6:40 pm on August 9, 2014. It is conducted by a detective with the Bureau of Crimes Against Persons. The assumption is that the interview is conducted at the residence of the witness, a female African-American that claims to have been driving in her vehicle immediately behind the police SUV driven by Officer Wilson, and to have been present at the point when the officer comes in contact with Michael Brown and Dorian Johnson. The interview concludes at 6:49 pm.

According to Witness #32, she has just left her apartment and is westbound on Canfield Drive and in the direction of West Florissant. She states she notices two young men walking along the yellow dividing line in the middle of Canfield Drive, heading into the apartment complex (towards Glen Owen) and coming from the direction of West Florissant. The vehicle driving in front of her is a Ferguson Police Department SUV.

As the police vehicle nears the two young men walking in the middle of the street, the two young men fail to yield. The witness states that the police vehicle stops alongside the two men and almost immediately a physical confrontation ensues between Michael Brown and Officer Wilson. She states that from the angle she has all she can see are Michael Brown's feet, but by the way the cab of the SUV is rocking back and forth, she assumes there is a physical struggle. In addition, she at this time notes that Dorian Johnson, who she describes as 'kinda short, kinda skinny … with dreads", is positioned to the front of and at a distance from the police SUV.

The witness reports she then hears a single gunshot. She notes that Michael Brown backs straight away from the driver's door of the police SUV. He has a surprised look on his face. She further states that Officer Wilson is still in the front seat of his vehicle and infers that the door is closed.

At this point, according to the witness, both Brown and Johnson start to run east. Officer Wilson then exits his vehicle. While Brown runs past the witness' vehicle, Johnson attempts to enter the witness' vehicle, but is unsuccessful.

According to the witness, following the first shot, she ducks down in her vehicle. However, she then sits up and looks into her rearview mirror. She sees Michael Brown to the rear of her vehicle. He is facing Officer Wilson. She states that Officer Wilson has run past her vehicle and he too is in her rearview mirror. She states she sees his back.

At this point she hears three more shots, after which Michael Brown hits the ground. The witness then states that she drives off heading west, and in the process almost runs head on into an arriving police vehicle, and instead drives up on the grass along the sidewalk on the south side of the road.

INTERVIEW WITH THE GRAND JURY, VOLUME 12

The Grand Jury interview with Witness #32 takes place on October 13, 2014, at approximately 11:03 am. The interview is conducted by Alizadeh and Whirley. All 12 jurists are present. It is also noted that the interview with the Grand Jury takes place before the interview with the FBI (below), which takes place that same evening.

According to Witness #32, she and her passenger, an unidentified male, are going for a leisurely drive. She identifies her car as a 1999, two-door white Monte Carlo. She states she is headed west on Canfield Drive, and as she is coming over the bridge, a police SUV driving at a normal speed and without his emergency lights on pulls in front of her from a side street.

As she is proceeding westbound on Canfield Drive, she notices two men walking in the middle of the street and in close proximity to the yellow dividing lines that run down the center. She describes Michael Brown as being considerably taller and larger than Dorian Johnson. She states Brown is wearing khaki-colored shorts and a baseball cap, dark in color. She describes Johnson's dreads.

Then the police SUV slows and stops in the middle of the road. The witness infers that Brown and Johnson continue walking as if ignoring whatever it is that Officer Wilson is saying to them at the time. Wilson then puts the SUV in reverse and comes back towards Brown and Johnson, braking the SUV at an angle and causing both Brown and Johnson to jump back and away from the vehicle.

The witness states the physical confrontation between Brown and Wilson, which she again describes only as the SUV rocking and having a view of Brown's feet tapping on the pavement, occurs almost immediately. She does not see his head. She then states that she hears a single shot. Michael Brown then moves away from the window of the police SUV and comes fully into view, according to the witness.

As Michael Brown runs past the car of the witness to the driver's side, the witness begins to duck her head to the passenger's seat. While her head is ducked down, she hears a second shot. She also states that due to her head lowered, she does not see Officer Wilson exit the truck. When she is again looking, she says Officer Wilson is running straight down the street. His weapon is drawn. She then looks in her rearview mirror. (There is no other car behind her.) Michael Brown is turned around and facing Officer Wilson. His hands are raised, but not all the way up. The witness hears three shots. Michael Brown falls.

At this point, Whirley and Alizadeh question the witness for clarity on specific details.

At a distance of about three to four car lengths, according to the witness, Michael Brown is turned so that she can see his face. He is raising his hands, palms out, but they are not all the way up. He is not moving towards the officer, neither walking nor charging. She then hears two or three more shots. Brown falls to the ground face first. Shortly after Brown falls, the witness states she drives off, almost collides head on with the arriving police vehicle, and ultimately steers up onto the curb on the south side of Canfield Drive. She then leaves the scene.

Upon further questioning, the witness acknowledges blacking out, but says it was only for an instant. She describes the incident as losing focus. The witness acknowledges that during this period of time, she is not aware of her surroundings or what is going on. She further states that she does not know if she lost consciousness, but that the episode lasts only one or two seconds.

INTERVIEW WITH THE FBI

The records show that Witness #32 is interviewed by the FBI on October 13, 2014, at 6:26 pm. The interview is conducted by a special agent and an attorney from the Department of Justice. The interview takes place at the FBI building at 2222 Market Place.

According to Witness #32, she has just left her apartment and is driving in her car, accompanied by a male friend she identifies only by first name, saying she doesn't recall his last name. She states she is driving behind a police SUV and is required to slow her speed when it came to a stop. She then goes on to state there is a physical confrontation between the police officer driving the vehicle and Michael Brown. She does not see the actual confrontation, but instead identifies the vehicle rocking back and forth and Michael Brown's feet "tapping" upon the pavement. During the confrontation, Dorian Johnson is out ahead of the front of the SUV and appears undecided as to whether he should keep his distance or come to the aid of Michael Brown.

The witness then reports hearing a shot. She then observes Michael Brown distance himself back from the driver's door of the police SUV. Then both Brown and Johnson start to run. Michael Brown runs past her vehicle. Moments later, Officer Wilson exits his vehicle and runs towards the witness's car. The witness states later in the interview that when Wilson runs past her car he already has his weapon drawn and pointed in the direction of Michael Brown.

According to the witness, she then immediately ducks her head down towards the passenger seat, which is occupied by her male passenger, and practically puts her head in his lap. She then states that she blacks out for a period of time. She also states upon questioning that at no time does she open the driver's door of the car, but that her passenger does open the passenger's door, and at one point he is actually hanging out of the car.

While her head is down, and the passenger door is open, she states that Dorian Johnson, ducking low and practically crawling, comes to the passenger door, gets partially into the car and asks the witness if she can get him out of there because it's crazy. She states her only response to him is to get down, and that he eventually moves away from her vehicle. She does not know where he goes from there.

When further questioned by the special agent, Witness #32 states that she hears the first shot while Officer Wilson is in the police vehicle and then three more shots while she has recovered from her blackout moment and is looking in her rearview mirror, and this is after Johnson comes to and leaves the vehicle. She states Michael Brown falls as a result of these three shots.

According to Witness #32, while she is looking in her rearview mirror, she observes Michael Brown stop running and "he's turned around". She then hears two or three more shots and Michael Brown goes to the ground. When asked further, the witness states that if there are other prior shots, they probably occur while she is blacked out.

ANALYSIS AND INTERPRETATION

The two key statements provided by Witness #32 are one, she "blacked out" for a period of time, and two, the number of shots she reports hearing and when. It is also interesting that she omits the presence of her passenger in the first interview and states she doesn't know his last name in the second interview.

AT THE POLICE SUV

While the witness' statement doesn't provide much detail about the confrontation between Brown and Wilson at the SUV, it does confirm that one does take place. It is also worth noting that the witness confirms that as the SUV is rocking back and forth Michael Browns' head is below the height of the vehicle, supporting the statements of other witnesses that his upper torso is at the least in position to be within the vehicle, as are his hands and arms.

THE BLACKOUT PERIOD

In her first statement, the witness mentions that she blacks-out and that this black-out period lasts for a measurable amount of time. She also states that while blacked-out—unconscious—she is unaware of any shots other than those that result in Michael Brown falling.

However, in her second statement, she changes her recollection of the events and states that she is only unaware for a second or two, and when she again looks up, she sees Michael Brown still running and then he is turned around and facing Officer Wilson.

In her third statement, which she makes only 6 hours after the second, she infers that she actually sees Michael Brown stop running and then turn around. She insists that she doesn't really black out, but only loses track of time for a matter of seconds.

Regardless, the witness clearly associates the moment she looks in her rearview mirror with the string of shots that kill Michael Brown, which indicates beyond a doubt that she does not see Michael Brown run as far as Coppercreek Court, does not see any of his movements at this time, and does not hear the first string of shots fired by Officer Wilson. The only conclusion, therefore, is that her head is down at this time, that she is not consciously aware of her surroundings, and that this lack of conscious awareness lasts for more than the second or two she claims.

THE SHOTS

It is clear that having blacked-out for a period of time that the witness inaccurately describes the actual sequence of events. The second shot she hears and associates with Officer Wilson pursuing Brown is actually the last shot of the first string he fires while Michael Brown is coming off of the curb at Coppercreek. The witness then sees the second string of shots, and that is when Brown falls.

A careful examination of the witness' statements reveals that she never actually says she sees Brown turn around, but instead that he is "turned around". It is the poor framing of the questions by the FBI agents, particularly, and their rephrasing of the witness' responses that fail to distinguish the difference.

PERSPECTIVE

While the testimony of Witness #32 provides clarification as to the color of the Monte Carlo, which others report as being blue or black, and the whereabouts of Dorian Johnson as the first rounds are being fired by Officer Wilson, her statements regarding the movements of Wilson and Brown from the moment they leave the SUV until the time Brown is fatally shot is unreliable as hearsay. She, therefore, is of no use to the Grand Jury in determining whether Brown does or does not act threateningly towards Officer Wilson, or whether or not Officer Wilson's choice to use deadly force is warranted.

HANDY MAN AND CONSTRUCTION WORKERS

WITNESS #10

INTERVIEW AT ST. LOUIS COUNTY POLICE DEPARTMENT

This interview takes place on August 11, 2012, at 11:39 am. Witness #10 is a black male. He states he is employed at a business located in a nearby industrial park, but that he is at the Canfield Apartments doing handyman work for an acquaintance at the time of the incident. His appearance at the police department is unscheduled. He self-reports to inform the police of information he has relative to the incident. He states his reason for coming forward is the amount of misinformation and false reporting which he is routinely hearing out on the streets, most of which is inconsistent with the incident as he witnesses it. He further states that he is hesitant about coming forward due to the degree of anger and verbally aggressive behavior to which he is subjected while at the scene of the incident and while taking his leave, and following sharing what he sees with some of those who have gathered. He states he is showered with racial epitaphs and with veiled threats as to his safety.

The desk officer immediately escorts him to meet with two detectives, both with the Bureau of Crimes Against Persons. The interview concludes at 12:16 pm.

According to Witness #10, he is working a side job doing repairs for a female resident of the Canfield Apartments. Physically, he is located in a parking field west of the incident on the south side of Canfield Drive, and proximate to a large open field to the west of the apartment building in which he is working.

He first notices Michael Brown and Dorian Johnson walking on the south side of Canfield Drive, coming from the direction of West Florissant and heading east along Canfield Drive. He states that his attention is drawn to the two boys due to Michael Brown's physical size. He states they pass within arm's reach of him. He then leaves the area to bring tools inside the apartment complex.

The witness then returns outside to retrieve additional tools and that is when he notices both the police SUV and Michael Brown in the same vicinity.

The police SUV is east of his position, front end pointed west, and parked on a slant in the middle of Canfield Drive. He states that Michael Brown is leaning in through the driver's side window of the SUV and appears to be involved in some sort of physical struggle. He then reports hearing a single shot fired, after which Michael Brown starts to run east along the middle of Canfield Drive. His first impression is that Michael Brown shot the officer. He attributes this impression to the approximately six seconds that he believes elapse before Officer Wilson exits the vehicle. He later adds that he thinks he hears something metallic hit the pavement once Michael Brown starts to run.

When Officer Wilson does exit the vehicle, he has his weapon drawn. He then begins pursuit of Michael Brown, who by this time "was quite a distance." Witness #10 then states that Michael Brown stops, turns around and "did some kind of movement", which the witness describes as pulling up his pants. He states that he at no time observes Brown raising up his hands or arms. He then states that Michael Brown charges Officer Wilson aggressively and in full stride. With Michael Brown approximately ten yards from the officer and in motion, Officer Wilson fires four to six consecutive shots. Michael Brown remains on his feet, giving the witness the impression that Officer Wilson's shots are off-target. At this point, Brown stops moving and Wilson stops firing. The witness then states that Brown again starts "charging" the officer, and again Officer Wilson fires an additional four to five shots. Michael Brown collapses to the pavement.

Asked by the detective to describe what happened next, Witness #10 identifies the Monte Carlo, which he describes as two-door and blue in color. He further states that the Monte Carlo is in close proximity to the police SUV. Following Michael Brown's collapse to the pavement, he observes the Monte Carlo make a left into the parking lot to the east of the complex on the south side of Canfield Drive and then exit around the other side, coming to stop in front and west of the police SUV. At this time, Dorian Johnson runs across the street from an unidentified point of origin. He is yelling, "Dog, they just killed him." The witness then states that Dorian Johnson runs off through the fields to the back of the complex. He states that at no time does Dorian Johnson get into the Monte Carlo.

At this point, the detective begins the process of reviewing with the witness his statement with focus on specific details.

According to Witness #10, Michael Brown is wearing tan short pants, a red baseball-type cap, and flip-flop-type sandals. He notes his socks are bright yellow and black with marijuana leaves. He describes Dorian Johnson only as having short dreads with bleached tips. He states that he has no previous knowledge of or contact with either Brown or Johnson.

With regard to the incident, the witness places himself approximately 100 yards from the SUV and on the same side of the road as the driver's side. He states he observes Michael Brown in direct relation to the driver's side front door, his feet firmly on the ground, and his upper torso fully inside the driver's side window. He notes the door of the vehicle is fully closed, and that he cannot see what is happening inside the car, but states that Michael Brown is in that position for a period of approximately 10 seconds, after which he hears the first gun shot. He assumes there is a physical confrontation due to the gun shot. He then states that Michael Brown flees east down the middle of Canfield Drive and looks initially to be heading left on what would be Coppercreek Court. He enters the driveway, but then stops, comes back, and starts moving in the direction of Officer Wilson, who by this time has exited the SUV.

According to the witness, having exited the vehicle, Officer Wilson is moving towards the direction in which Michael Brown has fled. The officer has his gun extended and pointed as if preparing to shoot. The witness states that he hears Officer Wilson issue a verbal command, but is at too far of a distance to make out what he said. It is at this point he observes Michael Brown turn and face Officer Wilson, then act with his hands as if pulling up his pants. Michael Brown is then observed moving towards Officer Wilson in what is described by the witness as "coming at an aggressive speed and just in a charge mode."

At the time of his first movement towards Officer Wilson, according to the witness, Brown is approximately 15 yards from the officer's position. He travels approximately five yards before Officer Wilson fires approximately five or six more rounds. The witness states that Michael Brown stops momentarily, then charges again, at which time Officer Wilson again discharges his weapon towards Brown, who then collapses to the pavement.

Prior to the conclusion of the interview, the detective asks the witness as to his opinion of the incident. The witness states that at first, based on his belief that Michael Brown is unarmed and Officer Wilson has the option of using a taser, he thought the officer's use of force is excessive. However, he then states that were he in the officer's position, giving the circumstances he observed, he too would have responded in the same way. When asked as to the time frame, the witness estimates two minutes elapse from the moment he sees Michael Brown involved in the physical confrontation at the SUV with Officer Wilson to the time that he collapses to the pavement.

INTERVIEW WITH THE GRAND JURY, VOLUME 6

On September 23, 2014, Witness #10 is interviewed by the Grand Jury. The procedure is conducted by Alizadeh and Whirley. All 12 jurists are present.

According to the witness, he is just finishing up a side job, returning tools to his vehicle, when he notices two males walking towards him within 10-15 yards of his position. Both are off the sidewalk and in the road (Canfield Drive). He states that he takes particular note of Michael Brown due to his size, his bright neon yellow socks with marijuana symbols, his black flip-flops, and his St. Louis Cardinals red baseball cap. He notes only that Dorian Johnson has short dreads, the tips of which appear to be dyed. He states they are not doing anything to draw attention to themselves, only talking.

For a two minute span to follow, Witness #10 states that he goes back inside the apartment in which he is working, and then comes back out to his vehicle to retrieve an item. Once by his vehicle, he notices the police SUV parked on Canfield Drive in a location he describes as between the two drive ways, one on each end, that form the horseshoe shape of Canfield Court, the road that encompasses the small parking lot across the street from the witness' location.

Witness #10 then goes on to describe the interaction as he sees it between Michael Brown and Officer Wilson. He states Michael Brown is leaning with his upper body inside the driver's side window and is engaged in a physical altercation with Officer Wilson. The witness estimates he is 50-75 yards removed from the location of the police SUV. He states the interaction "took place for seconds. I don't know how long." He then hears one shot. Michael Brown pulls away from the vehicle and starts to run. There is a lapse in time of anywhere between 10-15 seconds before the officer exits the vehicle. When the officer does exit the vehicle, he has his gun drawn and begins immediate pursuit of Brown.

At the point that Michael Brown nears Coppercreek Court, he appears prepared to turn off of Canfield, but stops. He then turns back towards the officer and makes some sort of hand gesture which the witness fails to describe, other than to say that he does not raise his hands. Michael Brown then "runs towards the officer full charge." Officer Wilson responds by firing five to six shots. Michael Brown continues to move towards the officer, leading the witness to believe the officer's shots missed Brown. Brown than slows and comes to a stop. In turn, Officer Wilson stops firing. After a brief pause, Brown "started to charge once more at him." Officer Wilson then fires three to four more shots. Michael Brown collapses to the ground.

The witness then accounts for the blue Monte Carlo and the actions of Dorian Johnson. He states Dorian Johnson appears from some unknown point on the south side of Canfield Drive, runs across the street, in front of the police SUV, and east towards the Monte Carlo. He yells, "He just killed him. He just killed him," and then runs off through the open field on the south side of Canfield Drive and beyond the apartment complex between Caddiefield Road. The Monte Carlo then bears to the right, up and on to the sidewalk to get around the SUV, makes a right onto Canfield Court, follows it around and exits back onto Canfield Drive heading west.

At this point in the interview, the attorney tells Witness #10 that he would like to clarify specific details.

According to Witness #10, Officer Wilson exits his vehicle and begins immediate pursuit of Michael Brown. He describes Officer Wilson as running in a fashion normally associated with running. His gun is drawn, held in his right hand and pointing as if prepared to shoot. The witness states that prior to Michael Brown stopping at the entrance to Coppercreek Court, Officer Wilson has started to close ground on him and is in line with the east entrance to Caddiefield Road when Brown stops. He further states that he does not hear any shots while Officer Wilson is in actual running pursuit of Michael Brown.

According to the witness, Brown stops running at the intersection of Coppercreek Court and Canfield Drive, and he is at this time on the sidewalk or perhaps a patch of grass by the sidewalk. Officer Wilson is in the middle of Canfield Drive and directly across from the east portion of Caddiefield Road.

It is at this point that Michael Brown makes a gesture with his arms. The witness expresses uncertainty as to the description, saying he may have shrugged his shoulders or pulled up the waist of his pants. He does state, however, "All I know it was not in a surrendering motion." He describes Brown's hands as low. He confirms Brown then charges Officer Wilson, by which, in response to the attorney, he equates a full charge to running. He states Brown runs to the back of a white car which at the time is stopped two car lengths behind the rear of the police SUV, and west of Coppercreek Court. He does not say how far the distance measures. The witness then hears five to six shots. Brown flinches but continues to run towards Officer Wilson. He then slows and stops. He pauses for two seconds before resuming movement towards Officer Wilson of five to six strides. The officer responds by firing three to four more times. Michael Brown collapses to the pavement. Officer Wilson stops shooting.

ANALYSIS AND INTERPRETATION

There are four key statements within Witness #10's testimony. The first is Michael Brown's physical position while beside the driver's side door of the police SUV. The second is his recollection of when the first shot is fired. The third is his recollection of when the first volley of five to six shots is fired. The fourth is his description of Michael Brown's forward movement towards Officer Wilson which results in all but the first shot fired by the officer.

AT THE POLICE VEHICLE

Contrary to both witness #12 and #16, neither who place any part of Michael Brown besides his arms inside the driver's side window of the police SUV, Witness #10 states most if not all of Brown's upper torso is through the window. However, it has already been speculated that Witness #16 did not actually see Michael Brown at the SUV, but only after he had already fled east down Canfield. Witness #12, at the most, saw only the final instants of the confrontation at the SUV, which would account for his seeing the head of Michael Brown and then Brown pulling away.

FIRST SHOT

That Witness #10 states the first shot was fired by Officer Wilson while he was seated in the vehicle with Michael Brown standing beside the driver's door supports the notion there had been a physical confrontation between Brown and the officer which results in Officer Wilson taking defensive action.

FIRST STRING OF GUNSHOTS FIRED

Contrary to the description provided by Witness #12 who states that the officer began firing as soon as he exited the vehicle, Witness #10 suggests there was initial pursuit during which Officer Wilson had his gun raised and pointed in a shooting posture. He states, however, that the officer did not start shooting immediately, but instead had first closed the distance between him and Brown, and did not fire until Brown had stopped and was moving back in his direction. The inference is that Officer Wilson did not fire at Michael Brown's back.

MICHAEL BROWN'S MOVEMENTS

It is Witness #10's contention that Michael Brown moved aggressively towards Officer Wilson two times, the first covering approximately five yards and the second 2-3 strides; a statement which is contrary to Witnesses #12 and #16, who both state Brown took only two short steps towards Officer Wilson. Such aggressive movement, if it did take place as described, would provide for Officer Wilson's decision to act defensively. It would also account for how Michael Brown's body collapses almost 50 feet from the intersection of Coppercreek Court where he first stops and turns, and for the two blood stains found on the road between the sidewalk and the middle of the road where Brown falls.

WHERE IS DORIAN JOHNSON?

There is one part of Witness #10's statement that is curious: His location of Dorian Johnson throughout the incident is not consistent with the recollection of Witnesses #12 and #16. He states that Johnson reappeared from an unspecified location on the south side of Canfield Drive and to the Monte Carlo. According to the statements of both #12 and #16, both Johnson and Brown immediately started running east down Canfield, and Johnson took cover to the rear of the Monte Carlo. In addition, Witness #10 states that Johnson fled through the open field to the back of the apartment complex, presumably to the north, while the other two witnesses state he jumped into the Monte Carlo through the passenger side door. The Monte Carlo then drove off.

PERSPECTIVE

Ultimately, Witness #10 is credible. His overall account of the incident is consistent with the events that make up the incident, the sequence of those events, and the location and chronology of those events. Small inaccuracies, such as describing the color of the Monte Carlo as blue, do not detract from his statement, but instead suggest that his attention was on the interaction between Michael Brown and Officer Wilson and not the peripheral elements. And to his credit, there were both white and blue cars present. He simply recalls their order inaccurately.

The statements provided by Witness #10 would not lead the Grand Jury to the decision to indict Officer Wilson on the grounds that he violates the civil rights of Michael Brown or that he acts criminally with regard to his duty as a law enforcement officer.

WITNESS #33

INTERVIEW WITH THE GRAND JURY, VOLUME 12

Witness #33 is one of two construction workers working on a drainage issue on the north-east side of the apartment complex between Canfield Court and Coppercreek Court. They are in proximity to the building and in the parking lot along Coppercreek Court. The interview with the Grand Jury takes place on October 13, 2014.

The two construction workers, Witness #33 and Witness #36, are seen on a video clip shot shortly after the incident and aired by multiple media outlets and via online sources. They are seen standing beside one of their trucks, which is parked parallel to the building. It is common knowledge that Witness #33 reaches out to various media sources to tell his story. The witness also acknowledges speaking to Michael Brown's mother by phone, a conversation that is arranged by a member of the media.

According to Worker #2, he first encounters Michael Brown earlier in the day, outside the apartment building. They speak informally for approximately 30 minutes. Michael Brown then goes up the stairs and into the apartments. He comes back shortly thereafter with Dorian Johnson. The witness states Michael Brown has a small amount of marijuana in his possession which he is wrapping in a piece of lined notebook paper. He tells Worker #2 that he is going to the store to get some skins or a blunt to smoke the marijuana.

Continuing, the witness states he and his partner have been working with a Mustang front-end loader—a period of approximately 15 minutes, and have just shut it down—it is loud, when the witness hears a gunshot. He shortly thereafter hears a second shot. According to the witness, he then observes Michael Brown come into sight and running straight down the street. The witness estimates the distance Brown runs (while in sight) as approximately 25'. Brown then appears to trip and uses his hand to catch himself before he falls. The witness states he does not see Brown's hand touch the ground. The witness then states that Michael Brown turned around with his arms up and his hands well above his head and started yelling "okay", which he does seven or eight times. The witness states he cannot see who Michael Brown is running from due to his line of sight, which is blocked by the apartment building (to the witness's right and east down Canfield Drive).

At this point, the attorney asks questions for clarification.

Witness #33 states there is a berm between where he is standing and Canfield Drive. The witness states he cannot see Michael Brown's feet. He can see him only to a point just below knee level. At the time Michael Brown turns around, the witness states he sees three policemen. The policeman closest to Michael Brown has his gun drawn and pointed to the ground. The other two officers, guns holstered, are to the back of the first and on each side.

Continuing, the witness states that when he first noticed the three officers, they were all running towards Michael Brown. When Officer Wilson started firing, the other two officers slowed. The witness then states that once Officer Wilson stopped firing, one of the other two officers then drew his gun for a few seconds until Michael Brown actually fell.

Upon further questioning, Witness #33 states that Michael Brown, after turning back west up Canfield Drive, takes four to five steps towards the officers, but "there was no gap between his heel and toe; he was just kind of staggering forward". At this point, according to the witness, Officer Wilson "just pulled up and started shooting". The witness states there was approximately 10' between Officer Wilson and Michael Brown when Officer Wilson started shooting, and about 7' when the last shot was fired. Witness #33 states he hears six to seven shots (not counting the first two fired earlier).

In addition, the witness states he sees smoke coming from both Officer Wilson's gun and Michael Brown's back.

According to the witness, he does not see Michael Brown actually fall, as the apartment building blocks his line of sight. He states that the gunshots have stopped prior to this point.

ANALYSIS AND INTERPRETATION

The number of contradictions and falsehoods throughout Witness #33's statement allow no other conclusion than he sees little to none of the actual incident.

Early in his statement, the witness states that due to the berm between his position and Canfield Drive he can only see Michael Brown from his head down to just below his knees. Later, he states that he sees no gap between Brown's heels and toes as he staggers forward towards the approaching officers. If he could only see just below knee level, it is not reasonable that he could see Brown's heels and toes. He also states that he did not realize Michael Brown had lost his flip-flops until he sees them in the road.

In addition, it is common knowledge there were no other officers present when Michael Brown was shot. Therefore the witness did not see three officers, nor did he see, as he states, another officer with his gun drawn waiting for Michael Brown to fall. The forensic evidence confirms Michael Brown was already in the process of falling when the last shot hit him.

Further, the witness states he could not see Michael Brown fall due to his positon further east up Canfield Drive and the apartment building serving as an obstruction. However, he states he sees Officer Wilson pull up and start shooting, which is not possible since Officer Wilson fired the second volley from a position further east than where Michael Brown fell.

Finally, the witness states that he saw smoke coming from Officer Wilson's gun and Michael Brown's back. It has already been established that he could not have seen Officer Wilson from his position, and therefore he could not have seen his gun. It also has been established that Michael Brown had not suffered any gunshots to the back. Witness #33 is also the only witness that states he saw Michael Brown stumble to the degree that he had to reach to the ground, and at a point others state Brown stopped running, looked down at this hand or side, and then turned back towards Officer Wilson.

Worker #2 is not a credible witness. For reasons known only to him, he provided details he himself fabricated or assumed, having heard rumors, media reports, or after speaking with others.

WITNESS #36

INTERVIEW WITH THE GRAND JURY, VOLUME 13

The interview with Witness #36, one of two construction workers, and the Grand Jury takes place on October 16, 2014. The procedure is conducted by Alizadeh and Whirley. The witness is a white male. He is college educated. He states he is in a supervisory capacity with the company installing the water lines, but on this day he is assisting in the actual labor. He states that he is present when Michael Brown first comes down from his apartment and as Brown is engaged in conversation with one of his fellow workers. He describes Michael Brown as wearing a grey t-shirt, blue-jean shorts, yellow and black socks with marijuana leaves, and wearing a St. Louis Cardinals baseball cap. He also identifies Dorian Johnson. The witness describes his location as east of the apartment complex between Canfield Court and Coppercreek Court and on the north side of Canfield Drive. He states he is 50-60 yards away from Michael Brown when he first comes into sight. However, his perspective does not allow him to see Officer Wilson when the incident begins, and he loses sight of Michael Brown as he falls.

According to Witness #36, he is working a Bob-Cat tractor, shuts down the machine, and as he does so, he hears a gun shot. Shortly after, he states he sees Michael Brown "come out behind the building, he was moving at a pretty good clip". When asked to define "clip", the witness states Brown is not running, but moving faster than a walk.

The witness then states that while Michael Brown is moving away from the officer he hears a second shot. He believes Michael Brown is wounded in the back. He states Michael Brown stumbles and then turns back to face Officer Wilson. At the time he turns, Michael Brown has his hands raised high and he is yelling, "Okay, okay, okay." He states Officer Wilson is stationary with his gun drawn and pointed at Michael Brown. Officer Wilson then, as he is taking steps backwards and away from Michael Brown, starts shooting. The witness states he hears six or seven shots, and at the third shot, Michael Wilson disappears from his line of sight and falls. The witness states he sees Michael Brown going down, but not actually fall, and at that time his hands have been lowered to a position at his belly. In addition, he states that when the final shots are fired, Brown and Wilson are approximately 15 feet apart.

ANALYSIS AND INTERPRETATION

Taken as a whole, the statement by Witness #36 doesn't hold together, and therefore is likely in part fabricated, and the rest derived from hearsay. The witness claims to see Officer Wilson in his line of sight. He states Wilson is stationary and has his gun drawn on Michael Brown. However, later in his statement, Witness #36 states that Brown falls, and when he does so, he falls in a location that is beyond his line of sight. The building is in the way. However, Officer Wilson at all times is in a position further west than Michael Brown, and as Brown ultimately falls in a location west of the witness' line of sight, the witness, therefore, by his own admission never has a line of sight that includes Officer Wilson. The witness cannot see Officer Wilson take steps back or start shooting. At best, he hears the shots, but doesn't know where they are coming from or who is firing them. In addition, there is a video clip in which the witness appears, and from where he is standing there is no line of sight to Wilson's position.

As a witness relative to the objective of the Grand Jury, Witness #36 is not credible.

The location of the two memorials illustrate the approximate locations where Brown is shot each time. The two dark spots in the road to the right of the memorial are blood stains.

CHANCE ENCOUNTERS

WITNESS #34

INTERVIEW WITH THE ST. LOUIS COUNTY POLICE AND THE FBI

The interview conducted by the St. Louis Police and the FBI with Witness #34 takes place on September 3, 2014 at 2:47 pm. Present are a detective with the Bureau of Crimes Against Persons, a Special Agent with the FBI, a member of the Justice Department, and a representative of the US Attorney's Office. The witness, a male African-American, is represented and accompanied by an attorney.

According to Witness #34, he is traveling (alone) eastbound in his truck, coming from West Florissant, when he encounters on Canfield Drive a police truck (he refers to it as a jeep) stationary and parked on an angle in the middle of the road.

At this time, the witness sees Michael Brown standing beside the driver's door of the truck. Brown and Officer Wilson are "tussling". The witness states that Brown and Wilson have hold of each other's shirts, and Brown "was throwing a couple of blows" and trying to get loose. (The witness states at least four times that Michael Brown punches Officer Wilson through the vehicle window, and that the punches are aimed at Officer Wilson's head or face.) He describes Officer Wilson as "trying to keep him blocked and was holding on [to Browns' shirt]", and at the time leaning towards the passenger seat. All of sudden, the witness says, he hears a single shot and Michael Brown starts to run.

The witness states that Michael Brown runs east down the middle of the road towards [Coppercreek Court] for two to three car lengths. At this point, the witness, wishing not to get involved, begins the process of turning around his truck to head back west toward West Florissant. He states as he is turning the truck, he sees Michael Brown stop running and place his hand on the back of a brown vehicle he describes as parked on the left. Michael Brown then turns and starts walking back at a fast pace towards Officer Wilson. The witness places Officer Wilson at the back of the police SUV and in relation to the passenger side. In addition, he states that Officer Wilson exits the vehicle following the first shot and moves in pursuit of Michael Brown at a pace he describes as "trotting". He states that there are no additional shots fired until after Michael Brown removes his hand from the brown car and starts forward towards Officer Wilson.

At this point, Witness #34 has backed up his vehicle towards a white car in the road behind him, turns his vehicle into a driveway on his left and to the north side of the street (Canfield Court), backs out to face westbound on Canfield Drive, and is in the process of driving away. It is at this time that he hears three shots, but he does not see the shots or any more of the incident.

As for Dorian Johnson, the witness places him ahead of and to the passenger side of the police SUV when Brown and Wilson are engaged in the initial confrontation at the police SUV, and reports seeing him run to the north side of the road and up on the grass following the first shot. He states that after that he loses sight of Johnson.

INTERVIEW WITH THE GRAND JURY, VOLUME 13

The interview of Witness #34 by the Grand Jury takes place on October 16, 2014, at 9:14. The process is conducted by Alizadeh and Whirley. All 12 jurists are present.

According to Witness #34, he is driving in his truck eastbound on Canfield Drive. He has one passenger, a male acquaintance with whom he occasionally works. He describes him only as African-American. The witness states that as he nears the apartments, there is a police truck parked on an angle in the middle of Canfield Drive. The truck appears to have been heading westbound towards West Florissant. The witness is forced to bring his vehicle to a full stop, and at the time he is separated from the police vehicle by a single car that is in front of his.

While stopped, the witness states he sees Michael Brown and Officer Wilson engaged in a physical struggle there at the driver's side of the police vehicle. The struggle goes on for two to three minutes. He states they have a hold of each other's shirts, their arms are pulling back and forth, Michael Brown is punching at Wilson, Wilson has his left forearm up to defend himself, and ultimately Wilson leans away from Brown and towards the passenger seat of the vehicle. According to the witness, he then sees Officer Wilson's right hand disappear and then hears a single shot. Michael Brown then runs from the vehicle. The witness states he then immediately starts to back up his truck in order to leave.

While in the process of turning his vehicle, the witness states Michael Brown runs "a piece off" eastbound on Canfield Drive. He then comes to a stop behind a brown car, perhaps a Mercury or Ford, parked along the north side of the road and perhaps belonging to a resident. Brown places both hands on the trunk and appears to be resting. He remains in this position for no more than two minutes.

At the same time, Officer Wilson has exited his vehicle with his gun down at this side, is perhaps talking into the walkie-talkie at his shoulder, and is pursuing Brown at a pace the witness describes as a trot. The officer is not pointing his gun at Brown at this time, and he does not fire.

As the witness begins to drive away, he states Brown has started walking back towards Officer Wilson and Officer Wilson is advancing towards Brown. He then hears, but does not see, three shots. He learns the rest while listening to the news.

ANALYSIS AND INTERPRETATION

There are two key statements made by Witness #34. The first is his assertion that Michael Brown is punching Officer Wilson through the window of the police SUV. The second is Michael Brown standing behind the brown car parked along the north side of the street with his hands on the trunk.

AT THE POLICE SUV

The statements by Witness #34 substantiate that Michael Brown, while beside the police SUV at the driver's side window, is involved in a physical confrontation with Officer Wilson, and that although they both have a hold of each other, Brown's intent is not to disengage from Wilson's grip, but to cause injury. It also substantiates that the confrontation goes on for a measurable period of time before Officer Wilson produces his weapon.

MICHAEL BROWN'S MOVEMENTS

Witness #34 is the only one to mention a brown car parked alongside the north side of Canfield Drive and in proximity to Coppercreek Court, and he is the only one to say that Michael Brown has his hands on that car. However, as the witness estimates Brown is in this position for as long as two minutes, which is improbable given the actual sequence of events, it is most likely that because the witness is at this time more preoccupied with turning his truck around, that he doesn't see what he thinks he sees.

The witness also confirms that Brown and Officer Wilson are at some point advancing towards each other. However, given that he's looking back over his shoulder or using the vehicle's mirrors, it is unlikely that he has a clear view of this movement and is unreliable in terms of distance and pace.

In addition, the witness substantiates that Dorian Johnson is not as close to the vehicle as Johnson provides in his own statements.

THE SHOTS

The witness directly substantiates at least one gunshot while Officer Wilson is still in the vehicle, and he indirectly substantiates that no shots are fired while Officer Wilson is in pursuit of Michael Brown. He infers that the first string of shots outside the vehicle are fired with Michael Brown advancing towards Officer Wilson at a fast pace.

PERSPECTIVE

In terms of the Grand Jury and their decision whether or not to seek indictment of Officer Wilson, the statements provided by Witness #34 suggest that Officer Wilson, based on Brown's actions at the SUV, has reason to consider Michael Brown a threat to his person. Brown's decision to advance on Officer Wilson "at a fast pace" does nothing to minimize that perception.

WITNESS #43

INTERVIEW WITH THE ST. LOUIS COUNTY POLICE DEPARTMENT

Witness #43 is a juvenile male, approximately 5'8" tall. The interview takes place at his father's residence on August 9, 2014, at 4:12 pm. The procedure is conducted by two detectives. Also present at the time is the juvenile's father, and the girlfriend of the father. The witness claims to have viewed the incident from his father's second floor apartment and through the sliding doors out onto the balcony. The doors are covered by vertical blinds. The interview concludes at 4:22.

According to Witness #43, he is listening to music on television. He hears "screaming and stuff" out towards the road and moves over to the sliding glass doors. At this time, the witness sees Michael Brown "with his hands in the police car and trying to snatch it away (his hands)". He then states Michael Brown successfully extracts his hand from the vehicle. The witness states he sees Officer Wilson attempt to use a taser on Michael Brown, but fails. He describes the taser as small and black. He then states that Officer Wilson pulls out his gun, opens the door of the vehicle, tries to shoot Michael Brown, and misses. Officer Wilson then runs down the street and shoots Michael Brown one time. Witness #43 then states that he stops looking, but hears four or five more shots. When he turns to look again, Michael Brown is lying in the street.

At this time, the detectives ask the witness to "break down" his statement. The witness clarifies he sees Michael Brown's hands extended into Officer Wilson's vehicle, but he does not see the actual engagement taking place, if any, between Wilson and Brown. He confirms Officer Wilson is alone within the vehicle. In addition, he confirms the presence of Dorian Johnson. He accurately describes both Brown (khaki cargo shorts and yellow and black socks) and Johnson (dreads).

Continuing, the witness states he turns from the incident because he thinks after the first shot it is over. In addition, he states there is an older model Pontiac G6 in close proximity to the incident. It is blue in color and has four doors. He also sees a four-door white Pontiac, but does not know the make.

There is a second interview that takes place with the FBI on October 22, 2014. The contents, however, are similar to and consistent with this first interview. However, the FBI agent conducting the interview does seek clarity as to why the witness turns away from the incident at the point that Michael Brown is fleeing. Ultimately, the witness states that Michael Brown runs down Canfield Drive to a point that he is no longer in view, and as there is a period of time in which no shots are fired, he makes the assumption that Officer Wilson has caught up to Brown, and that the incident is over. It is only when he hears the additional shots does he return to the balcony and sees Brown lying on the road.

INTERVIEW WITH THE GRAND JURY, VOLUME 16

Witness #43 is interviewed by the Grand Jury on October 27, 2014. The procedure is conducted by Alizadeh and Whirley. At the start of the interview, the witness states he lives with his mother and is visiting his father on the day of the incident. He states he does not know the address, and he cannot identify the location of the building on a diagram he is shown. The building is on the south side of Canfield Drive. He states it is only the second time he has been to the complex. The apartment has a single bedroom. The juvenile sleeps on the couch. He is alone in the apartment at the time of the incident.

According to Witness #43, he is listening to music on a Play Station 3, and he hears a scream outside. He states he cannot tell if it is a woman or a man screaming. He then walks over to the sliding glass doors and looks through the vertical blinds, some of which are missing. He does not move the blinds aside. He notes the police vehicle parked on an angle on Canfield Drive. His view is of the driver's side.

Prompted by the attorney, the witness states he sees Dorian Johnson standing on the sidewalk on the north side of Canfield Drive and to the passenger side at the back of the police SUV, but not close enough to touch it. In addition, he states he sees two cars trying to get past.

Continuing, he states he sees Michael Brown (a man) trying to pull his arm away from and out of the driver's side window of the police SUV. (The witness states later on that he sees both Brown and Wilson pulling back and forth at each other, and that perhaps Officer Wilson is trying to pull Brown into the vehicle.) The witness then states that he sees Officer Wilson attempt to use a taser, which he describes as yellow and black and which sends out a metallic string. He then states he sees Officer Wilson pull out his gun, which he describes as black, and while in the process of opening the vehicle door (he is half-way out), he fires. He states that Michael Brown has run towards the apartment complex by the time the first shot is fired. The witness further states that he does not hear any shots while Michael Brown is running from the police vehicle.

It is as this point, according to the witness, that he returns to the living room and sits down. He states he does so because he doesn't want to hear any more shots and he thinks Brown has already been apprehended. After a noticeable pause (five seconds), however, he states he then hears four to five more shots. He then returns to the window and sees Michael Brown prone in the street and Officer Wilson standing over Brown with his gun in his right hand and communicating via his shoulder walkie-talkie. The witness states he hears no other shots at this point or after. Additional police then arrive.

The witness describes Office Wilson as a white male, wearing a short-sleeved shirt, and with a yellowish-colored (blonde) beard (partial) and mustache.

ANALYSIS AND INTERPRETATION

The statement provided by Witness #43 is consistent with the general events of the incident, the sequence of those events, and the chronology of those events relative to the time between one event and the next. In addition, the witness is consistent throughout his testimony and has not been prejudiced or influenced by outside sources. He also is the only witness to this point who accurately describes Officer Wilson's features.

AT THE SUV

Pushed on his recollection as to the engagement at the police vehicle between Michael Brown and Officer Wilson, the witness maintains that Brown's arms are extended through the window and in contact with Officer Wilson. He also states Browns' head is level with the window, and that Brown and Wilson are pulling back and forth against each other. In addition, the witness provides for the probability that Officer Wilson has his gun drawn prior to the first shot, and that Wilson's right hand is free. The witness does insist, however, that he sees a taser, and then the gun. It is possible, though, that he confuses shattering glass with the wire he associates with the taser.

THE SHOTS

The witness' recollection of the first shot occurring at the vehicle is accurate. However, he continues to insist it takes place while Officer Wilson is exiting the vehicle and Michael Brown is fleeing. And while there is no other content to his statements that provide for his confusion, it is likely that he does not hear the first shot, which shatters the window, and which he associates with the taser, and then hears the second shot—he assumes it's the first, and then simply confuses the immediate sequence of events to follow. Michael Brown does take off running, but the shot that he is responding to has already taken place.

With regard to the shots to follow, after Michael Brown flees, it is reasonable to conclude that the witness does not accurately recall the exact number of shots—he says four or five, or in the process of returning to the living room and turning up the volume on the television, he doesn't hear the first volley. He does, however, accurately provide for the delay between shots at the vehicle and the collective shots that follow.

DORIAN JOHNSON

The witness places Dorian Johnson immediately behind the police SUV at the time of the second shot—the witness believes it is the first shot, and he states Johnson then runs off into the complex. These statements are consistent with other eyewitnesses, and suggest that Dorian Johnson is not telling the truth when he says he remains to Browns' left during the entirety of the incident at the SUV.

PERSPECTIVE

Witness #43 is a credible relative to the events that he sees, the sequence of those events, and the time periods between those events. However, his statements do not provide evidence that suggests Officer Wilson is criminal in the performance of his duties or in any way denies Michael Brown his civil rights.

WITNESS #44

INTERVIEW WITH THE FBI

The interview with Witness #44 with the FBI takes place on August 16, 2014, at 10:57. The procedure is conducted by two Special Agents. The witness is a female African-American with a residence in the Canfield Apartments off of Caddiefield Road. The interview concludes at 11:22. Early in the statement, the witness says that she has poor eyesight.

According to Witness #44, she is walking eastbound on the south side of Canfield Drive. She is returning to her apartment from the public library where she has selected various movies (videos). As she nears the leasing office, she observes a police SUV in the road. The officer is speaking with two boys alongside the driver's side of his vehicle. She states the officer then backs up and hits the two boys, describing the event as the officer backing past the boys and then angling his vehicle as to obstruct their path. She states the vehicle looks to have made contact with the two boys when it comes to an abrupt halt. (She infers the boys are hit by the driver's side of the vehicle.)

Continuing, the witness states that Dorian Johnson immediately takes off running, while Michael Brown "started like fighting with the officer through the window". She states Michael Brown's arms are going in and out of the car, and at one point his head and shoulders are inside the vehicle. She states the confrontation lasts approximately 15 seconds. She then hears a single shot—door of the vehicle closed, after which, she states, a gun falls to the pavement. She describes the gun as black in color and making a metallic sound when it hits the pavement.

Following the first shot, the cars in the immediate vicinity stop, and Dorian Johnson and Michael Brown start running. Johnson runs around to the back of the passenger side of the police vehicle. Michael Brown runs eastbound on Canfield and down the middle of the road. The witness states Brown runs a short distance—four steps (later she states 5 to 10 steps), stops and turns around. She says, "[He] took about a step back, then put his hands up, basically like I'm done". She then hears "the rest of the shots"—seven or eight in total. At this point, Michael Brown "stood there for a minute, then he just fell down". There are no shots fired after he falls.

Further questioned by the agents for clarification, the witness states that after Michael Brown stops running, he does not take any forward steps toward Officer Wilson, but is taking slow steps backwards. As he is backing up, according to the witness, Brown has his hands raised at shoulder level. She states approximately five seconds lapse from the moment Michael Brown turns and faces Officer Wilson and when Officer Wilson starts to fire. She states Officer Wilson is not firing while Michael Brown is running from the vehicle.

INTERVIEW WITH THE FBI, DEPARTMENT OF JUSTICE, AND ASSISTANT ATTORNEY

The second interview of Witness #44 by the FBI takes place on September 25, 2014, at the FBI building on 2222 Market Street. The procedure is conducted by a special agent of the FBI. Two additional attorneys are present, one from the Department of Justice and the other is the Assistant United States Attorney.

According to Witness #44, she is not wearing her eye glasses or her contacts at the time of the incident, and therefore her ability to see detail is compromised. She states she sees Officer Wilson's vehicle backup towards Michael Brown and Dorian Johnson. Brown, however, she describes as moving aggressively and as if with anger directly to the open window on the driver's side of the police SUV. She hears Brown screaming in anger, but cannot hear what he is saying. At this point, Dorian Johnson takes off running.

Continuing, the witness states that due to the size of Michael Brown, she cannot see what is happening at the vehicle, but all of Brown's upper torso is in through the window. She states the altercation goes on for about 15 seconds, and then she hears a gunshot. Brown then comes out of the window. She believes that he is checking himself over (as if he may have been shot). A moment later, Brown starts to run. He moves 10-12 steps, stops and turns around. He raises his hands about shoulder height. The witness describes the gesture as "you know, when somebody's scared, like they're backing away from something, like 'whoa'." She then hears the rest of the shots, at which time Michael Brown is "kind of scrunched up", and Michael Brown falls. She hears no further shots.

INTERVIEW WITH THE GRAND JURY, VOLUME 17

The interview with Witness #44 with the Grand Jury takes place on October 28, 2014. A specific time is not provided. The procedure is conducted by Alizadeh and Whirley. All 12 jurists are present. During the interview, the witness acknowledges her eyesight is not very good and rates her eyesight relative to the incident as a five out of ten.

According to Witness #44, she awakens at approximately 9:00 am in anticipation of the arrival of her boyfriend's son who is being brought to her by the boy's mother. Prior to his arrival, she has errands to run, including going to the public library. She rides the bus to the library but does not have money to take it back home, so she walks.

As she is walking eastbound on Canfield Drive she observes a police SUV in the center of Canfield Drive. The light bar atop the vehicle is on. She observes two boys—she provides an accurate description of both Brown and Johnson—who she believes are being addressed by the officer; however, they continue walking. As they reach the rear of the vehicle, the officer puts the SUV in reverse, by-passes the boys a short distance, and then angles the vehicle to obstruct their path. The witness states that both Brown and Johnson jump back from the vehicle as if startled, but she cannot say for sure if there is actual physical contact.

At this point, according to the witness, Michael Brown goes straight to the driver's window of the vehicle and "they (Brown and Wilson) got into it...it looked like they were fighting". The witness states Brown's hand and arms are within the car. The confrontation lasts a few seconds. Then, with Michael Brown still in the window, the first shot goes off. Michael Brown backs away from the vehicle. He appears to be checking himself for injury.

It is at this time, according to the witness, that she hears something metallic hit the ground. She assumes it is a gun. She states she does see the item on the pavement, but doesn't know what happens to it; she does not see anyone bend to pick it up.

Witness #44 then states that Michael Brown turns and runs eastbound on Canfield Drive for seven to ten steps. He then stops and turns with both his hands raised about shoulder level and with palms forward. The witness states she does not see Officer Wilson exit the vehicle, nor is she paying attention to him as she watches Michael Brown running. However, as Michael Brown turns around, he is facing Officer Wilson and they are in proximity. The witness states she then hears "the rest of the shots". Michael Brown then falls face-first to the pavement. She states he is never on his knees, but falls flat.

Upon further questioning, the Witness states she first hears two shots, but cannot identify when they happen; she doesn't see them. Further, she states that she interprets the position of Michael Brown's hands as a sign of surrender. She states Michael Brown does not take any steps towards Officer Wilson once he has stopped running and turns to face him.

ANALYSIS AND INTERPRETATION

Witness #44 is consistent in her recollection of the singular events of the incident, the sequence of those events, and in the way she describes them throughout the interview process. Her description of the physical engagement at the vehicle between Wilson and Brown is consistent with the statements of other witnesses, as is her recall of Officer Wilson's initial use of his weapon. Where she deviates is in her recollection of how far and to where Brown runs, where he turns, the distance he moves back towards Officer Wilson, and when he falls.

AT THE SUV

Witness #44 substantiates Dorian Johnson's claim that Officer Wilson reverses the SUV in an aggressive manner, and further that it is possible the SUV comes close enough to both Johnson and Brown for it to be perceived as having made contact. She also supports Wilson's claim that Brown becomes immediately aggressive and that he comes into the window of the vehicle. She is also the first witness who describes Brown as mad and confirms that there is a verbal component to the confrontation. The gun she sees go to the ground is more likely one of the bracelets that are recovered from the scene, or even glass from the broken window.

THE FIRST SHOT

The witness' recall of the first shot is consistent with Officer Wilson's version, in as much as Michael Brown straightens as if to check himself. However, the witness associates this sequence of events with Brown fleeing, which he does following the second shot, not the first. It is likely though, as the witness herself states, that as she herself is taking cover behind a tree following the first shot, she misses the sequence of events that happens between the first and second shots, and when she again looks, Brown is running from the vehicle.

BROWN'S MOVEMENTS

With regard to distance, the witness states Brown covers only four to ten strides—depending on which statement is more accurate, and at a pace less than running. Yet forensic evidence indicates Brown, from the event at the vehicle to the point where he falls, covers about 200 feet. Second, she equates Brown stopping, turning and falling essentially in the same spot, which does not account for his actions in proximity to Coppercreek Court. This inaccuracy is explained by the witnesses own movement, during which she is not maintaining sight of the incident. She only assumes that Brown moves to a certain point before he turns. However, her movement does not account for the inability to separate the two distinct strings of shots.

PERSPECTIVE

The statements provided by Witness #44 are most relevant to Officer Wilson's position that Michael Brown, while at the vehicle, establishes himself as a threat to the physical safety of Officer Wilson, and indirectly lends credibility to the claim that Brown attempts to take control of Officer Wilson's gun. However, she also supports the claim by other witnesses that prior to the fatal string of shots, Michael Brown provides a gesture suggestive of compliance, and his physical posture is one indicative of being injured more so than preparing to attack.

WITNESS: RESIDENT #1

INTERVIEW WITH THE GRAND JURY, VOLUME 11

Resident #1 is a male African-American. He is a resident of the Canfield Apartments. His complex is between Canfield Court and Coppercreek Court. The windows of his apartment face west and his apartment is to the east end of the complex. The view does not allow him to see as far as Coppercreek Court. At the time of the incident, he is at home with his girlfriend and at least one minor child. He is in the living room playing video games, having returned home early from work. His girlfriend is in the bedroom. There is some question as to whether or not she is sleeping. The minor child is in the same room and watching TV. The interview with the Grand Jury takes place on October 7, 2014, at approximately 10:15 am.

According to Resident #1, while he is playing video games, he hears three shots. At first, he believes the shots to be random. He then decides to investigate. He moves from the couch to the window where he observes Michael Brown in the middle of Canfield Drive. He is down on his left knee. His left hand is across his mid-section to the area of the ribs on his right side. His right hand is raised about shoulder level with his elbow at a 90° angle. The palm of his hand is forward. The witness states he hears four or five more shots, and with each shot he observes Michael Brown's head jerk back. Michael Brown then falls face first to the pavement. The witness states from his line of sight he cannot see Officer Wilson. He does see Dorian Johnson run south across the open field, presumably to the west of the Caddiefield complex. He then sees two Ferguson police officers in proximity to Michael Brown's body.

In response to further questioning by the attorney, Resident #1 confirms that when first observed, Michael Brown has his left knee in contact with the surface of the road and his right knee bent forward, with his weight upon the ball of his right foot. (He physically demonstrates the position for the Grand Jury.) Brown remains in this position during the second volley of shots fired, until he falls forward on his face. In addition, he states there is a pause of approximately 20-25 seconds between the two volleys fired by Officer Wilson.

ANALYSIS AND INTERPRETATION

There is no reason to believe that Resident #1 is reporting anything other than what he believes he saw. If there is a question, it is with regard to the amount of time the witness states takes place between the two volleys, which combined with his description of Michael Brown down upon one knee during the entire time of the second volley, seems to suggest that he either sees just the final moments when Michael Brown is falling, or perhaps gets to his window after Michael Brown has already fallen, and therefore did not see the events immediately prior.

The available forensic evidence suggests the final two shots fired, both of which hit Michael Brown in the head, were traveling parallel to the ground from the height at which they were shot. This would suggest that Michael Brown was standing, but with upper torso parallel to the ground.

Resident #1 is credible in as much as he was present in his apartment at the time of the incident, but his statement is questionable as to what he actually saw and what he may have been told or heard. His statement does not provide the Grand Jury with anything new or otherwise convincing.

QUESTIONABLE CREDIBILITY

WITNESS #12

FIRST INTERVIEW CONDUCTED BY DETECTIVE FROM THE ST. LOUIS COUNTY POLICE DEPARTMENT

This interview takes place on August 9, 2014, at approximately 4:40 pm, on Canfield Drive. The interview takes approximately three minutes, concluding at 4:43 pm. The witness resides in an apartment on Canfield Court to the north side of the street and west of the parking lot. His view of the incident is from the passenger side and across the hood of the police SUV.

According to the witness, he is in the bedroom of his apartment. He happens to look out the window and see a Ferguson police car and a young man standing beside the driver's side door and window. He notices a physical confrontation which he describes as arms being exchanged. He then calls his fiancé over to take a look.

Following the confrontation at the car door, the witness states that he goes outside on to his balcony. At this point he notices there are two young men, one who he describes as black and having dreads (Dorian Johnson). The first young man he had witnessed—Michael Brown, he now sees running down the middle of the street. He states that the officer exits the police vehicle and shoots. He states he hears six shots. He believes two of the shots hit Michael Brown, and as a result Michael stops running. Brown then turns and faces Officer Wilson. His posture is described as bent and curled forward. The witness states that Officer Wilson then fires three or four more times. Michael Brown falls to the ground.

Witness #12 then states that Dorian Johnson—he does not mention him by name—gets into a white car and leaves. The white car is one of two in the immediate area. He states both cars leave the vicinity. He stresses that everything happens too quickly for him to recall details, and that incidents of this sort (meaning gun shots) happen every weekend.

SECOND INTERVIEW CONDUCTED BY DETECTIVE FROM THE ST. LOUIS COUNTY POLICE DEPARTMENT

This second interview takes place on August 9, 2014, at approximately 4:45 pm, on Canfield Drive. It is a continuation of the previous interview, the witness approaching the detective to amend his initial statement. The interview is concluded at 4:47.

According to the witness, he misspoke while detailing his initial recollection. He changes his statement to say that it was not until after the initial shots that he comes out from his apartment and (onto his second story balcony). He states that while he is looking out his bedroom window, he witnesses Michael Brown running from the police SUV. He infers that he assumes there was some sort of struggle, and that he sees the last moments of it. He states, "When I saw the altercation...the guy (Brown) ran." According to the witness, "That's when [Officer Wilson] immediately hopped out the car and did his first two shots."

The witness then states he goes outside and sees Michael Brown has stopped running and has turned and is taking steps toward Officer Wilson. He is at the time curled up (bent forward), from which the witness assumes that Michael Brown has been wounded by the shots. The witness describes Brown as "kinda like walkin' towards [Wilson] just a little bit and he (Wilson) let go three or four more shots and that's when he (Brown) hit the ground."

THIRD INTERVIEW CONDUCTED BY DETECTIVE FROM THE ST. LOUIS COUNTY POLICE DEPARTMENT

On August 13, 2014, at 10:27 am, a third, more extensive interview is conducted with Witness #12 by the St. Louis County Police Department. The interview is conducted by a detective other than the previous one and takes place in the parking lot of DePaul Hospital. The purpose of the interview is to follow up on information that Witness #12 is in possession of evidence or information at the time of the previous interviews, namely video he records with his cell phone, of which he himself fails to inform that detective. He acknowledges having this material in his possession. The interviewing detective, after confirming that the witness is complying of his own free will, asks the witness to start his recall from the beginning. The interview concludes at 10:43.

The witness states that at approximately 11:30 am on the day in question, a friend appears at his apartment and wakes him. The friend stays only for a short period of time, after which the witness returns to his bedroom. It is then that he notices the developing confrontation outside his window between Officer Wilson and Michael Brown. He states that he sees Michael Brown standing beside the driver's side window of the vehicle, that there is some sort of physical confrontation, and that he believes that Michael Brown's hands and arms are inside the window and that it looks as if he is punching Officer Wilson. He states that Dorian Johnson is in front of the police SUV and at a distance, up to five feet away.

The witness then states that both Dorian Johnson and Michael Brown start to run east down Canfield Drive. Michael runs straight down the road. Dorian takes cover behind the car to the rear of the SUV, which the witness describes as a white two-door Monte Carlo. At some point, the passenger door of the Monte Carlo opens, Dorian gets in, and the car drives off. The witness states that he believes Dorian Johnson is afraid for his life.

At this point, according to the witness, Officer Wilson exits the police vehicle and fires off four rounds as he his walking the length of the SUV and towards its rear. Michael Brown is at this time approximately 25 feet down the road. The witness asserts that Brown's back is to Officer Wilson while these initial shots are being taken. He states that Officer Wilson is in the vicinity of the rear bumper of the police SUV when he takes the first four shots, and that he has finished the first round of shots by the time he reaches the rear of the vehicle. He describes Officer Wilson not as running but taking big (long) steps.

The detective then asks Witness #12 if Officer Wilson is yelling anything. The witness confirms that he is yelling, but does not remember what it is he is saying. He mentions that besides the white Monte Carlo, there is a second purple car, and that Michael Brown's body falls somewhere between the two.

The witness states that he does not come down from his apartment until after the shooting has occurred, that he is standing upon his balcony when Michael Brown is shot. He states that Michael has been shot prior to the point at which he stops running and turns back towards Officer Wilson. He states Brown has been hit "[because] he curls up and he's facin' the Ferguson officer." He further states that Brown is curling up due to having been shot, he assumes, in the stomach. He describes him as bent at the waist, as if he is ready to fall directly to the ground. Brown then takes approximately two steps in the direction of Officer Wilson. He states Brown may have had his hands, or just one hand, raised when he is shot—or at least that is what others are saying. The witness states that he remembers Brown raising his hands up after he is shot. He further states that Brown has his hands down when Officer Wilson fires the last four shots and Brown falls. He acknowledges that neighborhood people are saying Brown is already down when Officer Wilson fires the last four shots. But he says he only knows what he saw, and Brown is not shot after he falls. He says, "...before he (Brown) hit the ground, he (Wilson) let off four more shots." In addition, the witness says he does not recall if Officer Wilson or Michael Brown said anything.

FIRST INTERVIEW HEARD BY THE GRAND JURY, VOLUME 6

This fourth interview is a recording of an interview with Witness #12 conducted by the FBI. It is titled Grand Jury Exhibit #24. It takes place on September 17, 2014, at 1:06 pm at the FBI building, 2222 Market Street. The interview is conducted by a Special Agent and an unidentified Trial Attorney.

The witness starts by confirming that he, his fiancé and other family members had gone out for a meal and return to the apartment at 9:00, at which time he goes to his bedroom to take a nap. He is awakened by his fiancé at approximately 11:00 am. She tells him a friend is at the door. His friend leaves after a few minutes. At about 11:45, the witness returns to his bedroom to resume his nap, and that is when he becomes aware of the confrontation out in the street.

The witness states that he observes a physical confrontation taking place at the driver's side door of the police SUV vehicle. He describes it as some kind of tussling in which Michael Brown is punching Officer Wilson, or the officer was "grabbing on" Michael Brown. He then notices Dorian Johnson located in front of the vehicle, towards the passenger side and approximately five feet out ahead of the SUV. He states both Johnson and Brown begin to run east, to the back of and past the SUV. He confirms Johnson's location in proximity to the Monte Carlo, Brown is fleeing straight back from the SUV, and that Officer Wilson emerges from his vehicle and starts shooting. He describes Officer Wilson as taking long steps, ignoring Johnson, who the witness believes is afraid that he may be the intended target of the officer, and that Officer Wilson while walking is in a shooting posture.

The witness states he then exits his bedroom to put himself in a better position to witness the incident, stating that he is under the impression that Officer Wilson intends to shoot Dorian Johnson, and he doesn't want to miss it. He recalls that before going out [to the balcony of] his second floor apartment he goes back for his cellphone which is upon a small table beside the bedroom door. He states that when he does get outside, he sees Michael Brown facing Officer Brown, he has both his hands wrapped around his stomach, and he appears bent over and ready to fall forward. However, before Brown falls, the officer fires four or five more times. Brown hits the ground and is bleeding freely. At this point, Officer Wilson is four or five feet away from Brown and is talking on his walkie-talkie. The witness states that it is at this time that he starts recording the scene with his cellphone camera.

Following his testimony, Witness #12 is asked by the detective as to the video he recorded.

As Witness #12 is recording video of the scene with his cellphone and from his second floor balcony, he makes the statement, heard on the recording, that Michael Brown "ran up to the car and was punching it...all up in his (Wilson) car...up in his (Wilson) shit and punching on him." The witness clarifies at the interview, saying he was only making an assumption as to what is taking place based on his prior experience and perception of young people when confronted by police. He then states that what he sees might not have been a punching motion "because I just seen arms, you know, going through the window." He then states the Officer Wilson has Michael Brown by the arm.

Further questioned by the detective for clarification, the witness states he definitely sees Michael Brown's arm in through the driver's side window of the police SUV, he sees arm movements he interprets as aggressive by both men, and that he does not actually see Michael Brown approach and begin to punch the vehicle, stating that is the part he missed.

At this point, the detective acknowledges to the witness the understanding that the witness is probably feeling pressure and receiving stress from the community due to the intense nature of the incident. The witness acknowledges he has been interviewed by media, seen on television, and is routinely approached by members of the community. It is the detective's perception that the witness is being guarded and weighing his words in fear of reprisal from those outside influences.

The witness states that he has become very nervous and scared with his status. That he feels he should have a lawyer. In addition, he states that he Googles his own name which results in multiple references, at least one of which refers to him as a snitch and includes implied threats.

After the detective assures the witness he is safe and advises him on how to deal with the media, the interview resumes.

The witness states that when he first goes to his bedroom window, he is looking through vertical blinds which he parts to get a view of the street. His recollection of the initial events are consistent with his previous three interviews: Brown and Johnson running from the police SUV, Officer Wilson exiting the vehicle and moving the length of the vehicle to the rear while shooting, his physical stance, the location of Johnson relative to the Monte Carlo, and the sequence of these events.

The witness then describes leaving the window, losing his line of sight, and then moving out to the balcony. Here he sees that Michael Brown is no longer running, has stopped and is facing Officer Wilson. He has both hands held to his mid-section and is partially doubled over. The witness makes the assumption he is gut shot. He recalls Michael Brown then taking two small steps forward. Officer Wilson responds by firing four to five more shots at Michael Brown. The witness describes Michael Brown falling face-first to the ground with one hand still clutching his mid-section and the other down by his side. He does not recall which hand is which. When further questioned, the witness states at no time does he see Michael Brown's arms raised in the air.

At this point, the detective asks Witness #12 as to his activity immediately following the shooting and after which he comes down from his apartment to the street. The witness infers that he is joined by his fiancé and at least two of his young children. He also refers to a burgundy colored Bonneville and being told by its occupants, a guy and a girl, that Officer Wilson reverses his vehicle and runs over Michael Brown's foot. The witness also infers that male occupant is the primary source of the details he has as to what takes place between Brown and Wilson at the vehicle.

The detective then focuses on the witness' first interview on scene with the St. Louis County detective, at which time, the detective states, the witness claims he hears the first shot while Officer Wilson was still in the SUV, and which is contrary to his current statement that Officer Wilson does not fire until after exiting the vehicle. The witness states only that he may have been confused at that time, and has since had the opportunity to organize his thoughts. The witness then confirms that he does not hear any shots while Officer Wilson is still in the vehicle. He does, however, again acknowledge that the male occupant of the Bonneville might have told him that there was an initial shot while Officer Wilson was still in the vehicle, and it was that shot the sent both Brown and Johnson running. He describes the individual only has having dreadlocks. He states he was speaking with him from his second floor porch.

The interview concludes with the witness informing the detective of his growing unease with the process, adding that he constantly feels sick to his stomach, is not eating well, has lost weight, and is concerned about the safety of his family and himself.

SECOND INTERVIEW HEARD BY THE GRAND JURY, VOLUME 7

A second interview of Witness #12 takes place with the Grand Jury on September 25, 2104. However, the procedure is relatively brief and the witness does not provide any new information. He does, however, maintain that he sees Michael Brown and Officer Darren Wilson tussling in the vehicle. He also confirms that he did not see Michael Brown stop running and turn around—he assumes he does, and he believes Dorian Johnson drives off in the Monte Carlo because he at first doesn't see anyone in the passenger seat, then he does, and the car drives off.

ANALYSIS AND INTERPRETATON

The key statements by Witness #12 are those relevant to the events at the driver's side window of the police SUV, the points at which Officer Wilson is firing, and the point at which Michael Brown stops running and turns to face Officer Wilson.

AT THE POLICE SUV

Witness #12 provides multiple and conflicting statements as to what he sees prior to Michael Brown fleeing from the SUV. In his first statement he describes the interaction in general terms as "arms being exchanged". However, five minutes later, he informs the detective that he misspoke, and that he actually only sees Michael Brown running from the vehicle. Four days later, in his third statement, and after which he has already shared publically some audio he recorded on his cellphone, he states he sees Michael Brown leaning through the SUV window and punching Officer Wilson. A month later, while speaking to the Grand Jury, he amends his statement, saying he hears "tussling", and given his experience with young people and police, assumes there is a physical confrontation.

Closer to the truth is that Witness #12 comes to his apartment window only after hearing the first shots. By the time he gets there, he sees Officer Wilson already out of his vehicle and Michael Brown fleeing. He inaccurately associates the two shots with Officer Wilson's position outside the vehicle. All other details which he provides with regard to the actual physical confrontation come from other sources.

GUNSHOTS

Witness #12 makes the statement that as Officer Wilson is firing, he is watching Dorian Johnson. Johnson at this time is beside the Monte Carlo, and according to the witness, he appears visibly and physically distressed with each shot fired by Officer Wilson.

The question is why is the witness looking at Johnson and not Wilson and Brown? The answer is because he is in a location at his apartment which does not provide a line of sight down Canfield Drive. For this reason, the witness does not mention Brown reaching Coppercreek Court—he doesn't see him run that far, nor Brown's actions at Coppercreek Court—for example having his hands raised or moving back toward Officer Wilson, and why he believes Officer Wilson is firing while in pursuit and at Brown's back—Wilson is running when he last sees him.

BROWN'S MOVEMENTS

Witness #12 associates Brown stopping, turning and facing Officer Wilson with his location in the middle of Canfield Drive, and as a sequence of events which immediately occurs before Brown is fatally shot. The truth is, however, that this particular sequence occurs at Coppercreek Court and out of the line of sight of the witness. This is further evidence that the witness is using details he has since learned to complete the sequence of the incident, and that he is not being truthful in terms of what it is he himself actually sees.

However, the witness does confirm other eyewitness claims, including by Officer Wilson, that Michael Brown, at some point, does have his hands down around his waist.

PERSPECTIVE

Relative to its objective, Witness #12, although credible with regard to some of the details he provides, ultimately does not see the two key events that are of most interest to the Grand Jury: the confrontation at the vehicle and whether or not Michael Brown, while at the intersection of Coppercreek Court and Canfield Drive, has his hands in a position indicating he is surrendering to or complying with Officer Wilson. Therefore, his value as a witness is minimal in terms of establishing that Officer Wilson either violated the civil rights of Michael Brown or acted improperly in the performance of his duty as a law enforcement officer. In addition, given the number of discrepancies throughout his statements, Witness #12's credibility in the more formal setting of a court room is compromised.

WITNESS #25

INTERVIEWS WITH THE ST. LOUIS COUNTY POLICE AND THE GRAND JURY, VOLUME 11

The interview with Witness #25, a black female, takes place at 4:49 pm (the report list the time in error as 4:59) on August 9, 2014, in the apartment of the witness, which she shares with a roommate. She states her fiancé is present at the time of the incident. The interview concludes at 4:52.

According to the witness, she is in her kitchen eating with her younger sister, at which time her fiancé calls to her from the bedroom, directing her to look out the window. She looks out her patio window. She states she sees an

African-American gentleman running down the street and a police officer walking behind him and "steady opening fire."

At this point, she states that she loses sight of Michael Brown and assumes that he has gotten away. She then sees him walking in the direction of Officer Wilson. She exits her front door and goes out on the patio. She states Office Wilson is in the process of firing his weapon at the chest of Michael Brown. She then states she assumes Officer Wilson is using a taser because Michael Brown is not going down. She thinks Michael Brown "was resting". She says the officer then shoots Brown two more times and "that's when the guy tipped over [bent forward, but did not fall]." She then states that Officer Wilson "walked up and shot him three more times and the dude just tipped over head first and his head smashed into the pavement."

The witness further states that once Michael Brown is on the pavement and no longer moving, Officer Wilson steps away from the body.

Witness #25 is the girlfriend of Witness #12. She is a resident of the Canfield Green apartments, west of Canfield Court and to the north end of the parking lot. The apartment she shares with her boyfriend and her children is on the second floor. It faces Canfield Drive. The interview takes place on October 7, 2014. The procedure is conduct by Alizadeh and Whirley. All 12 jurists are present.

According to Witness #25, on August 9, 2014, while she is in the kitchen, there is a knock on the door. She answer to greet a friend of her boyfriend. She has to wake her boyfriend who is asleep in the bedroom. He comes out and meets with the friend outside the apartment for a few minutes. He returns to the apartment and goes back into the bedroom.

Moments later, with the witness speaking on the phone to her sister, the boyfriend calls out to her from the bedroom and tells her there is a shooting taking place out in the street. She immediately moves from the kitchen and to the living room, where she looks out the patio door. She observes Officer Wilson standing slightly beyond the open driver's door and to the rear of his vehicle. He is in a defensive posture with his gun in his hand. There is a black male running away. The witness states Officer Wilson's vehicle is facing "deeper into the apartments" (facing east towards Northwinds), and she has a view of the driver's side of the vehicle.

Questioned as to the presence of Dorian Johnson, the witness describes seeing a second black male. She describes him as having dreads. She further states that she sees him get into a white Monte Carlo, and then the Monte Carlo drives away.

Continuing, the witness states she first hears gun shots when Officer Wilson is taking long strides away from his vehicle and towards Michael Brown. At this point, Michael Brown has moved east on Canfield Drive and is no longer in her view. She then comes out on her porch and reestablishes sight of Michael Brown. She describes him as moving back in a direction towards Officer Wilson. His arms are raised approximately at a 90° angle, parallel to the ground, and his hands, palms out, are at head level. Michael Brown then takes four or five "big steps" towards Officer Wilson.

Upon further questioning, the witness states, "[Brown] was casually walking as if he had got shot and he started feeling the pain...where like he couldn't...pick up his pace because of the shot." Asked if she sees Brown get shot, the witness says, "Yes...as the officer is shooting...as the bullets were hitting [Brown], you saw like little smoke coming from his chest." She then states that Brown's steps "are ceasing" and he is ready to fall over. At this time, according to Witness #25, Officer Wilson is advancing on Michael Brown. He moves to within ten feet of Brown and he shoots him. Brown falls to the ground.

At this point in the procedure, Alizadeh conducts a review of the statement with Witness #25, which includes details she provides in previous statements.

The witness acknowledges that she does say in her previous statement to the FBI that at one point while Officer Wilson is advancing upon him and firing, Michael Brown does bring his hands down to his side as if he has been shot, and this just prior to the fatal shot from which Brown falls. In addition, she states she witnesses Officer Wilson firing his gun at the back of the fleeing Michael Brown.

ANALYSIS AND INTERPRETATION

Witness #25's statements are primarily a compilation of details she heard or was told by others, with some elements of the incident that she herself may have viewed. Given her recollection of when she first gets to the patio door and hears shots, it is highly unlikely that she saw any of the confrontation at the vehicle or Michael Brown running from it. If as she says, she reestablishes a line of sight only shortly after Michael Brown collapses in the street, most of what she claims prior to that point is either fabricated or from some other source.

Early in her statement, the witness states she observes Officer Wilson in proximity to the vehicle of his car, stationary and in a defensive posture. She then states that Officer Wilson while in pursuit of Michael Brown is firing his weapon. Both of these statements are inaccurate. Wilson does not assume a defensive posture until he moves beyond the rear of the vehicle. Second, Officer Wilson does not fire the first volley until he is to the rear of his vehicle.

Later, the witness states that she sees smoke coming from Michael Brown's chest following the shots that she claims to have seen. However, by the time she reestablishes a line of sight with Michael Brown, the first volley of shots has already taken place. She states it was these shots that she heard while moving to her patio, and while Michael Brown was out of sight. She does not see these shots, and she does not see smoke spiraling from the wounds.

Finally, the witness states she saw Officer Wilson advancing on Michael Brown, and within ten feet of him, fire the fatal shots. This statement, too, calls into question whether the witness actually saw the incident, is only repeating details she has heard or was told, or is fabricating. By this time in the Grand Jury process, it has been established through multiple eyewitness interviews that Officer Wilson was either stationary when shooting, or perhaps even taking steps backwards. The only witnesses that have reported otherwise have been unreliable and not credible.

Witness #25 is not credible as a witness. At best, she saw only part of the incident, and is repeating details she otherwise heard or was told after the fact; and at worst, she is fabricating details, the purpose of which is best known to her, and otherwise irrelevant.

WITNESS #57

INTERVIEW 2 WITH THE ST. LOUIS COUNTY POLICE DEPARTMENT

The interview with Witness #57, his second, takes place on November 6, 2014, at 12:10, in a conference room in the building of the St. Louis County

Prosecuting Attorney. The witness is responding to having received a Grand Jury Subpoena. Present are a detective from the police department's Bureau of Crimes Against Persons and a Special Agent of the FBI. Witness #57 is an unemployed African-American male residing in the Canfield Apartments. The detective and agent are interested in a pod-cast interview the witness did with Tommy Sotomayor, the host of the program. The interview the witness gives to Sotomayor is not consistent with the details he provides to the authorities. The interview concludes at 1:03 pm.

According to Witness #57, he is in his apartment, hears five or six shots, runs out to the street, and sees a police officer standing over a body.

At this point, the detective references both the cellphone recordings and a subsequent interview Witness #57 gives to Tommy Sotomayor. The witness then acknowledges that he may have told the host that he sees Michael Brown and Officer Wilson "tussling" at the police SUV. He tells the detective the tussling goes on for five or six seconds. He then states, "First I heard the shot. I heard one shot. I got up and looked out. And that's when I saw a tussle at the car." The witness then states he sees Michael Brown running down the street and Officer Wilson chasing after. He then says, "I got up and looked out...I heard the shots...and I saw the officer standing over the body." He states he then retrieves his cellphone, goes outside, and records.

Continuing, the detective asks Witness #57 to produce the recording from his cellphone, which he does. On the recording, the witness is heard saying, "[The] guy (Brown) was fighting him (Wilson) in the car."

Upon further questioning for clarification, the witness states, "I seen a guy push off the car and the officer had his shirt."

The detective then produces the witness' dialogue from the podcast in which the witness states, "[Michael Brown] was leaning up in the window [and] scuffling...It was a big scuffle...the guy (Brown) was inside the police car, when I heard the shot."

The witness then explains to the detective that what he means is that Officer Wilson has pulled a part of Brown's shirt into the car. He then states that he does not see Michael Brown doing anything specific with his hands.

Ultimately, the witness states that he hears a shot, sees Michael Brown push away from the vehicle and run east, sees Officer Wilson pursuing him, hears additional shots, and then sees Michael Brown's body in the street.

ANALYSIS AND INTERPRETATION

Witness #57 does not see any of the initial sequence of events. His podcast conversation with the host, Tommy Sotomayor, is a compilation of details he hears from other sources.

In his first statement, the witness says that he only goes to his window after hearing 5 or six shots. Therefore he does not see the confrontation at the police SUV between Brown and Wilson. Going by the words he uses, "push off the car" and "the officer had his shirt", it is likely that he derives these details from Dorian Johnson's take via local media. His other statement that Brown is fighting Wilson in the car is derived from another "witness" who is rejected by the Grand Jury and does not testify.

In all probability, Witness #57 does, as he says, hear a string of shots, but by the time he makes his way out of his apartment, the incident is over and Michael Brown is lying in the street. The witness, therefore, is not credible.

WITNESSES WITH NO CREDIBILITY

WITNESS #37

INTERVIEW WITH THE FBI

The interview with Witness #37 takes place on August 18, 2014, at 2:48 pm. There are two FBI agents from the Civil Rights Squad present and conducting the interview. The location is the office of the St. Louis County Prosecuting Attorney. The witness is a male, approximately 5'10" tall and 170 pounds. His first name is Michael (inadvertently left in the document). He is a plumber by trade. He states that he has been residing with his girlfriend in an apartment in the Canfield complex for the last eight or nine months, having been "put out" of his mother's house. In addition, he states that he has come forth as a witness following a conversation with his mother and his uncle. The witness also infers that he spoke at the scene with Michael Brown's mother. The interview concludes at 3:32 pm.

According to Witness #37, he is driving alone and eastbound on Canfield, having come from West Florissant, and is within the vicinity of the leasing office in proximity to Caddiefield Road. As he is driving eastbound, he comes across stopped traffic. A white pickup truck stops behind him. The witness states he sees Michael Brown and Officer Wilson already engaged physically. Officer Wilson has Brown by his neck and shirt, and Brown is struggling to free himself. The witness states he sees Michael Brown's upper torso inside the driver's window of the police vehicle as if he is being pulled in by the officer. The witness then states that he sees Officer Wilson point his firearm fully out the window with his right hand—he describes the gun as black—and still holding on to Michael Brown's shirt with his left hand fires the first shot. He states he believes the shot hit Brown in the left side of his upper chest. Michael Brown gets loose and runs ten to 15 feet down Canfield Drive. The witness then states that Officer Wilson fires three to four more shots before exiting the vehicle. (The witness infers that Officer Wilson has his arm out the vehicle window, is pointing eastbound on Canfield Drive, and is firing shots at the back of the fleeing Michael Brown.) He later states that he is sure at least one of the bullets hits Brown in the back and causes him to slow and stop.

At this time, the witness states, Dorian Johnson ducks between the back of the police vehicle and the vehicle stopped behind it. He then states that Michael Brown, having run a total of 25-30 feet straight down the middle of Canfield Drive, stops and "throw his hands up". (The witness later demonstrates a posture in which Michael Browns hands are one or two feet over his head.) At which time, Officer Wilson, in calm pursuit—he calls it "lazy"—walks up to him and from point blank range—two feet or less—fires three shots. The shots hit Brown in the face. Michael Brown then leans over and hits his head on the concrete. According to Witness #37, Officer Wilson "patiently took his time, stood over, [and] fired more shots." The witness states he hears [about] ten shots in total, four or five when Brown is already prone on the pavement.

Seeking clarification of the details, the witness is asked if he hears either Wilson or Brown say anything. The witness states he sees Michael Brown's mouth move as if he is saying, "Don't shoot me." The witness emphasizes, however, that he does not hear anything.

Following the shooting, Witness #37 states that he continues driving eastbound on Canfield Drive, and as he passes Officer Wilson he asks him why he shot him. According to the witness, Officer Wilson tells him to keep driving.

INTERVIEW WITH THE GRAND JURY, VOLUME 14

The interview with Witness #37 and the Grand Jury, conducted by Alizadeh and Whirley, takes place on October 20, 2014. A specific time is not provided.

According to the witness, he leaves his apartment in the Canfield complex around 8 or 9:00 in the morning, receives a call from his girlfriend to return to pick up some bills that need to be paid, and as a result is traveling eastbound on Canfield in a red two-door vehicle when he notices the confrontation already in progress between Michael Brown and Officer Wilson. He notes he stops his vehicle; there is a white pick-up truck immediately behind him. The witness further states that Officer Wilson's vehicle is approximately five car-lengths east of his position and parked on an angle in the middle of Canfield Drive in the vicinity of Caddiefield Road. (There are entrances to Caddiefield Road both to the west and east of the apartment complex on the south side of Canfield Road.) He states the vehicle is facing westbound. East of the police SUV and immediately to its rear is a small, four door black car.

At this point, the witness states he sees Michael Brown struggling to get away from the officer, who is holding Brown with both hands, one on the back of Brown's neck and the other grasping his shirt; Officer Wilson is pulling Brown towards the vehicle. The witness then states that he sees the first shot go off, sees the shot strike Mike Brown, and then Brown "gets loose and proceeds up Canfield." He is running slowly.

Upon further questioning, the witness states he sees Officer Wilson's gun—black in color—extend out the window of the vehicle and within six to 12 inches from Michael Brown's torso. The shot, according to the witness, hits Michael Brown in the left side.

Following the first shot, Witness #37 states that he ducks within his vehicle and that his female passenger was "scared out of her mind". He further states that he does not know her name; he picked her up and is giving her a ride. (In his previous interview, the witness states he is alone.)

Continuing, the witness states that Dorian Johnson, while Michael Brown is struggling with Officer Wilson, is standing immediately behind Brown. When Brown starts running east on Canfield, Johnson takes cover at the back of the police SUV and to the front of the black four-door car stopped behind it.

Then, according to Witness #37, Michael Brown stops running and turns and faces Officer Wilson with his hands raised. (Brown takes no further steps from this point on.) At this point, according to the witness, Officer Wilson is no more than two feet from Michael Brown when Brown begins to turn. The witness states he then hears a single shot and Michael Brown "hits the floor...the ground."

At this point, the witness is asked if any other shots have been fired up to this time and since the single shot the witness reports hearing while Officer Wilson is seated in the vehicle. The witness states he hears no other shots, only these two. He then states that he hears a third shot when Officer Wilson is standing over the prone body of Michael Brown, who has fallen face first. He states he believes Officer Wilson shoots Brown in the back of the head. The witness states he recalls only three shots.

Upon further questioning, the witness states that Office Wilson's back is to the witness when he shoots Michael Brown in the head. He then states that Officer Wilson, while talking into the walkie-talkie at his shoulder, walks around Brown's prone body so that he is now facing the witness, and then delivers the third shot into Brown's body.

Continuing, the witness states he drives past Officer Wilson while he is standing over the body and says, "Why in the fuck did you shoot him like that?" He states Officer Wilson responds by saying, "Mind your fucking business."

At this point, Ms. Whirley begins the process of comparing the details provided by Witness #37 during the Grand Jury interview with those he provides to the FBI. She reminds the witness he provides for significantly more shots in the previous statement and different times when he accounts for those shots. The witness states that after he was told by the FBI agents that his statement did not match the forensic evidence, he rethought his statement. He further makes a comment about perhaps 'hallucinating" and going into a "blur".

Pressed on the issue by Whirley, the witness then states he hears eight shots. He states there are two shots while Brown is running from the vehicle, one shot when Brown and Wilson are face to face, and then one or two shots when Brown is prone.

The witness then acknowledges that he does speak to Michael Brown's mother immediately following the incident. He states that Brown's mother asks him to tell her if her son is in the wrong. He states he tells her Brown is no threat at the time he is shot.

ANALYSIS AND INTERPRETATION

Video evidence from a television news segment confirms that Witness #37 is at the incident scene at the time when Michael Brown is lying prone in the street. He is identified and his presence acknowledged by Alizadeh and Whirley during the Grand Jury interview. However, given the inaccuracies throughout his statement, it is reasonable to question if he actually witnesses any part of the confrontation or the shooting to follow, and it is more likely that he drives into the scene only after Michael Brown is already deceased.

AT THE VEHICLE

The words Witness #37 uses to describe Michael Brown's activity there beside the police SUV suggest he has spoken to Dorian Johnson prior to making his statements, or at least has heard Johnson's comments to the media. And while it is likely that Officer Wilson does at some point have his hands on Brown's shirt, it is unlikely, and not logical, that he would be both trying to pull Brown into the vehicle while at the same time accessing his weapon to fend him off.

The witness also falsely claims seeing Officer Wilson's weapon fully extended from the vehicle while firing on Brown, and then remain in clear sight for three additional shots while Brown is fleeing. Forensic evidence clearly establishes that there are only two shots that occur while Officer Wilson is inside the vehicle. The first one is embedded within the interior door panel. The second one strikes Michael Brown in the hand. Both are fired while the weapon is fully within the SUV.

NUMBER AND SEQUENCE OF SHOTS

Claims by the witness that Michael Brown is shot in the left side of his chest and in the back are false. The forensic evidence establishes that Brown takes no gunshot wounds to either of those areas. In addition, no other credible witness reports shots fired while Brown is running east on Canfield Drive.

The witness also falsely claims that Officer Wilson, at a distance of two feet or less, fires three shots into Michael Brown's face, after which he stands over Michael Brown and fires a round into the back of his head. In his second statement, he adds that Wilson walks around Brown's prone body and shoots him twice more. The forensic evidences shows no shots to the back of the head, and no shots, other than the one that occurs at the vehicle (thumb wound), take place at point-blank range. There is only one gunshot wound to the face, and that is above the right eye.

OTHER INCONSISTENCIES

In the witness' second statement he makes no mention of Michael Brown mouthing the phrase "Don't shoot me", something he insists upon in his first statement. Given the potential significance of such a statement, it is logical to conclude that the witness fabricates this event. There are also no other witnesses who state seeing any vehicle approach Officer Wilson immediately following the shooting, and Officer Wilson himself makes no mention of it in his own statements. Therefore it is unlikely that the witness drives up to Officer Wilson or says anything to him from any location. Ultimately, to cover his false statements, the witness suggests he may have been hallucinating and the details as a result are a blur.

PERSPECTIVE

Relative to the objectives of the Grand Jury, Witness #37 is not credible. The number of false statements he makes far outweighs any value he may have in terms of any part of the incident he might have actually witnessed.

WITNESS #41

INTERVIEW WITH THE FBI

Witness #41 is an older African-American female and a resident of the apartments on Canfield Drive. She claims to be partially deaf in one ear and she wears glasses. She acknowledges that she has previous knowledge of Michael Brown and has spoken with him socially in the past. She also acknowledges knowing his grandmother. The interview takes place at the apartment of the witness on August 26, 2014, at 9:32 am, and is being conducted by two Special Agents from the FBI. The interview is terminated and then continues. The interview concludes at 10:08 am.

According to Witness #41, she is on the porch outside of her apartment and on the second floor. The porch faces out onto Coppercreek Court. The witness first states she hears one shot and goes down to the parking lot to see what is going on. She then amends her statement to say she hears two shots before going down to the parking lot. Once down at street level, she states she witnesses Michael Brown "on his knees with his hands up and he was being shot." She then states that Officer Wilson exits his vehicle, "stood over the boy and just emptied his clip."

Upon being asked for clarification, the witness states that Officer Wilson is walking towards Michael Brown—Brown is on his knees and has his hands up—and is firing his weapon. She then states that Brown eventually falls on his face and "that's when the policeman came over and just finished him up." She states that 'they' shot him in the head, but not the back of the head.

The agent then asks the witness to explain how Officer Wilson manages to shot him in the [forehead] if he is face down. The witness demonstrates, stating in addition that she hears nine shots in total, and then the gun 'click' twice upon empty chambers.

At this point, the detective reminds Witness #41 that lying to a federal officer is a criminal offense for which she could be prosecuted. The witness assures the detective she is telling the truth, adding that her uncle is an FBI Agent in Washington.

Ultimately, the agent informs the witness that he does not believe her statement, at which time the witness directs the agent to stop recording and erase her statement. The agent refuses. The interview concludes.

At 9:46, the agents continue the interview with Witness #41 upon her request. She tells them that she would like to modify her statement.

According to the witness, she did not see Officer Wilson approach Michael Brown and shoot him at any time. She states, instead, that she sees only the back of Michael Brown, but continues to insist he is down on his knees and has his arms raised. In addition, she states she hears two clicks, but cannot identify their origin, and counts nine shots, all of which occur while she is on her way down to the parking lot.

As for Michael Brown falling face first to the pavement, the witness states that while Officer Wilson is walking towards Brown, her attention is distracted by an unidentified person tapping her on the shoulder, and by the time she turns back to view the incident, Michael Brown is already prone to the pavement.

In addition, the witness states the right side of Officer Wilson's face is red "...just like a bruise".

INTERVIEW WITH THE GRAND JURY, VOLUME 16

Witness #41 is interviewed by the Grand Jury, Alizadeh and Whirley, on October 27, 2014, at 8:50 am. The witness confirms that her apartment faces Coppercreek Court. In addition, she states that she actually lives on the first floor, and that her godson's apartment is the one on the second floor. She also states that she changes her statement during the second part of her first interview with the Special Agents of the FBI to tell them what they want to hear.

According to Witness #41, around 11:00 am, she hears shooting. She claims she hears four shots before she comes out of her apartment and onto the second floor porch. She then goes down the stairs towards the parking lot. She states her godson is home with her at the time, but he remains up on the porch.

Once down in the parking lot, she states that she immediately sees Michael Brown. He is down upon his knees on the street on Canfield Drive. His arms are raised up over his head, but with a 45° angle to his elbow. She then states as Michael Brown is falling, the officer shots him again and that's when he goes down. She states she recalls 11 shots in all, but two may have been echoes.

Continuing, the witness states that the right side of Officer Wilson's face is red, as if bruised, or perhaps he is angry. She also notes that he is wearing a blue, short-sleeved shirt, does not wear a hat, and has light-colored (blonde) hair.

ANALYSIS AND INTERPRETATION

Although it is not reflected in the text above, Witness #41 has diagnosed mental and cognitive issues, is under the care of a physician, and takes multiple medications. As such, the approach of the Grand Jury is significantly more tolerant than that of the FBI agents, who initially are unaware of her mental issues.

Nevertheless, there is no reason to believe the witness saw any part of the actual shooting, and in all likelihood witnesses no more than Michael Brown's body, and even then probably only after having been covered by sheets. There are no details in her statement that are consistent with the sequence or chronology of the events as they are known by this time. The details which she does provide are by that time general knowledge, and it is probable that she learns of them through the news or conversation with others. To support this supposition, the witness changes the number of shots she hears while descending her stairs from one to four, with four being a number claimed by multiple witnesses as comprising one or both of the strings of shots fired by Officer Wilson.

Over all, Witness #41 is not telling the truth. Her statement is not credible.

WITNESS #42

INTERVIEW WITH THE FBI

The interview with Witness #42 takes place on August 16, 2014. A specific time is not entered on the document. The procedure is conducted by two Special Agents. The witness is an African-American male of mature age, perhaps 60 or older, and a resident of the Canfield Apartments. His unit is between Canfield Court and Coppercreek Court. He states he is outside his apartment and on his porch with his cellphone at the time of the incident.

According to Witness #42, he is speaking on his cellphone to an out-of-town caller and hears a shot. He states he does not see the initial part of the confrontation between Michael Brown and Officer Wilson, and by the time he has a visual, Michael Brown is running eastbound on Canfield Drive. He states Officer Wilson fires a shot while Brown is running away from him and has his back turned. The witness states Officer Wilson "shot the individual in the back".

Continuing, the witness states that Brown stops running and turns around with his hands in the air "in a fashion...that means surrender", and is stepping towards Officer Wilson. The witness states he hears Brown say, "Don't shoot." (The witness later states that he believes Michael Brown did not know how to properly surrender.) The witness then states that while Michael Brown has his hands up, Officer Wilson, at a distance approximately 20 feet from Brown, empties his gun into the chest of Michael Brown. As Officer Wilson then gets closer (the inference is that Wilson is also moving towards Brown; he later states that Wilson "close in on him"), Witness #42 says, "[He] let a round off in his head, his cheek, his head and he finished a round and stood over him." The witness states that Officer Wilson fires the final round, a head shot, from an arm's length away. Further, he states the head shot is delivered while Michael Brown is standing, and after which he has taken multiple shots to the upper torso and lower abdomen. The witness then states, "He (Brown) fell to the ground, and he (Wilson) continued to let the rounds off … [Brown] fell forward. The officer stood over him and finished him off."

Questioned by the agents for clarity of detail, the witness states that Officer Wilson is tall and with brunette hair. He has a slim build and is wearing a blue uniform.

INTERVIEW WITH SPECIAL AGENT, DEPARTMENT OF JUSTICE, AND ASSISTANT ATTORNEY

The interview with Witness 42 and the Special Agent takes place on September 30, 2014, at 9:50 am. Also present are a trial attorney from the Department of Justice and a United States Assistant Attorney. This is the second interview with Witness #42, the purpose of which is to clarify inconsistencies and discrepancies which surface during the first interview. The interview concludes at 10:23.

According to Witness #42, he is out on his porch speaking on his cellphone when he hears gunshots. He tells the person to whom he is speaking that he will call him back and then moves out further onto his porch where he can see down Canfield Drive. He sees Michael Brown, an individual he has met before and who is a friend to his nephew, but who he does not recognize at the time. Brown is running east on Canfield Drive. In addition, he also sees two construction workers.

The witness then states he hears an additional shot. Michael Brown stops and turns with his hands up. He begins to walk towards Officer Wilson. As Brown gets closer to Officer Wilson, the witness sees the gun going off, Brown continuing to move forward with his hands raised, and the bullets going into his chest. Brown is telling Officer Wilson "okay", and that he surrenders. He places Wilson at a distance of 8-10 steps from Brown when Brown falls. The witness says he screams out to Officer Wilson, saying, "He didn't pose a fucking threat."

At this point, the special agents asks questions to clarify specific details.

The witness states that his apartment is on the second floor and that his balcony, which is a shared balcony, provides him a clear view of Canfield

Drive. He states he has a clear view of both Michael Brown and Officer Wilson. He, however, retracts his previous claim that he sees Officer Wilson shoot Brown in the back. He states instead that Officer Brown fires steadily and without pause. The witness assumes Brown stops running because he his shot. He sees Brown turn around and move towards Officer Wilson. He then states that his balcony presents a blind spot and he loses sight of Brown. The firing stops, and the witness says he observes Brown get shot in the upper torso multiple times. He does not see him fall. He does hear more shots and assumes Brown falls at that time. He then states there is a time during the incident when he sees both Brown and Officer Wilson, although he acknowledges Wilson is always at a point further west than Brown. However, according to the Witness, Wilson is while firing backing-up and moving away from Brown.

Following further questioning, Witness #42 states he does not see Officer Wilson stand over Michael Brown and fire additional shots, does not see Michael Brown at any time on his knees, does not hear or see any additional shots after Michael Brown has fallen, nor does he at any time see Officer Wilson within arm's length of Michael Brown. He acknowledges these are assumptions he makes, details he hears from others, or what he believes to be common sense.

INTERVIEW WITH THE GRAND JURY, VOLUME 16

The interview of Witness #42 with the Grand Jury takes place on October 27, 2014. The proceedings are conducted by Alizadeh and Whirley. All 12 jurists are present. From the onset of the interview, Witness #42 provides significantly different details than he did with the FBI agents and acknowledges that he is aware of at least one autopsy report. In addition, he acknowledges he has poor eyesight and wears contacts. He states he is wearing his contacts at the time of the incident. As for his relationship to Michael Brown, he states Brown is a friend of his nephews and nieces and has been over their house to swim in the pool.

According to Witness #42, he has just finished preparing breakfast when he goes out onto his porch where the phone reception is better to continue a conversation he is having with a friend. He hears one or two gun shots. He then moves further out onto his porch and sees Michael Brown running eastbound on Canfield and towards Coppercreek Court. Officer Wilson is not in view at this time.

The witness then states that he sees Michael Brown, while in close proximity to Coppercreek court, stop running due to a bullet wound to his arm. Brown then starts to turn towards Officer Wilson's position and is raising his arms. He then starts to move back up Canfield Drive and towards Officer Wilson, who the witness states, is also moving towards Michael Brown. Both are walking.

Continuing, the witness states that Officer Wilson has his gun up, and as Wilson is approaching Brown, Brown is saying "stop shooting". (The witness affirms four additional times that he hears Michael Brown say 'stop shooting'.) Officer Wilson responds by shooting him and continuing to shoot him.

Upon further questioning, the witness states that Officer Wilson is within a few feet of Brown when he shoots him. The attorney then asks, "Who starts moving back?" To which the witness responds it is Officer Wilson; he is moving back while firing.

Further, the witness states that he sees Brown take two bullets to the upper torso and two bullets to the lower torso. He then states there is a blind spot upon his porch, and he does not see Michael Brown fall, nor does he see any shots to the head. He does state, however, he hears 10 shots in total.

At this point, the attorney, Whirley, starts the process of comparing the witness's previous statement to the FBI with the details he is now providing.

According to Witness #42, Officer Wilson is firing at Michael Brown while he is running eastbound on Canfield. He now says, however, that due to the autopsy report, he knows Michael Brown is not shot in the back, which is contrary to the information the witness provides in his first statement. He then states that he does not see Michael Brown fall, or Officer Wilson stand over Brown and shoot him. He states these are assumptions he makes.

At this point, Alizadeh address the witness. She states that he lies in his statement to the FBI. The witness acknowledges after each point that he lies, but that he interprets his actions as making assumptions.

ANALYSIS AND INTERPRETATION

Witness #42 is physically in a location during the incident that does not allow a line of sight west on Canfield Drive. The only sequence he actually witnesses is when Michael Brown comes into view in proximity to the intersection of Canfield and Coppercreek. It is possible, then, that he sees Brown turn with his arms raised and move back towards Officer Wilson. He does hear the first string of shots, and in all probability, does see Michael Brown flinch, as is reported by multiple other witnesses.

However, by his own acknowledgement, Brown, shortly thereafter, moves out of his line of sight. He hears, but does not see the second string of shots, and does not see, as he states, Michael Brown fall to the ground. The details he provides relative to this particular sequence of events are fabrications or come from other sources. Either way, they are not true. Michael Brown is not shot in the back or the back of the head, he is not shot multiple times in the chest; he is not shot after he falls, and he is shot at point-blank range only once, and that is within proximity to the police SUV.

While the witness' motivation for providing false witness are his own, when asked by Alizadeh, he says, "Because some individual getting shot by police, it was like, really, this didn't just happen." He also says that he believes Michael Brown poses no threat at the time to Officer Wilson, but acknowledges he does not see the confrontation at the SUV, and therefore is likely basing his impression on his opinion that Brown is "a well-mannered individual".

Witness #42 is not credible.

WITNESS #45

INTERVIEW WITH THE FBI

The interview with Witness #45, a female African-American, takes place outside the apartment of a male acquaintance on August 16, 2014, at 10:50 am. The interview is conducted by two Special Agents of the FBI. There are children present (in another room). The agent explains to the witness that they are there only to gather information and that they serve neither the police nor the victim. The interview concludes at 11:23.

According to Witness #45, she is in the area of the Canfield Apartments visiting a cousin. She is outside speaking with a male resident and a lady. She states that she sees Michael Brown and Dorian Johnson when they are walking to the store and then again when they are coming back.

The witness states Brown and Johnson are walking in the middle of the street. The police SUV backs up into them. The officer reaches out of the vehicle window and grabs Michael Brown by the collar. She then hears the first shot. Michael Brown tries to run. She hears the second shot. Michael Brown stops with his arms up. His arms remain up. Brown turns around. The officer fires. The shots continue ringing out. Brown falls. The officer goes over to the body, bends down to check on his condition, and then walks away. The witness states she sees two police officers in the vehicle.

As has been consistent with the process, at this point, the agent now takes the time to go over each of the details individually.

According to Witness #45, she actually stays (lives) around the corner. (She doesn't provide specifics.) At approximately 1:00 pm on August 9th, she is out driving and sees some neighbors in the parking lot of the apartment complex. (The witness is confused by the question. She has been in the parking lot for a least 30 minutes by this time.) She stops to ask for and smoke a cigarette. She doesn't know the name of the lady who gives her the cigarette, or the male with whom she is casually talking—only that he is upon his second floor balcony. (She points him out to the agent as they are speaking; he too is currently speaking with an agent.) She states she is standing in the vicinity of a dumpster in the Coppercreek Court parking lot east of the apartment complex. (Coppercreek Court, technically, is the entrance to the parking lot.)

The witness then accurately provides for the location and positon of the police SUV. She accurately establishes the direction in which the vehicle is heading, as well as for the eastbound direction of Brown and Johnson. She states that as the incident escalates at the vehicle between Brown and Wilson, Dorian Johnson takes cover beside the Monte Carlo, which she describes as black in color. She further states that Johnson runs off during the shooting.

Continuing, the witness states that Michael Brown is shot one time while at the vehicle. She sees him back away from the driver side door and notes blood staining his shirt at chest level. He then runs towards Coppercreek Court, at which point Officer Wilson fires a second shot. Brown then stops within the vicinity of the telephone pole within five feet of the driveway. Brown then turns and starts moving back towards Officer Wilson, whom she places at the back of and slightly to the side of the police SUV.

The witness then states that as Michael Brown turns back towards Officer Wilson he has his arms raised and she clearly hears Brown say, "I give up." She then states that's when Michael Brown "came back to him (Wilson), that's when he (Wilson) stood over him (Brown)...and emptied his [gun]." She states she sees eight or nine shots. However, she then states that the last shot is fired when Michael Brown, his knees bent but still upright, is falling. Officer Wilson then bends, checks Brown's pulse, and walks away.

INTERVIEW WITH THE GRAND JURY, VOLUME 17

The interview with Witness #45 and the Grand Jury takes place on October 28, 2014, at approximately 12:56 PM. The procedure is conducted by Alizadeh and Whirley. All twelve jurists are present.

According to Witness #45, she is riding through the Canfield Drive Apartment complex in a burgundy-colored car westbound towards Florissant to see a friend. The friend is not home. She states she recognizes people outside the complex on the corner of Coppercreek Court and Canfield Drive. She pulls into the parking lot and stops to ask for a cigarette.

The witness states as she and the male friend (he is up on his second floor balcony) are smoking and talking, she observes Michael Brown and Dorian Johnson walking on Canfield Drive and westbound towards West Florissant. (She is confused by directions. She later accurately acknowledges Brown and Johnson were walking towards the Northwinds Apartments, which are eastbound on Canfield Drive.) She accurately describes both, physically and relative to their clothing. She states she does not know either Brown or Johnson. She states she is on Coppercreek Court, near the dumpster in the parking lot, when both Brown and Johnson walk past her.

Continuing, Witness #45 states that Brown and Johnson separate to permit Officer Wilson's vehicle to pass by. Brown moves to the driver's side and Johnson to the passenger's side. The SUV continues westbound for an unspecified distance. Officer Wilson then backs up his vehicle in a straight line. The witness then states from her perspective from the passenger side of the vehicle she sees Officer Wilson reach out the window and grab Michael Brown by the shirt collar. Then Wilson and Brown start tussling. The witness estimates the struggle goes on for two minutes. Michael Brown then pulls away from Officer Wilson's grip.

According to the witness, as soon as Michael Brown moves back from the vehicle, she hears the first shot. She sees a red spot on Brown's shirt. Brown turns and runs straight in her direction and comes to a stop in the vicinity of the light pole on the north side of Canfield Drive and just west of the entrance onto Coppercreek Court. Brown then turns back towards the officer. He has his hands up and they never come down. At that point, the witness states, despite Brown surrendering and screaming "I give up", Officer Wilson opens fire on Michael Brown. Michael Brown falls upon his face in the middle of Canfield Drive. The officer then comes up, bends down towards the body, and checks Brown's pulse. The witness states at this time, however, that the officer that does so is not Darren Wilson. The face does not match the face she sees on television at a later date.

In addition, the witness states there are two officers in the police SUV at the time that Brown and Johnson are first engaged. The witness states she clearly sees the second officer in the passenger seat and that he does not at any time exit the vehicle to assist Officer Wilson.

During the process in which the attorney is reviewing with Witness #45 the details of her statement, the witness states that there is verbal engagement between Officer Wilson and Michael Brown and Dorian Wilson when Officer Wilson first encounters them on Canfield Drive, and after which he then backs up the vehicle to reengage. When Wilson stops his vehicle it is straight and not on an angle. She further states that the passenger side window is open and that's how she sees Officer Wilson grab Michael Brown by the shirt collar.

In addition, she states that Officer Wilson does not stand over Brown's body and fire any additional shots.

ANALYSIS AND INTERPRETATION

Given there are other witnesses who put a burgundy-colored car on scene in proximity to the time of the incident, it is possible that Witness #45 is present at the apartment complex. However, given the inaccuracies of her statement, it is obvious she is not only not telling the truth, but that she is lying both in regard to being a witness and as to what she claims to have seen. Included among her false statements are the following: Brown and Wilson move to opposite sides of the police SUV as Wilson approaches; Wilson immediately reaches out of the vehicle to grab Brown by the neck; Brown is shot in the chest there at the SUV; blood is visible on Brown's shirt there at the SUV; Brown turns at Coppercreek Court with his hands up and says, "I give up;" Officer Wilson stands over Brown and empties his weapon; Officer Wilson bends to take Brown's pulse; and there are two officers in the police SUV.

Witness #45 is not credible.

THE EXTREMISTS

WITNESS #35

INTERVIEW WITH THE ST. LOUIS COUNTY POLICE DEPARTMENT

The interview with Witness #35 takes place on August 13, 2014, at 1:50 pm. The witness is a 19 year-old African-American Male named Viron (inadvertently left in the document two times). The interview is conducted by a detective with the police department and a Special Agent with the Bureau of Crimes Against Persons. The witness is accompanied by a female attorney. The witness refuses to provide a telephone number and states that he is currently between residences, but is living with his sister in an apartment on Canfield Drive. The interview concludes at 2:32.

According to Witness #35, he is in his nephews' bedroom and talking on the phone with his girlfriend when he hears a gunshot. He moves to the window with a west-facing view and sees Michael Brown drop to his knees. He states "blood was rushing from either his shoulder or his rib cage" on his left side. In addition, he says at this time there are people on the street, families and kids—"a whole lot of traffic coming in and out."

Continuing, the witness states, "I seen Michael Brown, my best friend, drop to his knees, he dropped to his knees, he looked at my cousin (Dorian Johnson), and told him, 'Run for your life'." He states Dorian Johnson, both crying and in shock, is right next to Michael Brown when he is kneeling. Dorian Johnson then starts running. The witness then states that he sees Officer Wilson exit his truck and immediately shoot Michael Brown in the head while he is kneeling.

At this point, the detective reminds Witness #35 that he is speaking with an FBI agent, and that if he is lying he can be charged with a one-thousand one. The witness responds, "This is not a lie. I would never lie about this. This is my best friend." He then evokes God as his witness. He later states, "Everything I told you is one-hundred percent the truth."

Following a brief period of contentious dialogue between the witness and those conducting the interview, and in which the witness states that no one can tell him what he saw, the process continues. The witness immediately states, "I seen my best friend in the middle of the street with his hands in the air and he said, 'Please don't shoot me.' The officer got out of his car and shot him." The witness then states the officer shoots Michael Brown eight more times. After the first shot, Officer Wilson, who the witness states he cannot identify, shoots Michael Brown four more times, which the witness infers he sees, pauses for ten seconds, and shoots him four additional times; at which time, according to the witness, he is coming down a flight of stairs and does not see. All the shots are delivered at point blank range.

According to Witness #35, at the time Michael Brown is shot his back is to the front end of the police cruiser, to the driver's side, and Brown is approximately five feet from the cruiser. (During this exchange of dialogue, the witness is exhibiting significant resistance and will not provide details, and instead is permitting the detective to suggest details to which the witness agrees or disagrees. The witness is not being cooperative.) In addition, the witness states that Officer Wilson is standing in front of Michael Brown, approximately five to six feet away.

The witness then states that Officer Wilson walks up to Michael Brown, points his weapon directly at Brown's forehead and shoots. (When physically demonstrating the event, the witness places his finger [the gun] inches from his uncle's head, who is serving as the role of Michael Brown during the demonstration.) He then states that Michael Brown falls flat, then turns, and Officer Wilson shoots him four more times. According to the witness, those shots account for the wound Brown receives in his arm, and which the witness learns of watching the news on television.

The interview concludes with the detectives and attorney telling Witness #35 that his statement is not consistent with other witnesses. The witness states, "I need justice for my friend."

INTERVIEW WITH THE FBI

Witness #35 is a 19 year-old black male. He claims to be a cousin of Michael Brown. The interview takes place at the FBI Building, 2222 Market Place, on October 3, 2014, at 10:48 am. The interview is conducted by a Special Agent with the FBI, an attorney from the Department of Justice, and an additional federal attorney. The witness is accompanied by an attorney. It is apparent by the dialogue that the witness has given a previous statement.

According to Witness #35, at the time of the incident, Michael Brown, who he first refers to as one of his best friends—they went to high school together, is staying with him in his sister's apartment there on Canfield Drive. He states Brown had an argument with his grandmother about a week prior, who since that time is hospitalized, and as Michael Brown has no place else to go, he has been staying in the apartment since. In addition, he states he knows Dorian Johnson well, since he was a boy, and they are like cousins, but not by blood.

Witness #35 states that on the morning of the incident, he receives a call from his mother asking him to help put his nephews in the car. Instead, Michael Brown takes care of it. Brown then returns to the apartment and informs the witness that he and Dorian are going out to a local store.

According to the witness—he is still in bed and sleeping, approximately 15 to 20 minutes later, he hears the first shot. He states he leaves his bed and goes over to his third floor window. He states, "[What] I saw was that the officer had a gun drawn and Michael Browns' facing him on his knees. And then maybe about a few seconds later...I seen him shoot him in the head."

At this time, the witness states he leaves his window to go down to the street level. On his way, he hears four more shots. When he arrives at the bottom of the steps, he hears seven more shots.

The detective then asks how many shots he sees. The witness states only one. He then states that Michael Brown is kneeling with his back to him, and he only recognizes it is Michael due to his khaki-colored shorts, the black and white Nike flip-flops, and the yellow socks with the marijuana leaves.

Asked again if he saw the officer shoot Michael Brown, the witness states he did, and that Officer Wilson, while "at point blank range", shoots Brown in the head while he is down on his knees, apparently wounded, and "surrendering like". The witness then states that Michael Brown falls face first to the pavement, but that he is unsure where his hands are at this time. In addition, he states that the shooting takes place "about five to six feet" from the police vehicle.

Following this extent of the interview, the detective begins to question Witness #35 about Michael Brown's marijuana use. The witness states that Michael has only been using marijuana for about a period of four months, and then only during special occasions, such as holidays and birthdays. He states he does not believe Brown is in possession of marijuana at the time of the incident, and has no reason to believe Brown has used marijuana recently.

At this point, the detective refers to the previous statement Witness #35 gave to the FBI on August 13, 2014. In that statement, the witness states he sees Officer Wilson shoot Michael Brown in the head and then stand over his body and shoot four more times. He then says that after the head shot, Officer Wilson actually shots Michael Brown a total of eight times more.

The witness responds to the detective, saying, "More importantly it is what I heard." He states that he sees one shot and then hears nine more.

When the detective questions the witness' previous claim that he sees Michael Brown bleeding from his side or his shoulder, but on this date he states he did not see any wound on Brown, the witness states he was reporting something he had heard from an unidentified on-looker.

On further questioning, the witness then states that he hears Michael Brown, while on his knees and with his hands raised, say, "Please, don't shoot." When asked to clarify if Brown is pleading for his life, Witness #35 states yes.

At 11:26 am, the detective concludes the interview, saying, "We certainly don't want you to talk to us anymore."

INTERVIEW WITH THE GRAND JURY, VOLUME 13

Witness #35 is interviewed by the Grand Jury on October 16, 2014, at 1:11 pm. The interview is conducted by Alizadeh and Whirley. Prior to the actual interview, Alizadeh expresses confusion about the witness' choice of first names, as it is not the name he uses in prior interviews. The witness states he has recently started using the name, having learned about his heritage from his uncle. He states a preference for using his given name during the interview.

According to the witness, Michael Brown has been living with him at his sister's apartment for about two or three weeks prior to and until the incident. He further states that Brown is related to him. (However, the witness is actually related by blood to Brown's step-father.)

In response to questioning, the witness states that his sister's apartment is on the north side of Canfield Drive, on the third floor and facing west towards West Florissant. (This statement doesn't appear to be accurate.)

However, there is a bedroom with a window overlooking Canfield Drive to the south.

The witness states that the morning of August 9, 2014, Michael Brown helps his sister bring her young children down to her mother's waiting car. Brown returns and asks the witness to use his cellphone. It was about 11:00. After he uses the phone, Brown tells the witness he is going to the store with Dorian Johnson.

According to the witness, while Brown is gone, he is lying in bed and talking to a lady friend on his cellphone. He then hears a gun shot and goes to his bedroom window. The witness states he sees Michael Brown on his knees with his hands up in the air and "smack dab in the middle of the street down the yellow line". He states he is looking at Brown's back and into the face of Officer Wilson. (He later describes Wilson as wearing a black police hat and glasses.) Brown and Wilson are approximately four to five feet apart. The witness refers to the distance as "point blank" range. He also states that the police vehicle, which he says he doesn't see until he comes down to street level, is no more than five feet away from Brown's position in the street.

Upon further questioning, the witness states that Michael Brown is kneeling and has his hands raised. While demonstrating for the Grand Jury the position, it is noted that the witness has his hands about shoulder level with his palms pointed up. At this point, according to the witness, Officer Wilson has his gun pointed at Brown's skull. The witness states he sees Wilson shoot Brown in the head, and Brown fall to the pavement. The witness then exits his apartment, and by the time he is out the door and on the porch, he hears three to four more shots. By the time he gets to the end of the steps, he hears several more shots.

At the conclusion of the interview, Witness #35 states he did not hear Michael Brown pleading for his life; it was something that he was told by someone else.

ANALYSIS AND INTERPRETATION

The issue with Witness #35 is his ignorance—perhaps 'naïveté' is a kinder word—as to the reliability of forensic science to uncover some of the facts, and therefore he believes he is free to concoct a sequence of events that places Officer Wilson in the wrong, regardless of the fact that all of what he says is contradicted by forensic and witness-generated evidence. Later, when challenged by the FBI as to the implausibility of his claims, he resorts to modifying his statements to provide vague and less verifiable details—he hears, not sees, or his told by others. When that tactic fails, he stubbornly insists despite the counsel of his representation that no one can tell him what he sees.

Nevertheless, his statements are included to illustrate the challenges with which the Grand Jury are presented in their task of determining the facts having only second person accounts to rely upon. And while Witness #35 is so extreme in the false statements which he provides, and therefore easily discounted as not credible, there are other witnesses who clearly have seen particular events or sequence of events, but who then try to fill in the rest using details they learn from other sources—some as false as Witness #35, and are thereby tainted in terms of what they actually see and what they think they see.

However, in terms of the overall process, Witness #35 is of some use to the Grand Jury. He serves as a cautionary warning as to the extent that some witnesses will go to further an objective of their own. And his statements are so extreme that they establish both a sequence of events that is not possible and an increased probability factor for one that is.

WITNESS #40

INTERVIEW WITH THE FBI AND THE GRAND JURY

Witness #40 is a white female who claims to have pulled into the Canfield Green Complex looking for directions. She is interviewed by the FBI on October 22, 2014, at approximately 2:14 pm. The interview takes place at the FBI building on 2222 Market Place. The procedure is conducted by a Special Agent and a prosecuting attorney from the Department of Justice. The interview as presented in the documents, however, first appears in Volume 15 of the Grand Jury.

The witness is an unidentified white female (?) of middle age. She claims to have been driving on her way to a friend's house when she becomes lost. Eventually, she sees residents outside the apartment complex between Caddiefield Road, pulls in the west entrance and drives around to the east side.

She exits her car and approaches a heavy set African-American male wearing a green shirt and sporting braids. She then lights a cigarette. It is at this time she observes the police SUV driven by Officer Wilson. Her perspective is to the driver's side. She states she is somewhere towards the center of the apartments.

According to the witness, when she first observes the police SUV, Officer Wilson is addressing both Michael Brown and Dorian Johnson. She states Dorian Johnson is the first to exchange words with Officer Wilson. She does not hear what is said. She then states Officer Wilson continues to roll past both Brown and Johnson for a couple of tire rotations and then backs up to reengage them. She states almost immediately Michael Brown physically engages Officer Wilson, putting himself waist deep into the vehicle through the driver's side window.

Prior to the actual physical engagement, the witness states that Officer Wilson twice attempts to open the door to the vehicle. She states Michael Brown uses the heels of his hand to push the door closed on the first attempt, at which time Dorian Johnson with a closed fist pushed against the side view mirror. She states that at this time a gold-colored bracelet falls from Johnson's wrist and to the pavement below the driver's side door. On the second attempt, Michael Brown uses his body weight to close the door, and that is when he then puts his entire upper body through the window.

Continuing, the witness states that she clearly observes Michael Brown punching Officer Wilson multiple times. She states she assumes the punches are to Officer Wilson's face or head, but she can't be sure. At this time, Officer Wilson is leaning away towards the passenger seat of the front of the vehicle. She states Dorian Johnson has moved from her line of sight, and that she is not sure where he is located at this time.

According to the witness, she then hears a single shot. At this point, Michael Brown moves away from the car, pulls up his sagging pants, and begins to run eastbound down Canfield. His arms are moving in a normal runner's motion, and he at least once more pulls his pants up.

Officer Wilson then exits the vehicle. He has his gun drawn in his right hand and he is holding his left hand to the side of this face. The witness reports Officer Wilson takes one unsteady step with each foot—wobbling, according to the witness—and appears confused or dizzy. She states he then says something, the only part of which she recalls is "or I'll shoot".

At this time, the witness states, Michael Brown stops running, turns around and faces Officer Wilson. The witness then states that Michael Brown puts his hands in position somewhat higher than his waist, his fists are clenched, and are out and away from his body. The witness describes it as "a football thing" and with attitude, as if Michael Brown is saying, 'What are you going to do?'

By this point, according to the witness, Officer Wilson is positioned to the back of the police SUV, is stationary, in a defensive posture and has his weapon pointed at Michael Brown: "The hand was on the trigger; he was ready to go. He was focused. He no longer had that confused, just got smacked look."

Continuing, the witness states Michael Brown "bent down in the football position...and began to charge at the officer". She states Michael Brown "looked like he was on something". In addition, she states Officer Wilson says something—she doesn't know what—and Michael Brown may have been saying something, but to her it sounds only like grunting. Officer Wilson then starts to fire, shooting at Michael Brown at least four times. According to the witness, it looks as if the bullets have no effect: "He didn't flinch...he just kept going." The witness then reports there is a pause that seems like a lifetime, but is probably only a few seconds, and then Officer Wilson, while backing up and Michael Brown continues to "charge"—bent lower than before, fires at least twice more. On the first shot, Michael Brown pitches forward. On the second shot he falls flat to his face. The witness said she sees blood (and stuff) come from Michael Brown's head.

At this point, the witness returns to her car and leaves the scene.

Following her statement, the detective and agent follow-up on specific details.

Using the provided diagram of the related streets and the apartment complex, the witness provides a means out of the complex that is not possible. The detective states he does not believe she is actually ever there at the scene. He states, "You are telling us that you...were able to get out...without going back the way you came ... [and] there is no way out that way."

In addition, the witness cannot explain how her car does not appear anywhere in available video, has been found to have researched the incident extensively on-line, and posts the following on Facebook: They need to kill the fucking niggers. It is like an ape fest. In addition, she acknowledges creating an organization to raise funds for the benefit Officer Wilson. It also becomes apparent that the witness has mental issues for which she has been medicated in the past.

During the Grand Jury interview, which takes place the next day, October 23, 2014, the following is also revealed: The witness states that she observes multiple pairs of African-American boys and girls walking on Canfield Drive. She reports that she drives immediately behind both Michael Brown and Dorian Johnson as they walk in the road, and that they move aside. She incorrectly states that Brown and Johnson are walking towards West Florissant. She also states that she does not recall if Officer Wilson has a short or long-sleeve shirt, or whether his shirt and pants are the same color. Further, the witness states she does not remember seeing a blue pick-up truck or a mini-van. She states she sees a two-door white car.

ANALYSIS AND INTERPRETATION

Witness #40 is exposed by the Grand Jury as not credible. There is no evidence that she is actually present on or near Canfield Drive or any of the neighboring apartment buildings or complexes during the incident. Police photos of the separate parking lots at the time fail to show her vehicle in the area she claims. The roads she claims to have used to exit the complex don't exist. She does not accurately describe the complex, nor is she capable of providing any details about the buildings. And there are no residents who remember her in the area she claims to have been in. The witness is clearly motivated by her desire to support Officer Wilson, and she is found to have emotional and psychological issues that may be contributing to her behavior. The details she claims to have seen are derived from online resources and newspaper articles.

PART 3: EXPERT WITNESSES

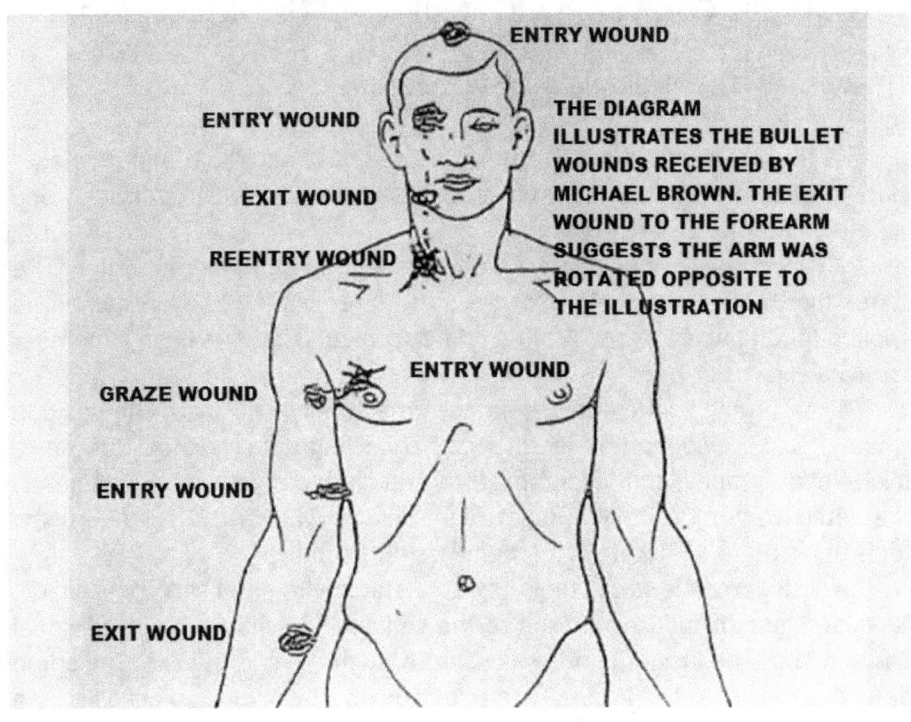

THE CRIME SCENE

ST. LOUIS COUNTY POLICE CRIME SCENE DETECTIVE #1

INTERVIEW WITH THE GRAND JURY, VOLUME 2

The interview with the crime scene detective and the Grand Jury takes place on September 3, 2014. The procedure is conducted by Alizadeh and Whirley. All 12 jurists are present.

The crime scene detective is a policeman with specialized training. He states that he has a bachelor's degree, and after serving as a policemen he applied for and was accepted to the crime scene unit. He has been a member for five years.

According to the detective, the primary responsibility of the position is crime scene evidence, which includes collecting data, creating diagrams, taking photographs, and videotaping. In order to complete his assignments, the detective works out of a department vehicle which is supplied with the tools of his trade. He is one of 17 members of the unit.

The detective states the procedure starts with a call to a crime scene. He arrives and introduces himself to the individual in charge. That individual fills him in on the incident and walks him through the crime scene. The crime detective then uses this information to decide on a beginning point to his own investigation.

Typically, the investigation starts with the crime scene detective creating a video walk-through of the scene from his own perspective. The video is not narrated. The next step is the still photographs. These photos are of the existing scene. Nothing is fabricated or re-arranged to replicate what may have been in place before the detective arrives. After the photos, the detective then does a more formal walk-through of the crime scene placing placards—pieces of hard plastic with numbers—and other markers in spots where evidence is found. That evidence is then photographed in place, removed as necessary—placed in individual plastic bags, and then documented—referred to as the paper trail. At that point, the process starts all over again and is repeated until all evidence is uncovered.

According to the crime scene detective, on August 9, 2014, at approximately 1:00 pm, he receives a call to report to the scene of the incident between Officer Wilson and Michael Brown. At the time, the detective is driving in his van on I-270. He is switching between channels of his official radio when he hears the report of shots fired near the crime scene. He states he immediately pulls over to the side of the road and puts on his Kevlar vest. He is then told the shooting involves a Ferguson police officer, and that the Ferguson police are requesting the St. Louis County Crime Scene to respond.

The detective states that he turns onto West Florissant to head east on Canfield Drive. He immediately encounters an unusual volume of traffic, which he is directed around by officers controlling the scene. He states as he nears the actual scene, there are 300-400 on-lookers that have gathered.

Upon his arrival to the actual scene, the detective states that he joins a group of officers who have assembled and is told there was an assault on a law enforcement officer (LEO), and as a result, there was a fatal shooting. He has Michael Brown's body pointed out to him, as well as the location of Officer Wilson's vehicle. Brown's body is considered the east end of the crime scene. Wilson's vehicle is the west end. It is situated so that the driver's side door is facing towards West Florissant. The tire on the rear left of the vehicle is over the double yellow line.

The detective states that he is given a walk-through by a Ferguson sergeant and that the process starts in proximity to Brown's body. There is evidence that has already been marked by other officers, and this, too, is common.

After the initial walk-through, the detective prepares to do the formal video. However, while at his van writing notes, there is a volley of near-by gunshots. The procedure is delayed while other officers investigate and make sure the crime scene is secured. Police officers, approximately 50 in number, are established at 5-10 foot intervals around the perimeter of the crime scene, which at this time is taped off, to keep back the gathering crowd.

Once secured, the detective begins to video record the scene. He starts in the south-west corner and moves counter-clockwise around the perimeter, establishing himself physically in certain points and then panning with the camera to record his surroundings from that particular perspective. He does not narrate what he is seeing; however, the video does have audio and picks up the ambient sound. Following the video, the detective takes 161 still photos. The photographs are digital JPG format.

In response to a specific question asked by Alizadeh, the crime scene detective states there are no photographs to document that Wilson's vehicle has left any tire marks in the street, or that there is reason to believe the car skids to any degree. However, photographs for that purpose are taken.

Following the photographs, the detective states he diagrams the scene. In the diagram, he places circles to denote areas where evidence is located. There is a legend on the diagram which serves to label and identify each circle and the evidence it denotes. Some of the evidence listed are a black and yellow bracelet, a red baseball cap, .40 caliber shell casings, and a black bracelet. The shattered driver's window is also indicated, as well as glass from the window that is found within the vehicle. The detective also states that there is a defect noticeable on the outer surface of the driver's door from which the paint has peeled away, but there is not a hole. There is a hole on the inside of the door panel.

Continuing his description of the process, the detective states that shortly after photographing image 68, a member of the Brown family tears down some of the crime scene tape and a number of the on-lookers move into the crime scene. At this point, it is deemed necessary to discontinue his normal procedure and focus on the body so that it can be removed as soon as possible from the scene. As the detective moves to the body, he states there are hundreds of people lining the balconies and roofs of the nearby apartments and a large crowd has gathered just east of where Michael Brown lay. Some of the crowd has started chanting "kill the police". In addition, the detective remarks on how close the buildings really are to the streets, and in general, how enclosed the whole area is.

Describing a series of photos (78-86) documenting Michael Brown's body, the detective identifies a wound to the right hand, the right forearm, the right upper arm, and tattoos on both his right and left arms. He makes no other specific references to any other wounds.

In addition, the detective establishes the distance between Michael Brown lying prone in the street and Officer Wilson's van as 159' 9". He states he documents no evidence of blood anywhere within that space. However, image 125 provides evidence of two blood splatters east of Michael Brown's body and in the vicinity of Coppercreek Court. The splatter is consistent with the type of evidence the detective has encountered at other shooting scenes.

According to the detective, the weapon used by Officer Wilson is a Sig Sauer semi-automatic pistol. The ammunition is contained within a magazine. The magazine holds 12 bullets. There is a 13th bullet in the chamber. The weapon ejects spent casings each time it is fired. After the incident, Officer Wilson has one live chamber remaining in his gun; twelve rounds have been fired. Ten casings are recovered at the scene during the first phase of the process. Two remain missing. A casual and visual examination of the inside of the vehicle is then performed. (The detective does not touch or remove any item within the vehicle as not to contaminate the scene.) The shells are not found. However, during a second sweep of the area, the two missing casings are found by the detective and an assistant in the grass alongside the sidewalk to the north side of the Canfield Drive and east of Officer Wilson's vehicle. The detective states they hit the pavement of the road upon rejection and skip off into the grass. In addition, a possible bullet hole in the structure of an adjacent apartment is investigated. The bullet is not found.

ST LOUIS COUNTY POLICE DEPARTMENT CRIME SCENE DETECTIVE #2

INTERVIEW WITH THE GRAND JURY, VOLUME 5

The interview of Crime Scene Detective #2 with the Grand Jury takes place on September 16, 2014. It is not the first interview of the day for the Grand Jury. The procedure is conducted by Alizadeh and Whirley. All 12 jurists are present. The detective states he has been with the St. Louis County police for eight years, and has been a detective for two and a half years. Detective #2 is provided the task of interviewing Officer Wilson with regard to the shooting of Michael Brown.

According to Detective #2, the interview procedure with Darren Wilson is cursory. The objective is to understand the sequence of events of the shooting incident. The interview procedure is not taped in any way. The detective makes written notes.

The detective states that when he arrives at the Ferguson Police station, Darren Wilson is in an office with three other individuals. They are a Lieutenant, an attorney, and another detective. Officer Wilson is wearing his full uniform and has present his duty belt. Officer Wilson has already bagged his weapon. The envelope containing the weapon is currently present. The detective states this is not the procedure followed by the St. Louis Police Department, which requires the officer to keep his weapon in the holster until it can be downloaded in full view of the crime scene detective. The download procedure requires the ejection of the magazine, a formal inventory of the number of rounds still in the magazine, and the ejection of the round in the chamber. Photographs of the gun are then taken. The weapon is then seized by the crime scene detective.

The detective states at the time he meets Officer Wilson he notes reddening to the left and right sides of his jaw; the right side of the jaw is swollen. By this point, Officer Wilson has been directed by the Lieutenant to report to the hospital for medical treatment. The detective drives himself to the Christian Northwest Hospital and the process resumes there.

In the trauma room of the hospital, the Ferguson Police detective takes photographs of Darren Wilson's facial injuries.

Following the photos, the detective states that he requests that the Lieutenant and the Ferguson detective leave the room so that he may conduct the interview. The attorney remains present. The interview takes approximately 30 minutes.

According to the detective, Officer Wilson provides the following summarized statement:

Officer Wilson has left a previous call and is traveling west on Canfield Drive. He hears a call on his car radio not intended for him about a stealing in progress. The only description is of a black male wearing a black shirt and brown pants, and there is further mention of a box of cigarillos.

Continuing west on Canfield Drive, Officer Wilson spots two individuals coming from the direction of West Florissant. They are walking in the center of the road. He describes one subject as about 5'5" tall, black with a dark complexion, with short dread-lock hair, and wearing a black shirt. He describes the second subject as black with a light complexion, approximately 6'3" tall, weighing approximately 270 pounds, with a red baseball cap, gray shirt, khaki pants, and black and yellow socks.

Officer Wilson stops his vehicle and allows the two individuals to approach. They do so on the driver's side of his vehicle. The window is down. As the two individuals approach, Officer Wilson says, "Hey, why don't you guys walk on the sidewalk?" Dorian Johnson replies, "We're almost to our destination." Michael Brown says, "The fuck with what you have to say." Both continue to walk east on Canfield.

Officer Wilson gets on his radio and tells dispatch that he is going to be conducting a pedestrian check. He requests an assist car. Officer Wilson than places his vehicle in reverse and backs up toward Johnson and Brown. He then puts the car in park. As he attempts to exit the vehicle, he says, "Hey, come here."

As Officer Wilson is opening the door, he feels Michael Brown push the door closed. He directs Michael Brown to step back and attempts to open the door a second time. Brown pushes the door closed. Michael Brown has both hands against the lower frame of the window. Officer Wilson directs both Brown and Johnson to "get back" and "move".

At this point, Michael Brown comes through the window with his upper body and both arms. Brown begins to swing wildly, striking Officer Wilson in the chin, face, shoulders and chest. Officer Wilson is deflecting the strikes with his left hand. Michael Brown then takes his left arm and hand from the vehicle, says, "Here, take this," and hands the cigarillos to Dorian Johnson. Brown then brings his left hand back into the vehicle and punches Officer Wilson in the right side of his face.

While continuing to protect himself with his left hand, Officer Wilson goes through his options, rejecting for various reasons the use of mace and his asp. He decides escape of the vehicle through the passenger side is not viable due to his computer, radio and shotgun situated in the center console.

Ultimately, Officer Wilson decides on the use of his weapon. He draws it with his right hand from this holster, raises it in the direction of Michael Brown and yells, "Stop, or I'll shoot."

Michael Brown reaches for the gun, encompassing the top slide with his hand, and says, "You're too much of a pussy to shoot me." Brown then forces the muzzle of the gun down and into Officer Wilson's left hip. Officer Wilson shifts to the right so that the gun is now pointing down and into the seat. Using his left hand, his right hand on the gun's grip, he pushes the barrel towards the door and pulls the trigger. Due to Michael Brown's hand on the slide and interfering with the hammer, the gun misfires. Officer Wilson pulls the trigger again. The gun goes off, the bullet passing into the driver's door and shattering the window. Glass flies into the car and Officer Wilson sees blood on his hand, but he is unsure if it is his or Brown's. However, Brown's hand is still on the gun. Officer Wilson pulls the trigger two more times. The gun misfires both times.

(At this point in the narrative, it seems that the detective's notes become disjointed and are not accurately sequential. For example, the notes make no mention of Michael Brown removing himself from the window, but provide for him reentering, and there is no mention of a second shot, which would have been the one that wounds Michael Brown's thumb and palm.)

Michael Brown then reenters the vehicle and punches Officer Wilson in the face several more times before fleeing east on Canfield Drive.

Officer Wilson uses his radio to inform dispatch that shots have been fired, and exits the vehicle in pursuit of Michael Brown. Either during or after the pursuit, Officer Wilson is providing loud verbal commands for Brown to stop and get on the ground. Brown stops and turns. He has "an intense and psychotic look on his face". Brown then takes his right hand and moves it towards his waistband on the right side. (Wilson does not describe the position of Brown's left hand.) Brown screams something and begins to charge Officer Wilson. (Wilson uses the word 'charge'.)

As Brown is charging, Officer Wilson continues to give him verbal commands to stop. Wilson is at this time backpedaling as to keep his distance from Brown. Wilson states that if Brown were to reach him, "He would be done," referring to having been over-powered by Brown at the vehicle. As Brown closes from 30' to within 15' feet of Officer Wilson, Wilson discharges five rounds of ammunition. The rounds have no visible effect and Brown continues forward. Officer Wilson then discharges two additional rounds, again with no seeming effect. Brown then lowers his head. Officer Wilson believes he is going to be tackled. He again fires. The bullet, Wilson believes, hits Brown in the head. Officer Wilson then uses his shoulder walkie to notify the dispatcher. He says, "Send me every car you've got and the supervisor."

Following the summary, the detective is asked and responds to multiple questions.

He states that although he is not a firearms expert, he knows from experience that a firearm can misfire for various reasons, including an object impeding with the hammer's ability to cycle. He states that Officer Wilson's gun could have misfired due to Michael Brown's hand over the slide and pushed down on the hammer. In addition, if the weapon is hampered in this way, the round would not discharge and the casing would remain in the gun. The round in the chamber remains live. The detective also states that when fired, the round casing is ejected from the top of the weapon.

The detective states that Officer Wilson does not state that he fires his weapon at any time while in actual pursuit of Michael Brown, and that he does not fire his weapon following the events in the police SUV until Michael Brown stops (at Coppercreek Court) and starts back in his direction.

ST. LOUIS COUNTY POLICE DEPARTMENT DETECTIVE #3

INTERVIEW WITH THE GRAND JURY, VOLUME 3

This witness is a crime scene detective with the St. Louis County Police Department's Bureau of Crimes Against Persons. The interview with the Grand Jury takes place on September 9, 2014, at approximately 1:00 pm. The procedure is conducted by Alizadeh and Whirley. All 12 jurists are present.

The detective has been with the police department for 33 years, the last 14 of which has been as a crime scene detective. In addition, he has 27 years of experience as a field training instructor. He holds multiple formal certifications related to his profession.

According to the detective, at approximately 1:00 pm, on August 9, 2014, he receives a call from his supervisor to report to the home office, retrieve a van outfitted for the demands of his position, and then contact another detective presently at Christian Northwest Hospital. He reports he arrives at the hospital at 2:20 pm. Once at the hospital he reports to the awaiting detective. Also present are the assistant chief of police for the Ferguson Police Department, Officer Darren Wilson, and an attorney from the fraternal order of police representing Darren Wilson.

The detective states that the awaiting detective provides him with an overview of the Darren Wilson/Michael Brown incident. He then states his role is to document any visible injuries to or complaints of injuries by Officer

Wilson, to seize his clothing and his weapon, and eventually, to process Officer Wilson's police vehicle.

The detective states he first encounters Officer Wilson in the emergency room, and that he has no previous knowledge of Officer Wilson. Officer Wilson is wearing his uniform pants, a t-shirt and his boots. He does not have his fire arm or his duty belt.

In response to specific questions as to his physical condition, the detective states that Officer Wilson indicates pain or discomfort to his face, neck and his head. The detective states that he notes visual areas of injury. He then follows protocol for completing the required photo documentation, which in this case, consists of 50 photos.

Responding to specific questions by the Grand Jury, the detective states that Officer Wilson suffers no injuries resulting in bleeding, complains of no other injuries than those already stated, has blood stains on the left leg of his uniform pants, and the uniform pants are seized following Officer Wilson's return to the police department. The detective states Officer Wilson has no other clothes to wear, and it is the detective's decision to seize the pants back at the police department and not there in the hospital. He states Officer Wilson's uniform shirt and weapon are both seized at the police department, and have been taken from him and bagged prior to Officer Wilson going to the hospital. Both are in possession of other detectives during the interim. In addition, the detective states there are red stains on two places on the gun— including the slide (A swab for DNA was processed). He states that the choice is to swab for DNA because there is no reason to believe definitive fingerprints would be available, and the performing of one procedure precludes the performing of the other.

FBI AGENT INTERVIEW WITH OFFICER DARREN WILSON

INTERVIEW WITH THE GRAND JURY, VOLUME 5

The interview of the FBI agent that interviews Darren Wilson by the Grand Jury takes place on September 16, 2014, at approximately 2:00 pm. The procedure is conducted by Alizadeh and Whirley. All 12 jurists are present. The interview concludes at 3:20.

The agent states she has been with the FBI for three and a half years and works out of the St. Louis County FBI building on Market Street. Prior to coming to the FBI, she was a civilian crime scene examiner for the Baltimore County Police Department. She was not a commissioned police officer. Her experience with the FBI has been investigating federal violations, which do not include violent crimes. She is brought into the Michael Brown case on August 11, 2014. Her responsibility, among others, is to interview Officer Darren Wilson. The Grand Jury is interested in that interview.

According to the agent, she interviews Officer Wilson on August 28, 2014. She states she is aware that Officer Wilson has been interviewed by other agencies by this time and she has listened to and read the transcripts of these interviews. Her objective, however, is concerned with civil rights, and her job is to see if Officer Wilson is in violation of his sworn duties. It is an investigation separate from the county's homicide investigation. The interview is conducted at the FBI building. Darren Wilson is accompanied by two attorneys. Also present are two attorney's representing the government, one from the Federal Government and the other from the Department of Justice. A second detective is also present. The interview is not recorded; however, written notes are taken. At no time is Officer Wilson issued his Miranda rights, or is there intention to place him under arrest. The interview takes approximately one hour.

The FBI agent, reading from her notes, provides the following summary of Officer Wilson's recollection of the events of August 9, 2014:

After responding to and clearing a sick call concerning an infant, Officer Wilson, while in his car and traveling eastbound on Canfield Drive, hears a call for a stealing in progress. He hears the suspects are walking towards Quiktrip, steal cigarillos, and one suspect is wearing a black shirt. Shortly after, Officer Wilson sees two individuals in the middle of the road, walking single file, with Dorian Johnson out ahead of Michael Brown. Both are moving towards Officer Wilson's vehicle.

Officer Wilson pulls up next to Dorian and asks him and Brown why they are not walking on the sidewalk. He describes his tone as non-confrontational, due, he says, to his desire to go for lunch. Johnson answers by saying they are near to their destination and continues to walk. Wilson states that he acknowledges Johnson, but adds, "Okay, so what is wrong with the sidewalk?" Michael Brown, who is in proximity to the sideview mirror, responds by saying, "Fuck what you have to say."

At this point, Officer Wilson notices that Michael Brown has a handful of cigarillos and that Dorian Johnson is wearing a black shirt. He makes the call to dispatch and puts the vehicle in reverse, passing in front of the path of both Johnson and Brown as to cut off their advance and contain their movement. His intent, he says, is not to question or arrest, but merely to stall until backup arrives. Officer Wilson states he bases his decision on the fact he is outnumbered and on the size of Michael Brown, who he believes would overpower him.

As he puts his vehicle in park, Officer Wilson attempts to exit his vehicle, and in the process—his window already down—he tells Brown to come over for a minute. Michael Brown pushes the door closed and says, "What the fuck are you going to do about it?"

Officer Wilson then attempts to open the door a second time. Brown again pushes the door closed, ducks his head down and then comes in through the window with both arms swinging wildly. Officer Wilson is struck in the left side of his face. As Officer Wilson is using his left hand to block Brown's assault, Brown turns and hands the cigarillos to Dorian Johnson, and then comes back in through the window and again hits Officer Wilson in the face with his left hand.

At this point, Officer Wilson describes going through the force triangle in his head. The force triangle, according to his formal training, allows him to use one level of force higher than the threat level to his own safety. He first considers using mace. However, his mace is off his left hip, which he can't reach, and from his experience in the academy, he knows he has a poor reaction to mace. He is concerned that in such tight quarters, were he to spray the mace he will be as equally, if not more, incapacitated than Michael Brown, thereby increasing and not lowering the threat to his own person. He then rejects both the baton and the flashlight, believing that reaching for either will further expose him to Michael Brown's assault, and that neither will be effective in closed quarters. He does not carry a taser. Believing that Michael Brown can beat him to death, he decides on using his sidearm.

Officer Wilson pulls out his gun and tells Michael Brown that he will shoot. Michael Brown responds by telling Officer Wilson he is too much of a pussy to shoot. Brown then grabs the gun and forces it downward towards

Officer Wilson's left hip. Wilson describes only that Brown had his right hand along the top part of the gun and in contact with his own hand. Wilson manages to level the gun barrel in direction of the door and at Michael Brown. He pulls the trigger. The gun fails to fire. He pulls the trigger again. The guns fails to fire. On the third attempt, the gun fires. The round goes into the door panel and the glass from the window shatters, flying throughout the vehicle. Officer Wilson notices blood on his hand and assumes he is injured by the flying glass.

When the shot goes off, Michael Brown pulls away from the window. He puts his hands down by his right hip. Officer Wilson assumes the round passes through the door and hits Michael Brown in the hip. Brown's face then takes on an enraged expression, which Office Wilson likens to a demon. Brown reengages Wilson. Both of Brown's hands come back into the vehicle, and Wilson responds by putting up his left hand to deflect the assault. With his right hand, he brings up his gun and pulls the trigger. The gun misfires. Assuming the round stovepiped—the round is unsuccessfully ejected, thereby jamming the gun and interrupting the cycle, Officer Wilson blind racks the gun in an attempt to clear the round. (Officer Wilson does not explain how he performs the maneuver, whether with both hands, or using some part of the vehicle, such as the steering wheel.) He then fires the gun successfully. He immediately notices dirt kick up and assumes the bullet misses Michael Brown and hits the ground across the street.

Following the gunshot, Michael Brown moves away from the vehicle and starts to flee along Canfield Drive.

According to Officer Wilson, he remembers making a call that shots are fired and assistance is needed. He does not remember if he uses his shoulder walkie or the radio in the car.

In direct response to a prompt by the FBI investigator, Officer Wilson describes his reason for pursuing Michael Brown.

He states Michael Brown is a fleeing felon who has just assaulted him and tried to kill him with his own duty weapon. He believes that Michael Brown is capable of assaulting other officers or witnesses, and that he believes Brown to be an immediate danger to others in the area. He feels it is his responsibility to know where Michael Brown is going and to assist in his apprehension once other officers respond.

Officer Wilson explains that while he is in active pursuit of Michael Brown, he is under the impression that Brown would run for a while, and therefore Wilson has his gun down by his side because it makes running easier. He does not believe Michael Brown is a threat at this time, and therefore he has no reason to keep his gun pointed at him. He does state that as he is pursuing Brown, he is telling him to stop and get on the ground. Wilson states that as he pursues Brown, he passes three cars which are lined up in the street and stopped. He recalls only a green Pontiac. Wilson states he does not fire any shots during the pursuit.

At some point, according to Wilson, Michael Brown stops running, turns and faces him, grunts, hops, and with his hand down by his waistband on the right side, starts towards him. He states he believes Michael Brown may be armed and is reaching for a weapon. Brown's left hand is clenched in a fist and down by his side.

Wilson states that as Brown is running towards him, he starts firing, his eyes trained the whole time on Brown's right hand. Wilson describes it as tunnel vision. Unaware if any of his shots have hit Michael Brown, Officer Wilson notes that at one point Brown's body jerks and flinches. Brown stops running briefly, but starts up again shortly thereafter. Wilson describes Brown's chest as being puffed up and his hand still down by the waistband at his right side.

Officer Wilson, as Michael Brown is moving towards him, begins to back up. He states that as Michael Brown is within 8 feet of him, he fears that his own life is in danger. He recalls firing only one more time—admits he could have been more—and states he sees the bullet strike Michael Brown in the head. He sees blood splatter. Michael Brown then falls face first to the pavement. He says that Brown has so much forward momentum, when he hits the ground, both his feet kick up with the heels moving towards his head.

Officer Wilson makes the statement that if Michael Brown had at any time stopped moving towards him, he would not have fired. However, Michael Brown at no time complies with Officer Wilson's directives, and he at no time has his hands up in the air. Officer Wilson further states that when the sergeant arrives, he tells him, "[Brown] grabbed my gun and I shot him."

At this point, the sergeant directs Officer Wilson to sit in his (the sergeant's) vehicle, but Wilson refuses, not wanting to be singled out as the shooter there at the scene, which he considers unsafe given the reputation of the area, the lack of respect for police in that community, and the fact that the police at the time are outnumbered 300 to 1.

The sergeant then directs Officer Wilson to take his car and drive back to the police station, which Wilson describes as unconventional procedure. However, while driving back, he checks his shoulder walkie and realizes it is on channel 3 and not channel 1. Channel 3 is not an appropriate channel for communication with dispatch.

Back at the station, Officer Wilson states that he washes the blood from his hands concerned with possible hazards. No one at the station photographs his hands prior to washing. He then states that he makes his gun safe and packages it as evidence. He does not wait for anyone else to do so, because he sees blood on the gun, believes it belongs to Michael Brown, and wishes to preserve the DNA evidence. He then contacts the appropriate attorney. After the attorney arrives, he and the lieutenant, both noticing Wilson's face is red and swollen, direct Officer Wilson to go to the hospital for examination.

Towards the end of Officer Wilson's statement to the FBI Agent, Officer Wilson states that he has been assaulted before as an officer, but not to the extent as with Michael Brown. He explains that no one else has ever tried to take his weapon before, and that he has been trained to use physical force when a physical threat is present. He states that Michael Brown becomes a physical threat once he comes into Officer Wilson's vehicle, when he goes for Officer Brown's weapon, and when he turns to charge towards Officer Wilson.

DARREN WILSON'S TRAINING OFFICER

INTERVIEW WITH THE GRAND JURY, VOLUME 22

The interview of the training officer with the Grand Jury takes place on November 11, 2014. The procedure is conducted by Alizadeh and Whirley. All 12 jurists are present. The primary topics of concern for the Grand Jury are Officer Wilson's general demeanor and performance as an officer, his interaction within the community he serves, and protocol relative to the use of force as an officer and under what circumstances.

According to the training officer, he has the responsibility of mentoring new officers to the department. These new officers can be recent graduates of the academy or transfers or new employees from other police departments. The process consists of approximately six weeks of ride-along training in which the new officer and the training officer are partnered in the same vehicle. During this period of time, it is the responsibility of the training officer to reinforce all formal policy and protocol and to produce routine evaluation reports of the new officer. At the end of this six week period, the training officer decides whether or not the new officer qualifies for a car of us own or is in need of extended reinforcement.

The witness states that in his time as a training officer, he has mentored approximately ten policemen, none of whom were required to undergo extended evaluation. Officer Darren Wilson is one of those ten policemen.

According to the training officer, Officer Wilson, who he trained in 2009, was one of his most qualified and competent trainees, and that Officer Wilson met all benchmarks in terms of evaluation. He found him to be concerned with developing a vested interest in the community in which he was working, which was primarily African-American. He states that Officer Wilson told him that he has little experience interacting with African-Americans. The training officer also states in response to direct questioning from the Grand Jury that he never saw Officer Wilson employing excessive force during an arrest, demonstrating bad temper, engaged in any behavior he would deem racist or inappropriate, abusing his authority, bullying, or using poor judgment. In addition, he states that he is aware of no civilian complaints brought against Officer Wilson or any negative comments, either during his training period or after. The training officer states they continue to work on the same shift.

Discussing the Use of Force Triangle or Continuum, the training officer states it is a protocol for determining how to best control a situation, and that the options are generally dictated by the response or actions of the suspect. The objective is to use the most appropriate level of force to affect compliance. The process is considered reactive.

According to the training officer, the primary components of the Force Triangle are compliance, threatening resistance, non-threatening resistance, and deadly force. Compliance is the center of the triangle, and the other three levels are the corners. Compliance is defined as full cooperation. The suspect responds appropriately to officer directives. Non-threatening resistance is defined as a lack of cooperation, but without the threat of physical violence from the suspect. Threatening resistance is non-compliance on the part of the suspect that includes the threat of bodily harm by the suspect to the officer. Deadly force implies the suspect is a threat to the life of the officer.

Responding directly to a question by Alizadeh, the training officer states that in a situation in which an officer deems necessary the use of his gun, all officers are trained to aim towards center mass to terminate the threat. The officer defines center mass as the greatest area that presents as a target at the given moment. He states that the heart is typically considered the center mass on a suspect, but he adds that individuals shot in the area of the heart may continue to pose a threat for thirty seconds or more before succumbing to the injury. In addition, he states that officers are not trained to shot to wound, for example, in the leg, but instead to incapacitate the suspect. The goal is to strike the central nervous system.

With regard to permitting a suspect to "get away" as to be picked up at a later time, the training officer states that all officers are trained to pursue and apprehend. He uses as justification a situation in which a suspect demonstrates the willingness to attack and assault a police officer who the suspect knows is trained and armed, stating further that such a suspect would be expected to not hesitate to attack and assault a defenseless civilian. However, he also states that the specific situation and setting often dictate the actions an officer takes depending on the risk involved both to himself and to others in the surrounding area at that time. For example, police officers are trained not to engage speeders in high speed pursuit due to the potential dangers to other motorists. He then qualifies his statement by illustrating the risks officers face due to unknown factors. He cites, for example, pulling over a driver for something as simple as speeding, unaware that the driver is actually fleeing from a robbery and is armed. In a situation of this sort, the suspect is likely to react in a way that the officer is not expecting.

Finally, the training officer, in response to direct questioning from Whirley, states that he would consider a suspect who is fleeing a direct threat to both his person and the community, and that he would continue pursuit until the suspect is subdued or apprehended. In addition, he states that officers are permitted to use their vehicles to halt the progression of suspects, and that he knows of circumstances in which it has been done.

PHYSICIAN'S ASSISTANT

INTERVIEW WITH THE GRAND JURY, VOLUME 22

The interview of the physician's assistant by the Grand Jury takes place on November 11, 2014. The procedure is conducted by Alizadeh and Whirley. All 12 jurists are present.

The physician assistant is the medical care specialist working at the Northwest Health Care Emergency Department, which is affiliated with Christian Northeast Hospital, who tends to Officer Wilson following the incident with Michael Brown. Officer Wilson is accompanied by two other officers.

According to the witness, she has a master's degree which allows her to diagnose, treat and prescribe non-narcotic medications to a patient. In her position, she sees certain patients in need of non-emergency care following an initial examination by a triage nurse. A doctor is consulted as needed.

According to the physician's assistant, she examines Officer Wilson with regard to his complaint of jaw pain, scratches to his neck, and minor headache. She states that Officer Wilson informs her only that he was punched twice in or about the face while engaging with an arrest subject. She states that she notes redness and swelling on the right side of his face and linear marks and slight puffiness on his neck which she associates with fingernails. She states that the swelling to Officer Wilson's face is minor and involves only superficial tissue. Officer Wilson reports his level of discomfort in terms of pain as a six on a scale of one to ten. She states that upon examination, Officer Wilson's injuries are superficial, but consistent with impact injuries such as those that would result from being punched or scratched. She prescribes a treatment of ice and Naprosyn, 500 milligrams of which Officer Wilson receives during the examination.

MEDICAL EXAMINERS

MEDICAL EXAMINER: FIRST AUTOPSY

INTERVIEW WITH THE GRAND JURY, VOLUME 3

The interview of the medical examiner with the Grand Jury takes place on September 9, 2014, at approximately 2:00 pm. The procedure is conducted by Alizadeh and Whirley. All 12 jurists are present.

According to the medical examiner, he is a forensic pathologist. He received his undergraduate degree from Xavier University in Louisiana, followed by four years of medical school at Louisiana State University, four years in medical school in New Orleans, and then four more years of residency at St. Louis University. He states he is certified in both forensic and anatomical pathology. He is currently employed as the assistant medical examiner at the St. Louis County's Medical Examiner's Office. He has been in that position for two years.

According to the medical examiner, he examines Michael Brown's body on August 10, 2014. Prior to the examination, he speaks with a department detective who provides him with the basic details of the encounter between Officer Wilson and Michael Brown.

The medical examiner states Michael Brown receives eleven bullet wounds from seven bullets. Seven are entry wounds, one is a reentry wound, and three are exit wounds. Two of the entry wounds are tangential or graze wounds, meaning the wound is a surface wound in which the bullet does not pass fully through a body surface, but instead travels parallel and in contact with the surface. Of the entry wounds that are not graze wounds, two are to the right arm, one is to the chest, and two are to the head. The entry wounds to the arm are to the back of the forearm, approximately 16 centimeters below the elbow, and to the bicep, approximately 6 centimeters above the elbow. The entry wound to the chest is to the lateral right side. The entry wounds to the head are to the forehead and just above the right eye and to the top of the skull and just right of center. The exit wounds are to the forearm, the back of the upper arm, and beneath the right side of the jaw. Each is the result of the trajectory of the bullet from the corresponding entry wounds. The reentry wound is to the right chest and just above the right nipple. The graze wounds are to the lateral right arm, up by the shoulder, and to the palm and thumb of the right hand.

The only wound which occurs at close proximity is the graze wound to the thumb. The medical examiner prefers the term tangential to describe this specific wound, inferring that the bullet plows more deeply through the skin throughout its trajectory, causing more damage than the typical graze wound. This wound is the only one received by Michael Brown that contains both soot and stippling. Soot is associated with gun powder. Stippling is damage done to the skin by other solid matter expelled from the gun along with the bullet and which becomes lodged in the tissue. According to the medical examiner, soot is rarely evidenced when a bullet travels more than 12 inches after having been fired, and is more common from 6-9 inches. Stippling can be detected on shots from as far away as two feet, and perhaps somewhat further depending upon the caliber of the bullet and the gun from which it is shot. The medical examiner is confident that Michael Brown receives this wound in proximity to Officer Wilson's vehicle. No other wound received by Brown shows any indications of soot or stippling, meaning Officer Wilson and Michael Brown are separated by three feet or more at the time the gun is being fired.

At this point in his explanation, the medical examiner states that it is impossible to determine the particular order of the remaining six bullets that hit Michael Brown, or even the specific angle in which each bullet traveled, with the exception of the last two. The bullets to the head suggest that Michael Brown's upper torso is leaning significantly forward, and at some point is parallel to the ground.

The wound to the forearm enters to the back side of the arm. Upon entry, the bullet hits and fractures the ulnar bone. The course of the bullet is then altered, and it exits from the inside of the forearm, creating a wound greater in size than the original entry wound. Due to the complexity of the elbow and wrist joints—rotation and angle, the medical examiner states it is impossible to determine the angle or level of the arm at the time of the entry wound, but he conceives it is possible the entry wound occurs with Michael Brown's back to Officer Wilson. However, he does state that when diagraming injuries on a two-dimensional surface (paper), the arms are down to the side with the palms facing forward. The wound is not considered debilitating (during the incident) or fatal.

The wound to the bicep enters to the medial (inside) part of the bicep and exits through the back side of the upper arm and just below the armpit. The bullet's trajectory is not interrupted by bone. The track of the bullet is back and slightly to the right. The wound is not considered debilitating (incident) or fatal.

The wound to the lateral part of the upper arm, just below the outside head of the shoulder, is a graze wound. The bullet is not found. The wound is not considered grave.

The entry wound to the lateral right side of the chest enters high up on the rib cage and in proximity to rib number three. According to the medical examiner, it passes upwards and fractures the clavicle. It then is deflected downward where it fractures rib number eight. Rib number eight splinters and punctures the lower lobe of the lung. The bullet then passes through and is lodged in the soft tissue of the back without doing any further damage to bone or organs. The bullet is recovered during the autopsy. The wound is considered grave and would have eventually been fatal if not treated due to the accumulation of blood which would eventually interrupt blood and oxygen flow to the heart. However, at the time of the incident, Michael Brown would not have been incapacitated.

The entry wound to the forehead most likely occurs when Michael Brown is bent at the torso and close to parallel to the ground. The bullet enters the forehead just above the right eye, travels downward, rupturing the right eyeball, fracturing the orbital socket, and exits beneath the right side of the lower jaw. No other bone damage is incurred. This wound is also not considered fatal by the medical examiner, and as a result, Michael Brown is still capable of mobility.

The reentry wound to the chest above the right nipple is the continued trajectory of the bullet that hits Brown in the forehead. It passes beneath the lower jaw, and due to the angle of Brown's torso, enters the chest. The bullet moves through the upper lobe of the right lung and is recovered during the autopsy from the chest cavity.

The entry wound to the skull is just right of dead center and would have had to occur when Michael Brown's torso is bent forward and nearly parallel to the ground. The medical examiner states the shot is the same as if the gun is aimed at the skull from a point directly above. The bullet passes completely through the lobes at the right side of the brain and is lodged in the soft tissue beneath the brain and towards the back of the head. The wound is instantly fatal.

In addition, the medical examiner notes multiple abrasions, particularly on the left elbow and left wrist. However, there are no abrasions on the neck or the face. There are no injuries to Michael Brown's back, the back of his legs, or his buttocks.

INTERVIEW WITH THE GRAND JURY, VOLUME 20

The interview of the medical examiner with the Grand Jury takes place on November 6, 2014. The procedure is conducted by Alizadeh and Whirley. All 12 jurists are present.

According to the medical examiner, he has since the first interview, more closely examined a skin sample from the graze wound on Michael Brown's palm and thumb area, right hand. He explains the examination process to the Grand Jury and states that in his professional opinion, and based on his experience, that gun powder, among other matter expelled from a gun muzzle when fired, is found embedded in both surface (skin) tissue and the muscle tissue beneath. He concludes the wound suggests the shot was fired within 12inches or less, and probably within 6-9 inches. He further states that he does not do a chemical analysis of this foreign matter, as he is confident in his visual assessment that it is in fact, gunshot related.

The medical examiner then verifies that either of the two shots to the head would have immediately incapacitated Michael Brown. However, he states that the shot that enters through the top of the skull and goes through to the back of the brain, more so than the shot that passes through the forehead and exits at his lower jaw, is the more significant of the shots. The shot through the top of the head would have rendered Brown incapable of putting his hands out in front of him to cushion his fall. As evidence, he points out that Michael Brown's left hand falls beneath his mid-section and his right to his side and at a slight angle away from the body. The palm of his right hand is facing up.

Then addressing a second sample of tissue which is removed from the exterior of the door, the medical examiner states that the cell DNA matches that of Michael Brown, and that due to the relative lack of pigmentation of the skin, he associates the tissue with the palm of Michael Brown's hand.

Further, with regard to the gunshot wound to the palm and thumb, he states the direction of the skin tags around the wound (the direction in which the damaged tissue is pointing) would suggest the path of the bullet is upwards. In addition, the medical examiner cannot state whether or not Michael Brown touches Officer Wilson's gun.

In response to a specific question as to the possibility that Michael Brown's feet are run-over when Officer Wilson backs up his vehicle (the situation is inferred by the question), the medical examiner states there is no evidence of trauma to Michael Brown's feet.

FORENSIC PATHOLOGIST, BROWN FAMILY:
SECOND AUTOPSY

INTERVIEW WITH THE GRAND JURY, VOLUME 23

The interview with the Forensic Pathologist recruited by Brown's family takes place on November 13, 2014, first thing in the morning. The procedure is conducted by Whirley and Alizadeh. All 12 jurists are present.

Prior to the actual interview, the pathologist explains that pathology is a science of chemistry which is concerned with finding out what is wrong with the body and not how to treat it. The role of the pathologist is to determine if there is evidence of disease, illness or trauma within the body, the organs, or the blood, among other areas. Pathologists generally run blood and tissue tests, such as biopsies. He defines the autopsy procedure as a systemic external and internal examination of the human body to determine information as to the cause of death.

According to the pathologist, there are three fields of pathology: anatomical, clinical and forensic. The role of the forensic pathologists is to look into the cause of unnatural deaths due to accidents, suicide and homicide. Unnatural deaths make up approximately 8% of all deaths in the United States.

The Forensic Pathologist states he is licensed in New York State. He is certified in all three fields, and he has conducted more than 20,000 autopsies related to forensic pathology. He has served as a forensic pathologist for more than 50 years, and at one time was the chief medical examiner in New York

City. He states that he is working for the Brown family, pro bono, and that his travel and related expenses are being paid by the attorneys representing the Browns.

This particular pathologist performs an autopsy on the remains of Michael Brown on August 17, 2014. A prior autopsy has already been performed by St. Louis County.

According to the pathologist, when he first has a chance to examine the body it has already been embalmed. Embalming, he states, does change the way the wounds appear, as well as affecting any toxicology specimens he may think to obtain. He states that due to these variables, he is confident that he can make only approximate findings as to the specific details which contribute to the death of Michael Brown.

Discussing the individual bullet wounds (after embalming), the pathologist states, "[Some] bullet holes may be difficult to tell entrance or exit." In addition, because by the time he sees the body, the organs and the bullets have been removed already, the appearance of the wounds change, and he cannot see where the bullets became lodged. Further, due to the dissection of the organs, there is no way for him to observe the actual wounds themselves.

As a result, during a follow-up autopsy, the pathologist relies primarily on photographs and x-rays. The x-rays, in particular are useful. They show fractures that may have occurred prior to the autopsy—bones are often damaged in the procedure, and they show where the bullets are lodged. As for the photos, the pathologist states that, in this case, most are taken after the autopsy, but he is able to examine those taken by the police before the procedure. These are helpful in terms of entrance and exit wounds, and the proximity of the individual shots.

As for the actual second autopsy, the pathologist is assisted by an individual he has not met prior to this time. The autopsy is performed at the funeral parlor where Michael Brown's remains are held. To perform the re-autopsy, the pathologist removes the sutures put in place after the initial autopsy, as well as the ribs and skull bone. The dissected organs are stored in plastic bags.

According to the pathologist, his primary concern is the wound paths of the individual bullets that struck Michael Brown.

However, prior to discussing his findings in this area, the pathologist states that there are scraping or rubbing abrasions and bruising around Michael Brown's right eye that have no connection to the gunshots. He states, also, that generally when people fall face-first damage is done to the nose area, and that the area around the eyes is generally protected. He does not conclude that the damage seen around Michael Brown's right eye is related to his fall. In addition, the doctor notes minor bruising and a linear abrasion on one of Brown's wrists. He cannot state when they may have occurred, but he does not rule out during the incident.

At this point in the interview, the pathologist begins to discuss the individual bullet wounds. Prior to doing so, however, he states that once a shot is fired beyond three feet to the target, it is no longer possible to determine the actual distance. He states that beyond four or five inches, the powder expelled from the muzzle of the gun begins to disperse at a rapid rate to the point that it dissipates without a reliable forensic trace. With these variables as his basis, he states only one shot hits Michael Brown within the prescribed range, and that is the one which wounds his hand.

The doctor refers to the hand wound as a graze wound. Further, he states that due to the flexibility of the wrist he cannot determine the position of Michael Brown's hand at the time of the wound, or the angle of the shot. He does state the muzzle of the gun is within four to five inches, and that this particular wound is most probably responsible for much of the blood found on his shorts and his socks, as it is the type of wound that would bleed freely. The doctor is certain this wound is the first wound.

The doctor then describes the head shots. He states he believes there are, or may have been—he states that rarely does an autopsy reveal the order of the shots—three shots fired in rapid succession, two of which are the fatal head shots, and the third the shot to the chest.

The first wound he describes entails a shot that hits Michael Brown in the top of the head and just to the right of the center of the skull. The pathologists believes Brown's head is bent forward almost parallel to the ground and with his eyes up so that his head is aligned with the right clavicle (collar bone). The bullet enters the skull, travels a straight path at a 5 to 10° angle through the face, through the right eyeball—damaging the orbital bones around the right eye, exits out the lower jaw on the right side, reenters the body at the upper chest in the area of the clavicle and is recovered in or near to the lungs. The second wound, the bullet that hits Michael Brown slightly above the right eye, passes through the brain, but does not exit. The bullet is recovered at the back of his head during the autopsy. The third wound is to the right side of the chest. The bullet enters just above the nipple, by-passes the third rib, travels through the lung, and fractures the eighth rib. The bullet is recovered from the back. There is also a fourth wound to the upper-right biceps, with the exit through the back of the arm. There is no damage to bone. The autopsy also determines that Michael Brown is not shot at any time in the back.

The next wound discussed by the pathologist is a graze wound to the upper right arm. The doctor describes a graze wound as one associated with a bullet that strikes a body but does not cause any anatomical damage. In this instance, the bullet strikes Michael Brown's upper arm, leaves enough tissue evidence to verify the strike, but then disappears and is not recovered.

The wound the doctor then discusses is the one he terms controversial. It is the wound to the forearm, and specifically the ulnar bone. It is the doctor's belief, due to the point of exit, that the shot enters from the back of the arm, which would suggest that Michael Brown's back, at the time of the shot, is to Officer Brown. However, he does state that again due to the general flexibility of the arm, he cannot be sure with any degree of certainty, and that he is basing his findings on the fact that upon exit, the bullet does not reenter the body at any point, meaning the bullet goes in and straight out with the arm not being aligned to any other part of the body. He acknowledges that line could be straight down, straight up, or even at some angle up or down and away from the center of the body.

The pathologist also discusses the possible effect that the marijuana found in Michael Brown's body may have had in terms of his behavior. The amount is 12 nanograms, which by definition, is legally impaired. However, the doctor states that in his many years of experience, a vast majority of people under the influence of marijuana tend not to act aggressively. He states a more effective barometer of Michael Brown's state of mind at the time would be his general behavior. The pathologist does not believe Michael Brown's behavior relative to his incident was overtly influenced by marijuana.

MILITARY FORENSIC PATHOLOGIST: THIRD AUTOPSY

INTERVIEW WITH THE GRAND JURY, VOLUME 20

The interview of the military forensic pathologist with the Grand Jury takes place on November 6, 2014, at approximately 1:30 pm, and immediately following the medical examiner. The military forensic pathologist performs a third autopsy on Michael Brown's remains, and at a time after the second autopsy performed by the family's specialist.

According to the military forensic pathologist, he graduated from LaSalle University in 2003, Georgetown University in 2007, and completed further studies and training at the University of North Carolina at Chapel Hill in 2012. He has been employed at Dover Air Force Base since that time. He is a commissioned officer in the Air Force, serving as a Major. He holds all relevant certifications and has significant experience performing autopsies, including secondary procedures. He performs the additional autopsy of Michael Brown at the request of the Department of Justice. He is assisted by a naval pathologist—no further identification—with 15-20 years of experience.

According to the military forensic pathologist, prior to beginning the autopsy procedure, he is provided with and views all available x-rays and photos. He also reads a brief description of the physical scene at the time of the incident. He states he is not provided any photos related to the previous autopsies or the investigation until after he performs the third autopsy.

Overall, the pathologist believes there are eight gunshot wounds, two of which he concedes may be reentry wounds—the bullet enters the body in one spot, exits, and then enters the body a second time in a different spot. If this is the case, it would suggest that of the 12 shots fired by Officer Wilson, six hit Michael Brown and six miss—one of which is lodged in the door of the vehicle.

It is also possible, according to the pathologist, that seven bullets actually hit Michael Brown, with only one of the wounds being a reentry wound. The particular wound in question is the bullet that enters Brown's rib cage in the region of the lateral chest on his right side. The pathologist suggests that this bullet may have been one of the three successive shots associated with the two head wounds. He also infers it may be a reentry wound caused by the bullet that passes through Michael Brown's forearm.

The eight wounds—eleven counting three exit wounds—identified by the pathologist are to the right thumb and palm (tangential), the back of the right forearm approximately 7 inches below the elbow (entry), the front of the right forearm (exit), the lateral part of the upper right arm (near the shoulder)(graze), the right biceps (entry), the back of the right arm (exit), the forehead (entry), the top of the head (entry), beneath the right side of the jaw (exit), above the right nipple (reentry), and the right lateral side of the chest (entry/reentry).

With regard to the thumb wound, it is the only wound with powder, stipple, and thermal evidence, suggesting the gun was fired in close proximity to Michael Johnson, but not in direct contact. Michael Brown does not have his hand on the gun at this time. However, according to the pathologist, given the complexity of the arm and hand in terms of mobility and angles, it is impossible to determine the position of the hand at the time of the wound. The skin tags—the way the skin is damaged and the direction it is facing— suggests the gun is fired at an upward angle.

The graze wound to the upper shoulder is superficial damage only. The bullet does not enter the body. The pathologist states there is no way of knowing where the bullet goes after grazing Michael Brown.

The wound to the upper right bicep exits the back of the arm (area of the triceps) in a fairly straight trajectory.

The wound to the forearm, according to the pathologist, is the most difficult to assess. The bullet enters the back of the arm (backhand side), fractures the ulna bone, and exits through the palm-side of the forearm in a manner that creates a hole measurably larger than the entry wound.

The bullet to the top of the skull enters just to the right of center, fracturing the upper skull, and traveling downward and to the right. It passes completely through the right hemisphere of the brain, through the parietal and temporal lobes, and to the base of the skull beneath the brain, causing additional fractures, and comes to a stop. It is removed during the autopsy.

The bullet to the forehead enters just to the right of center and above the right eye. It then travels downward at a slight inward angle, passes through and destroys the right eye, fractures the bones around the orbital socket of the right eye, exits beneath the lower right jaw, reenters just above the right nipple, fractures the right clavicle and a rib, and pierces the lung resulting in approximately a soda can of accumulated blood in the chest cavity. The bullet is recovered during the autopsy.

The wound to the lateral right chest, in the area of the ribs, according to the pathologist, is the least certain in terms of entry when compared to the other bullets. The pathologist states that he believes the bullet is a direct entry and is fired during the final volley of shots by Officer Wilson and just prior to Michael Brown collapsing. The bullet enters nearer to the third rib, which is higher up on the cage, and moves down and back where it fractures the eighth rib—which pierces the lung, and then lodges in the soft tissue of the back. This bullet, too, is recovered during the autopsy.

With regard to this chest wound, the pathologist does not discount the possibility that it is a reentry wound, and may be the bullet that passes through Michael Brown's forearm.

Ultimately, the pathologist concludes that only the two wounds to the head would have incapacitated Michael Brown. He states that Michael Brown would have had full mobility as a result of the other wounds. He adds that the wound to the chest, if it occurs in isolation, would have allowed Brown to raise his hands and arms, but not without pain. He does, however, state that given the intensity of the moment and the role of adrenalin, an individual, despite significant bullet wounds, is capable of continuing on in terms of mobility and conscious actions.

In response to specific questioning by the Grand Jury, the pathologist additionally states there are no indications the Michael Brown collapses to his knees; under normal circumstances the bullet passing through Brown's forehead and rupturing the eye would be sufficient to stop him and probably would have resulted in disorientation and staggering; the bullet to the top of the head would have resulted in instantaneous death, resulting in immediate collapse and without control of the extremities; and, there are no overt abrasions or bruising on or around Brown's neck.

ANALYSIS AND INTERPRETATION

There are three times and two locations during the incident in which Officer Wilson fires his weapon and wounds Michael Brown. The first time and location is while he is seated in the police vehicle. The second and third times are when he is standing on Canfield Drive. The first string of rounds is fired while Michael Brown is in proximity to the intersection of Canfield Drive and Coppercreek Court. The second string of rounds is fired after Michael Brown has moved from the intersection and back towards the middle of Canfield Drive.

As for the toxicology report, the questions remain is the quantity of marijuana detected in Michael Brown's system a contributing factor to his behavior, and if so, to what degree; and at what point in his day does Michael Brown smoke marijuana.

AT THE POLICE SUV

The forensic evidence leaves no doubt that Officer Wilson fires two rounds while in the car, the first of which penetrates the interior panel of the driver's door, and does not penetrate but does damage the exterior panel. The glass of the widow, which is down and concealed within the door panel at the time of the shot, is shattered. The glass is found within the panel and the interior of the car.

Logic dictates that a police officer trained in the discharge of firearms, and who is required to recertify on a routine basis, is not likely, outside of accidental discharge, to fire such an errant shot unless he is being impeded or interfered with. Combined with the gash to the underside of Brown's left arm and near to the elbow—caused by the broken glass, and which the medical examiner describes as severe enough as to require treatment, there is little doubt that Michael Brown's arms and hands are within the vehicle and he has partial control of Officer Wilson's weapon. Either through direct or indirect contact, Brown is the cause of this errant shot.

All three autopsy reports state that there is soot and stippling present in the wound to Brown's right thumb and palm, confirming that the gun is within 6 to 9 inches when fired. Combined with eyewitness reports which place the gun within the vehicle at all times while Wilson and Brown are engaged, it is clear that Brown, at some point in time, has both hands and arms within the vehicle. The angle and trajectory of the bullet suggests Officer Wilson is leaning away from Brown, is firing the weapon at an upward angle, and that the palm of Brown's hand is more parallel to the ground than perpendicular.

THE FIRST STRING

—According to the Ferguson sergeant, the preferred term to use when referring to consecutive shots fired by a single officer is "string". The term "volley" is used when two or more parties are shooting back and forth at each other.

According to Officer Wilson, he fires his first string of rounds—five to six shots—as Michael Brown is moving off the sidewalk, and both back towards his position and to the middle of the road. Given that position, Michael Brown would then be at an angle exposing his right side to Wilson—the body mass at which Wilson has been trained to aim. Wilson's eyes are also focused on Michael Brown's right hand. It is reasonable to conclude, therefore, that this first string of shots accounts for the three wounds which Brown receives to the right arm: beneath the shoulder, through the bicep, and through the forearm. This would also account for why Brown flinches, but is otherwise undeterred. It also suggests that at least two to three shots are off target.

THE SECOND STRING

Up to this point, the combined narratives of both Officer Wilson and the forensic experts account for seven or eight rounds. Twelve rounds in all are fired. All twelve spent casings are recovered.

With regard to the second string, Officer Wilson states that he fires definitely twice more, and perhaps a third time. Evidence clearly shows that at least two of these rounds hit Michael Brown. One is to the forehead. One is to the top of the skull. The round to the skull is immediately fatal.

Undetermined by the autopsies is whether the entry wound suffered by Michael Brown to his chest occurs during the first string or the second string, and whether or not it is a reentry wound or a direct entry wound. Given the path of the bullet, entering high up on the rib cage and then moving downward and deeper into the body, it is logical to assume that Michael Brown is leaning forward at the time. If this is the case, it is reasonable to conclude the wound is a result of a round fired during the second string, and if it is the wound that accounts for Brown staggering momentarily and "scrunching over" that it occurs prior to the two head wounds.

The chest wound and the two head wounds would account for three additional rounds, making the total number of rounds accounted for ten or eleven. One or two rounds, then, are unaccounted for in terms of the narrative.

Also unaccounted for, are the distances separating Wilson and Brown when each shot is fired. However, forensic evidence provides for blood near to the sidewalk at Coppercreek Court more than 150 feet from the police SUV and near to 25 feet from where Brown's body ultimately falls. There is no doubt that Brown, after fleeing the vehicle, moves back towards Officer Wilson.

IMPAIRMENT

The toxicology laboratory report with regard to Michael Brown is performed by St. Louis University at the request of the St. Louis County Police. It confirms the presence of 12 nanograms of Delta-9-THC, the active ingredient of marijuana responsible for its hallucinatory effects. The report concludes "detection in the blood defines impairment." Brown is also found to be in possession of approximately 1 and one-half grams of marijuana contained in a knotted plastic bag.

With regard to his impairment, the pathologist hired by Brown's family denies the presence of marijuana accounts for Michael Brown's behavior. It is his opinion based on 50 years of experience that individuals under the influence of marijuana are as a rule not prone to aggressive or violent behavior.

Notwithstanding, the detectives from the St. Louis County Police do not rule out the effects of marijuana as a contributing factor in Brown's behavior. They are under the suspicion that Brown and Johnson may have smoked a potent form of marijuana referred to as "wax", and that the source of this marijuana may have been Witness #36, one of the two construction workers present the day of the incident.

Lending to this suspicion is the allegation by Dorian Johnson that Witness #36 asks both him and Brown about wax, and the inference by Johnson that Witness #36 may have shared the substance with them. Witness #36 vehemently denies the charge and volunteers to undergo tests to prove as much, as well as allow the detectives to search his vehicle. However, neither Johnson nor Witness #36 sufficiently account for the events between 7:30 am and 11:30 am at which time Johnson claims to have been with Brown. The speculation by the detectives is that Brown, Johnson and Witness #36 smoke marijuana together, and that the impairment experienced by Brown is a contributing factor to his behavior. Their rationale is that marijuana impedes the brain's ability to properly interpret sensory stimuli.

Dorian Johnson, for his part, denies smoking marijuana that morning, denies he is aware that Michael Brown smoked marijuana that morning, and refuses to provide any samples for toxicology testing—although he is first interviewed several days after the incident, and at a time when it would be impossible to make any connection between current test results and the incident.

PERSPECTIVE

The autopsies do nothing to dispel any claims or eyewitness reports that Michael Brown has some part of his body, including both arms and hands, inside the police SUV or that he is engaged in a physical confrontation with Officer Brown. The physical evidence supports Officer Wilson's claim that Michael Brown reenters the vehicle following the first shot, and therefore suggests that Michael Brown is instigating a physical confrontation. It is not until he is actually shot that Brown extracts himself from the vehicle and flees.

Further, the physical evidence provides clearly that Michael Brown moves back towards Officer Wilson, and that he continues to advance on Officer Wilson even though he has been wounded by as many as three shots. It is only then that Officer Wilson fires the fatal shots.

In terms of the objective of the Grand Jury, the evidence provided by the autopsies and the corresponding physical evidence do not indicate probable cause to indict Officer Wilson.

DNA ANALYSIS

FORENSIC SCIENTIST: DNA

INTERVIEW WITH THE GRAND JURY, VOLUME 19

The interview of the forensic scientist from the St. Louis County Police Department takes place on November, 4, 2014. The procedure is conducted by Alizadeh and Whirley. All 12 jurists are present. The interview is specific to the process and does not provide any insight into any of the samples that are collected.

According to the forensic scientist, she has been working for the police department and at her position for nine years. Her job is to collect bodily fluids from crime scenes, primarily blood, saliva, and semen, which are then tested for DNA, and to produce related documentation, such as written reports. She also looks for and identifies trace evidence, which are indications left behind when an individual makes contact with a surface, including clothing, and in this case, weapons. Typical types of trace evidence are fingerprints, footprints, hair, fibers and DNA. Most fluid samples are collected from surfaces by swab, while trace evidence is collected by a variety of means and is then packaged.

This particular forensic scientist is assigned to the Michael Brown case.

According to the forensic scientist, she takes a DNA sample from Michael Brown's blood. The DNA sample she has for Officer Darren Wilson is from a buccal sample, meaning saliva.

The forensic scientist explains that she takes samples from the surface of all of Michael Brown's clothing, seeking possible DNA not only from Brown, but from Officer Wilson also. The same procedure is performed relative to Officer Wilson's clothing, and again, to test for Michael Brown's DNA and trace evidence. She notes there are no blood stains on Officer Wilson's shirt, but there are blood stains on his pants.

She notes that she also takes three specific DNA or trace samples from Officer Wilson's vehicle. The first is what appears to be dried nasal mucus found on the exterior surface of the back seat door on the driver's side. The second is blood on the interior door handle of the vehicle. The third sample is blood found on the exterior of the driver's door.

The forensic scientist also notes what appears to be blood on the surface of Officer Wilson's gun. The swab sample she takes tests positive for blood. There are also two bracelets which are found at the scene. One is rubber with yellow, black and white coloring. The second is dark brown in color and beaded (wood). They too are processed for DNA. The same is done for the baseball cap and the flip-flops.

DNA TECHNICAL LEADER, ST. LOUIS COUNTY POLICE DEPARTMENT

INTERVIEW WITH THE GRAND JURY, VOLUME 19

The interview of the DNA technical leader by the Grand Jury takes place on November 4, 2014. The procedure is conducted by Alizadeh and Whirley. All 12 jurists are present.

According to the leader, he has been employed with the St. Louis Police Department for four years. He also has 6 years prior experience with the St. Louis Metropolitan Police Department Crime Laboratory. In addition, he has a master's degree in biology from Washington University. In all, he has been involved in over 1400 DNA-based cases.

According to the leader, everyone on earth has a unique forensic DNA profile (except exact twins). In addition, the DNA profile is the same regardless of the sample used, meaning that a strand of hair will provide the same DNA profile as a finger nail or a blood sample. However, a DNA sample will not provide evidence related to time, meaning that there is no way of telling simply through the DNA sample when the evidence may have been left at the scene.

Speaking from a legal perspective, the leader states that the process seeks to provide a probative match. A probative match is based on a statistical measure intended to give weight to evidence as a really strong match, a good match, or a so-so match. When a sample comes from a single source, the statistical model used is called a random match probability. When the sample comes from a mixed source, meaning more than one possible DNA profile — Officer Wilson and Michael Brown both making physical contact with the surface of Officer Wilson's duty weapon, for example, the measure is referred to as a likelihood ratio.

Ultimately, a determination is made as to whether or not an individual is a major contributor or minor contributor to the sample, and this determination is made comparatively in terms of any random or unknown person in the general population. In terms of providing for probability, the leader explains that ratios are used, and that these ratios are 1 to nonillion (10 followed by 30 zeros), then million, billion, trillion, quadrillion, quintillion, sextillion, septillion, and octillion.

In discussing Michael Brown's case, the leader states that the nasal mucus-like substance, for example, tests highly probative for Michael Brown as the source, as do the reddish-brown stains found on Canfield Drive. The ratio the leader provides is a 1 in 36 nonillion chance that the DNA belongs to someone other than Michael Brown. (There are approximately 7 billion people in the world.) The same is true of the blood found on Officer Wilson's pants.

Addressing the DNA profiles discovered on the surface of Officer Wilsons' gun, the leader states the testing suggests three or more contributors, with Officer Wilson and Michael Brown being the major contributors, and a third minor trace contributor not identified. The odds of the trace DNA belonging to Officer Wilson and some other person and not to Officer Wilson and Michael Brown is 1 in 2.1 octillion.

With regard to Michael Brown's shirt: the DNA samples tested indicate one major contributor—Michael Brown—and one or more trace contributors. Officer Wilson is not one of those contributors.

SPECIFIC DNA ANALYSIS FINDINGS

The DNA test of Michael Brown's t-shirt indicates a mixture of two or more individuals. The major component profile is consistent with Michael Brown. There are one or more trace contributors. Officer Darren Wilson is not a trace contributor.

The DNA test of Michael Brown's shorts indicates a mixture of three or more individuals. The major component profile is consistent with Michael Brown. There are two or more trace contributors. Officer Wilson is not a trace contributor.

The DNA test of Michael Brown's left hand indicates a mixture of two or more individuals. The major contributor is Michael Brown. The minor contributor is consistent with Officer Wilson. The probability ratio is 98 times more likely that the mixed material is from Michael Brown and Officer Wilson than Michael Brown and some other individual.

The DNA test of Michael Brown's left hand fingernail scrapings indicates a mixture of three or more individuals. Officer Wilson is excluded as a contributor.

Michael Brown is the source of DNA for the nasal mucus substance found on the vehicle, the blood found on the rear driver side door of the vehicle, and the two blood stains found on Canfield Drive in proximity to Coppercreek Court.

The DNA test of blood from Officer Wilson's uniform pants indicates a mixture of two or more individuals. The major contributor is Michael Brown. The minor contributor is Officer Wilson.

The DNA test of the top exterior of the left front door of the police SUV indicates a mixture of three or more individuals. Michael Brown and Officer Wilson are major contributors. The probability ratio is 6.9 million times more likely that the mixed material is from Brown and Wilson than Wilson and some other individual.

The DNA test of the interior left front door handle of the SUV indicates a mixture of two or move individuals, with a major contributor and one or more minor contributors. Michael Brown is the major contributor. The minor component is insufficient to indicate Officer Wilson as a contributor.

The DNA test of Officer Wilson's duty weapon indicates a mixture of three or more individuals, two of whom are major contributors, and one or more who are trace contributors. The two major contributors are Officer Wilson and Michael Brown. There is insufficient data to determine the trace contributors. The probability ratio is 2.1 octillion times more likely that the mixed material is from Wilson and Brown than Wilson and some other individual.

In addition, the DNA tests suggest that the black, yellow and white rubber bracelet belongs to Michael Brown and that it came off during the physical confrontation. Officer Wilson's DNA profile was included. However, the brown, wood bead bracelet does not indicate the presence of Michael Brown's DNA, or that of Officer Wilson. In all likelihood, the bracelet belongs to Dorian Johnson.

PART 4: THE GRAND JURY

THE SEQUENCE OF EVENTS BASED ON THE EVIDENCE

It is well established by psychologists and other experts that memory is selective. People as a rule recount their experiences the way they remember them and not necessarily how they actually occur. For this reason, many of the witnesses offer different perspectives on what may have happened on Canfield Drive on August 9, 2014. And many of these same witnesses modify their statements multiple times over the days and weeks that follow. The brain's need to fill in the empty spaces in order to form a more complete and logical picture is largely responsible for these modifications, and the details required are derived from the variety of sources available. However, modifying statements does not in and of itself imply lying or the intent to deceive. Those "witnesses" willing to do as much expose themselves early in the process and are readily discounted. Relying, then, solely on the statements provided by those witnesses most credible and the physical and forensic evidence, here is the most likely sequence of events that take place on August 9, 2014.

Dorian Johnson exits his apartment. His intent is to go across the street, Canfield Drive, and over to the apartment complex between Coppercreek Court and Canfield Court to drop in on a friend who he believes can provide him with the cigarillo he desires to smoke his marijuana. As he crosses the parking lot outside his complex, he sees Michael Brown. Michael Brown is helping his friend Viron's sister and mother by getting a couple of toddlers into the car.

It is not known whether Johnson and Brown get together at this time. What is known is that sometime around 11:00 am, and as many as three and one-half hours later, Michael Brown comes down to the parking lot a second time and spends as much as a half-hour in the company of Witness #33, and to some degree, Witness #36. It is also known that Dorian Johnson is not with Michael Brown at this time.

At no time during his statement to authorities does Johnson account for his own whereabouts, nor does he say that he is not at all times with Brown. In all likelihood, he goes to see the friend he sets out to see in the first place. It is possible also that Brown is with him at some point, and before he is with Witness #33. It is at this time that Brown smokes the marijuana that accounts for the toxicology report.

At approximately 11:30, Brown leaves the company of Witness #33 and climbs the stairs up to the apartment complex. It is likely at this time that he speaks to Viron, returns to him his cellphone, and asks if he wants to go to the store. Viron declines. When he again comes down to the parking lot, which according to Witness #33 is approximately 10 to 15 minutes later, he is accompanied by Dorian Johnson, which suggests Johnson may have been with Viron, and it is then that he and Brown smoke marijuana. Whether Witness #36 offers the wax to and smokes with Johnson and Brown is debatable, and there is no concrete evidence to support such speculation.

Brown and Johnson then take the walk to the Ferguson Market. Despite Johnson's claim to the contrary, by their actions once in the store, it seems that both Brown and Johnson are aware of Brown's impending behavior. Brown reaches over the counter, takes the cigarillos and hands them to Johnson, who is standing there to Brown's back. After grabbing the loose cigarillos, both immediately head for the door. Johnson does place the box of cigarillos on the counter.

On the way out, Brown reaches the door before Johnson does. The door is being held open by an unidentified man. The store clerk arrives to the door before Brown and moves to close it before Brown can exit. Brown pushes the clerk away from the door. Johnson exits. Brown moves threateningly towards the clerk, who backs away. Brown leaves the store with the cigarillos.

While Johnson and Brown are walking eastward together down the middle of Canfield Drive, Officer Wilson approaches from the opposite direction and heading west towards West Florissant. He observes both Johnson and Brown in the road. He slows his vehicle to stop and directs them both onto the sidewalk. Johnson, while still walking, tells Officer Wilson they are nearing their destination, but makes no move to comply. Brown responds dismissively, using the word "fuck".

Officer Wilson, at this time, decides to forego his lunch, and instead do a pedestrian check. He calls into dispatch. It is only after doing so that he checks his sideview mirror and makes the connection between Johnson and Brown and the stealing incident he hears over the radio. Based on the elevated conditions of the situation, he reverses his vehicle aggressively intent on the element of surprise and hoping to contain their movements before they can run. In doing so, he comes close to but does not hit either Johnson or Brown.

Johnson then backs away from the vehicle, but Brown responds aggressively, pushing back the door of the vehicle as Officer Wilson, having issued a verbal directive, attempts to exit. Officer Wilson then issues a verbal warning, and again attempts to exit. Brown again pushes the door closed and places his hands upon the door. Officer Wilson responds by attempting to physically remove Browns' hands. Brown responds by coming in through the window and attempting to assault Officer Wilson. In the process, Brown does strike Officer Wilson on or about the face multiple times. At some point early in the assault, Brown ceases momentarily, and only long enough to hand the cigarillos to Johnson. Johnson is positioned to Browns' back. Brown again enters the window and goes after Officer Wilson.

Failing to halt Michael Browns' assault, Officer Wilson draws his gun and warns Brown that he will fire. Brown fails to acknowledge the warning and continues the physical engagement. He places his hands on the weapon, which Officer Wilson is attempting to point in Brown's direction. Wilson attempts to fire the weapon, but Brown's hands are interfering with the slide or the hammer or both. Twice the gun fails to fire. On his third attempt, the gun fires, but as Brown is pushing down on Wilsons' right arm, the barrel fails to rise to the level of the window. The round is fired and pierces the interior panel of the door. Dorian Johnson takes off running.

In response to the first shot, Brown exits the window. He checks himself to see if he is wounded. Seeing no wound, he returns to the assault of Officer Wilson, at which time he receives a gash to his left forearm near to the elbow from the shards of glass of the window shattered by the first shot. He again attempts to go for Wilson's gun. Wilson, however, is leaning away towards the passenger seat, and is using his left hand to ward of Brown's assault. His right hand free, he fires his weapon, but it again fails to discharge. He manages to clear the obstruction and fire again. This shot hits Brown's right hand while the hand is still inside the car.

Unnerved by the second shot, Brown exits the vehicle. Realizing he has been injured, he begins to flee from the vehicle heading east on Canfield Drive and towards Coppercreek Court. He is heading towards Viron's apartment.

Meanwhile, Officer Wilson takes a moment to call in his situation. He then exits his vehicle in pursuit of Brown. Brown, who has lost at least one of his flip-flops, is in the vicinity of Coppercreek Court and near to the sidewalk. Officer Wilson, while in pursuit, tells Brown to stop. Brown stops just before the corner. He turns back towards Officer Wilson, his wounded right hand raised to shoulder level and his left hand somewhat lower. He briefly assesses the injury to his thumb, considers his options, and for reasons unknown, makes the decision to present himself in a manner which does not suggest compliance: he lowers his arms, forms a fist with his left hand, makes some sort of verbal sound, and begins to move assertively towards Officer Wilson.

Officer Wilson, at this time, holds his ground and fires multiple shots, as many as five to six. In all probability, at least three of these shots strike Brown, all in the right side and in some part of his right arm. Despite his wounds, none of which are considered incapacitating, Brown continues forward. Officer Wilson again provides a verbal warning. Brown fails to comply. Officer Wilson, this time taking steps back, again fires. The first found hits Brown in the right lateral area of the chest. Brown flinches and halts momentarily. He then staggers another step, his upper torso leaning close to parallel with the ground. Officer Wilson, interpreting Browns' posture as preparation to tackle him, fires twice more. Both rounds hit Brown in the head. Brown falls dead.

ANALYSIS AND INTERPRETATION

THE INITIAL ENGAGEMENT

Johnson's statement that Brown doesn't say anything isn't reasonable. While it may be possible that Wilson isn't adverse to a confrontation at this time, that he keeps going and doesn't wait for compliance is indication that he is initially satisfied with making his point. If Brown doesn't say anything, odds are Wilson doesn't reengage.

VEHICLE REVERSAL

The only witnesses that say Officer Wilson reverses so aggressively that his tires screech upon stopping are Johnson, Witness #11, and Witness #16. However, it has already been determined that neither of these witnesses hear a screech. Witness #16 doesn't hear anything until the first string of shots, and Witness #11 is more than 200 feet away, and in all likelihood talking on her phone. Only Johnson is close enough to hear the approach of the vehicle, and it is he who describes the sound as a screech, and then shares that description with #11 and #16.

WHO'S THE AGGRESSOR?

Johnson's claim that Officer Wilson, for no apparent reason, reaches out the window of his vehicle and grabs with the weaker of his two hands an individual who is 6' 5" and weighs 289 pounds makes no sense, and therefore has no merit. Multiple times, and without being asked directly, Johnson insists Brown, at no time, is trying to keep Wilson from exiting, and that Brown is simply trying to pull away. That too makes no sense. There is just no way for Wilson to maintain control of Brown simply by pulling on his t-shirt. Brown's size and superior leverage give him a distinct advantage in the described position. In addition, as Brown is free to turn and hand the cigarillos to Johnson, he is free enough to back away from the vehicle, if he so chooses. He chooses not to.

BROWN'S HANDS

Johnson's claim that Brown's hands never enter the vehicle and that Brown's only intention is to free himself from Wilson's grip fails to account for Wilson's gun misfiring three times. The gun has since been checked for defects and found to be operating correctly. It is possible that Wilson doesn't experience three misfires and that he fabricates this claim to support the sense of threat imposed by Brown. However, the explanation would not account for the bullet shot into the interior panel of the door. A much more reasonable explanation is that Brown has his hands on the gun and is pushing it down into the car as claimed by Wilson. There are also significant DNA samples belonging to Michael Brown that are recovered from within the vehicle and upon Wilsons' gun, which is only in proximity to Brown while Brown is next to the vehicle. And there are the superficial impact injuries to Wilson's right cheek and jaw.

POINT-BLANK RANGE

There is no other reasonable explanation for the gash wound to Brown's left arm than it coming from reaching through the window and the broken glass, which means it occurs after the first shot, and a time at which, if he chooses to do so, Brown can distance himself from Officer Wilson. That he instead reenters the window of the vehicle, which he definitely does of his own volition, further substantiates that he is the aggressor. The point-blank range of the shot that injures his hand is additional evidence that he is inside the vehicle, and that he is continuing to assault or attempt to assault Officer Wilson.

HANDS UP

Brown stops running either because he can't run any further, is confused and frightened, or because he considers complying with Officer Wilson. When he turns, his hands are in full view but not up in the way to suggest surrender. It's possible he may just be looking at the wound to his hand. Perhaps because he is mad or perhaps due to the effects of the marijuana, he then uses poor judgment, and despite the directives by Officer Wilson, starts back towards Wilson with purposeful strides.

DECISION TO USE DEADLY FORCE

Officer Wilson, aware first-hand of Brown's willingness to engage him in physical confrontation despite his authority as a law enforcement officer, interprets Brown's actions as a continued threat to his personal safety. He makes the decision to fire to stop Brown before he can get within arm's reach.

FIRST STRING OF SHOTS

As Brown's movement both towards Wilson and the middle of Canfield Drive put him at an angle to Wilson, and thereby minimizing the degree of body mass exposed, Wilson's first string of rounds either miss Brown altogether or hit him in the arm. One is to the outer arm just below the right shoulder. One hits the right bicep and passes through the back of the arm. The thirds hits him in the forearm just below the elbow and exits out the other side. This third shot, given the angle of entry and exit, suggests Brown's right arm is down towards his waistline and the elbow extended out and away from the body, thereby exposing the forearm to the round and providing for the bullet exiting cleanly without reentering body mass elsewhere. Two significant blood stains, both with Brown's DNA, are found approximately 22 feet east of where Brown falls, and approximately twenty feet west of his position near Coppercreek Court. Brown, therefore, takes a number of steps back toward Wilson to account for more than 40 feet.

FATAL SHOTS

As this first string of shots fails to stop Brown, Wilson fires again. However, there is sufficient circumstantial evidence that Brown has been slowed by this time, and it is likely that he would have stopped at this point if directed more sternly or if Wilson continues to move back while assessing the effects of his first shots. Wilson, though, has the moment speedup on him, and as the distance between him and Brown has narrowed considerably, he interprets Brown's slumping posture as the onset of a charge. The first bullet hits Brown to the lateral side of his right chest. This causes Brown to double-over. However, Wilson is already pulling the trigger again and again. The next shot hits Brown above the right eye. His head and eyes drop. The last shot hits Brown in the top of the head, and he falls. The threat to Wilson and others is terminated.

JURY DELIBERATIONS AND THE LAW

POSSIBLE INDICTMENTS

Deliberations on the case begin on November 21, 2014. According to Alizadeh, the Grand Jury has the following indictments to consider: Murder in the first degree—a class A felony—and armed criminal action—an unclassified felony; murder in the second degree and armed criminal action; voluntary manslaughter—a class B felony—and armed criminal action; involuntary manslaughter in the first degree and armed criminal action; and, involuntary manslaughter in the second degree and armed criminal action. The standard of proof for all possible indictments is probable cause. The task of the Grand Jury is not to decide guilty or not guilty. Probable cause is sufficient to bring the case to trial.

Whirley then refers the members of the Grand Jury to a written clause dealing with assault of a law enforcement officer, and the varying degrees: first, second and third. She then reminds the members that Officer Wilson's claim is that he is making an arrest based on assault. She also reminds them that law enforcement officers are permitted to use force while making an arrest.

According to Whirley, the Grand Jury must, in order to decide on a true bill, find probable cause that Darren Wilson commits the offense or offenses established by the indictments, he does not act in lawful self-defense, and/or he does not use lawful force in making an arrest. She reminds them, also, that all it takes to indict and move for trial is any nine of the twelve jurists finding in favor.

Alizadeh then explains that the Grand Jury must find probable cause for both charges, as either defense, in and of itself, is a complete defense to any offense. In other words, the Grand Jury has to find probable cause that Officer Wilson does not act in lawful self-defense in response to Michael Brown's actions and that he does not use lawful force in his attempt to arrest Michael Brown. If he is found to have acted lawfully in either application and not the other, he is still justified in using lethal force, and is therefore not accountable in terms of the charge for which probable cause may be established. She references the case of Garner vs. Tennessee.

As part of her final words, Alizadeh encourages the Grand Jury to make a decision based on the evidence heard and the law as explained, and not based on the media, public opinion, or their individual fears.

DEFINITIONS BY LAW

Murder in the first degree is defined as an unlawful killing that is willful, deliberate and premeditated, meaning an element of planning is required. In some states "malice aforethought" is also required, indicating an extreme indifference to human life.

Murder in the second degree is defined as an unlawful and intentional killing that is not premeditated or planned, or is caused by dangerous conduct and an obvious lack of concern for human life. Second degree murder is perceived as impulsive, with malice aforethought, an intent to cause serious bodily harm, and demonstrates depraved indifference.

Voluntary manslaughter in the first degree is defined as an intentional killing without prior intent to kill, and under circumstances that would cause a reasonable person to become emotionally or mentally disturbed. Malice aforethought is not applicable. The charge of voluntary manslaughter often applies with regard to the mistaken belief that the killing is justified, for example based on the defendant's belief that the situation requires lethal force.

Involuntary manslaughter in the second degree is defined as an unintentional killing that results from recklessness or criminal negligence, or an unlawful act that does not rise to the level of a felony. The act is considered criminal if it is inherently dangerous to others or with reckless disregard for human life, and if the defendant knows or should know his conduct is a threat to others.

Armed criminal action is defined as the committing of any felony by, with, or through the use, assistance, or aid of a dangerous instrument or deadly weapon.

Probable cause is defined as apparent facts that would lead a reasonably intelligent and prudent person to believe that an accused person has committed a crime.

THE STATE OF MISSOURI STATUTE ON THE DEFENSE OF JUSTIFICATION

According to statute 563.046 of Missouri state law, a law enforcement officer need not retreat or desist from efforts to effect the arrest, or from efforts to prevent the escape from custody, of a person he reasonably believes to have committed an offense because of resistance or threatened resistance of the arrestee. The use of physical force, however, requires the officer to reasonably believe it is immediately necessary to make the arrest or to prevent the suspect's escape. Further, the officer must reasonably believe the arrest is lawful. Deadly force is justified only if the officer reasonably believes the suspect has committed or attempted to commit a felony, is attempting to escape by use of a deadly weapon, or may otherwise endanger life or cause serious physical injury unless stopped. The clause also states that the defendant has the burden of proving the arresting officer unjustly uses physical or deadly force.

TENNESSEE VS. GARNER

On October 3, 1974, and just before 11:00 pm, two Memphis police officers responding to a burglary call chase a fleeing subject. The subject, 15 year-old Edward Garner, attempts to escape pursuit by scaling a 6 foot chain-link fence. Officer Elton Hymon, who is closest in pursuit, using his flashlight, correctly determines that Garner is unarmed. However, as Garner refuses the directive to cease in his efforts to flee, Officer Hymon shots him in the back of the head. Garner is found to be in possession of ten dollars and a lady's purse. He dies in the ambulance on his way to the hospital.

According to the existing state statute, Hymon is justified in using deadly force to subdue a fleeing suspect. That statute is based on common law developed at the time when most felonies were punishable by death and most law enforcement officers did not carry guns. However, Garner's father brings a law suit against local law enforcement to the United States Supreme Court under the Civil Rights Act of 1871, which states:

> Every person who, under color of any statute, ordinance, regulation, custom, or usage, of any State or Territory or the District of Columbia, subjects, or causes to be subjected, any citizen of the United States or other person within the jurisdiction thereof to the deprivation of any rights, privileges, or immunities secured by the Constitution and laws, shall be liable to the party injured in an action at law, suit in equity, or other proper proceeding for redress (Andrew Branca, lawofselfdense.com, 2014).

Ultimately, the Supreme Court finds for Garner and against the city of Memphis and the State of Tennessee, stating they fail to present evidence that its interest in shooting fleeing suspects outweighs the suspects own right to life, and that because Officer Hymon has no reason to believe Garner is either armed or dangerous, the use of deadly force is not warranted. The case is then remanded for the determination of liability.

CONCLUSION

At the conclusion of the Grand Jury process in the case of Officer Darren Wilson, the jurists are provided with a very specific task. They must find or not find probable cause for indicting Officer Wilson on any one of five charges. Three of those charges require the Grand Jury to find probable cause to indict Officer Wilson on the intentional murder of Michael Brown. Of these three, two require unlawful actions on the part of Officer Wilson which are taken with the express intention of taking Michael Brown's life, one requiring premeditation and indifference, and the other impulsiveness and indifference. The other requires intent due to a disturbed state of mind on Wilson's part to kill Michael Brown. The involuntary manslaughter charges require differing degrees of recklessness and negligence on the part of Officer Wilson, and probable cause that he acts with knowing disregard for the safety of others. Further, the Grand Jury, in order to do so, must simultaneously find that Officer Wilson does not have probable cause to believe Michael Brown is a credible threat to himself or others, and that any other reasonable individual under the same conditions would have acted differently.

FIRST DEGREE MURDER

With regard to the first degree murder charge, there is no credible evidence which suggests that Officer Wilson plans to kill Michael Brown. There is nothing to suggest the death of Michael Brown is a premeditated act, nor an act of willfulness on the part of Officer Wilson. To the contrary, Officer Wilson, according to numerous witnesses (#14, #26, #30 and #48) more than once directs Michael Brown to cease and desist in his actions, and pauses intentionally between the first and second string of shots in the hope that Michael Brown will comply. Were Officer Wilson to have shot Michael Brown while his hands are raised demonstrating an intent to comply, as suggested by witnesses who otherwise are not credible (#33, #35, and #45), there would be probable cause for indifference. However, general consensus (#10, #26, #30, and #48) is that Michael Brown does not have his hands or arms raised in a fashion or for a period of time that requires Officer Wilson to interpret his intent as surrender. In addition, physical evidence, regardless of statements to the contrary, clearly shows that Brown continues to move towards Officer

Wilson and without any physical gestures or verbal indications of intent to comply.

SECOND DEGREE MURDER

With regard to the second degree murder charge, there is no credible evidence which suggests that Officer Wilson engages in any dangerous and unlawful conduct or acts impulsively with regards to his actions leading to the death of Michael Brown. His actions, according to multiple expert witnesses, are consistent with his training and the duty of his position. His decision to use deadly force is dependent upon the Use of Force Triangle (or Continuum) as dictated by Michael Brown's actions, which include physically assaulting Officer Wilson with blows to the face and attempting to overpower Officer Wilson and take control of his weapon. His decision to pursue Michael Brown is based on the expectations for the performance of his duty, including eliminating perceived threats to the general populace. Michael Brown's willingness to engage in unlawful and potentially dangerous behavior provides for that threat.

VOLUNTARY MANSLAUGHTER

With regard to the charge of voluntary manslaughter in the first degree, there is no credible evidence that Officer Wilson kills Michael Brown as a result of any emotional or psychological disturbance. There is only one (somewhat) credible witness, Witness #16, who attributes any emotion to Wilson's actions. She says the redness of his face is due to anger. However, Witness #16 is of questionable motive, changes her statements multiple times, and in all likelihood sees much less of the incident than she claims.

The more difficult challenge—Officer Wilson's perception of Michael Brown's actions as justification for the use of deadly force—requires concrete evidence that provides clear insight to Officer Wilson's thought process throughout the sequence of events and leading up to his decision to use deadly force. Since there are no measurable or objective means by which to obtain such clarity, the Grand Jury is therefore tasked with finding probable cause to the contrary: Michael Brown's actions are in no way a threat to the safety of Officer Wilson or anyone else.

However, outside of a handful of witnesses whose statements are obviously contrary to the physical evidence, there is no such evidence. The facts are that Michael Brown willingly engages in a physical confrontation with Officer Wilson (#10, #11, #14 and #44), attempts to physically overpower him, reaches for and tries to take control of Officer Wilson's weapon, and ultimately, chooses not to comply with verbal directives to cease and desist, and instead advances on Officer Wilson (#10, #14, #17, #26 and #48) thereby creating the perception he is willing to again be physically confrontational. It is reasonable, then, that Officer Wilson perceives Brown as a threat to his safety and the safety of others—for example, the responding officers he summons.

INVOLUNTARY MANSLAUGHTER

With regard to the charge of involuntary manslaughter, there is no evidence which points to probable cause in terms of negligence or reckless behavior. Officer Wilson follows police department procedures, accurately identifies the suspect, verbally communicates his expectations of the suspect, and takes reasonable precaution in firing his weapon. No other persons are at any time in danger, and no other persons are injured or property damaged.

THE GRAND JURY'S DECISION

Within the interpretation permitted by the cold and dispassionate language of the law, free of the influence of a family's love of a son, the bonds of friendship, social belongingness, cultural and class disparity, and the contemporary phenomena of media sensationalism, the members of the Grand Jury tasked with deciding the Darren Wilson case have no other recourse than find for lack of probable cause, and therefore must not bring forth a bill indicting Officer Wilson for the unlawful taking of Michael Brown's life. Given the weight of the physical evidence and the statements of those witnesses that are deemed credible—and there are a good number of them, Officer Wilson's actions are not unlawful, and by definition, reasonable.

AFTERWARD

The Grand Jury's decision to not indict Officer Darren Wilson on any of the charges specified is not an indictment of the legal process nor of society at large. Held to a specific set of laws—and the animating purpose of those laws, there could have been no other possible outcome. Had they made the choice to indict, regardless of the specific charge, there is little doubt, if any, given the collective credibility and statements of the witnesses, combined with the forensic and physical evidence, that a formal trial would have eventually exonerated Officer Wilson of all charges.

The Grand Jury's decision, however, does not mean that Officer Wilson was justified in killing Michael Brown, or that Michael Brown's actions called for the use of deadly force. Unfortunately, each failed to show empathy for the human condition of the other, lost his sense of self in a moment that escalated quickly and became surreal, and became unsuspecting victims to identities and roles which have been distorted by the social settings in which they have taken root and been nurtured.

Nevertheless, both Officer Darren Wilson and Michael Brown are accountable for their actions on that day. Michael Brown was mature enough and educated enough to know right from wrong, two concepts—regardless of where or how we grow up—which are pretty much inherent in all of us. As for Officer Wilson, had he allowed the moment to slow down, especially following the first string of six shots, and taken the time to access the situation, there is little doubt that he would have realized that those final four shots were unnecessary.

What has been done, unfortunately, is—as always—inalterable.

www.ingramcontent.com/pod-product-compliance
Lightning Source LLC
Chambersburg PA
CBHW071341280526
45787CB00001B/171